D1255600

# THE NEWS AS MYTH

**Recent Titles in**
**Contributions to the Study of Mass Media and Communications**

# THE NEWS AS MYTH

*Fact and Context in Journalism*

**Tom Koch**

Contributions to the Study of Mass Media
and Communications, Number 17
Bernard K. Johnpoll, Series Editor

**GREENWOOD PRESS**
New York • Westport, Connecticut • London

**Library of Congress Cataloging-in-Publication Data**

Koch, Tom
   The news as myth : fact and context in journalism / Tom Koch.
     p.  cm.—(Contributions to the study of mass media and
communications, ISSN 0732-4456 ; no. 17)
   Includes bibliographical references.
   ISBN 0-313-27268-9 (lib. bdg. : alk. paper)
   1. Journalism—Objectivity.  2. Journalism—Technique.  I. Title.
II. Series.
PN4756.K63  1990
070.4—dc20      89-27371

British Library Cataloguing in Publication Data is available.

Library of Congress Catalog Card Number: 89-27371
ISBN: 0-313-27268-9
ISSN: 0732-4456

First published in 1990

Greenwood Press, 88 Post Road West, Westport, CT 06881
An imprint of Greenwood Publishing Group, Inc.

Printed in the United States of America

The paper used in this book complies with the
Permanent Paper Standard issued by the National
Information Standards Organization (Z39.48-1984).

10 9 8 7 6 5 4 3 2 1

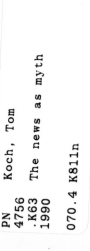

**Copyright Acknowledgments**

The author and publisher gratefully acknowledge permission to use the following:

"Death Sets Off Alarm" (February 3, 1987) and "Fatal Slip Unnoticed," by Holly Horwood (February 11, 1986) are reprinted by permission of *The Province*.

"Two-year-old Dies After Operation in Dental Office," by Robert O. Boorstin (June 6, 1986), copyright © 1986 by The New York Times Company. Reprinted by permission.

"Surgeon Says Shintaku Took a Bad Beating," by Lee Games and Charles Memminger (October 8, 1981) is reprinted by permission of *The Honolulu Star-Bulletin*.

"Death Probed After Teen's Heart Stops During Dental Surgery"—Sun Staff, *The Vancouver Sun*.

"Media Ruined Reputation. Cleared Dentist Says"—Wyng Chow, Pat Leidl, *The Vancouver Sun*.

*Money and Class in America* by Lewis Lapham. Copyright © 1988 by Lewis Lapham. Used with permission from Weidenfeld & Nicolson.

For Denis,
Who insisted

# Contents

# Illustrations

# Acknowledgments

Like all those with the temerity to write at book length, I have incurred numerous debts in the research and preparation of this manuscript. As a professional journalist writing about the news, I would be remiss in not acknowledging first the assistance of those who so thoroughly instructed me in the form and procedures of daily news work. My most critical tutor was *Springfield Union* city editor Jane Maroney who, in the early 1970s, taught a generation of reporters the basic rules of urban reportage. Alumni of her Massachusetts city room have gone on to posts from Greece to Beijing the better for that instruction. In Vancouver, Canadian Broadcasting Corporation producer Curtis Albertson introduced me to the techniques of radio production and, with show hosts Ann Petrie and Patrick Monro, tutored me in public affairs reportage on a superbly produced and expertly conceived afternoon radio program. My interest in medical reportage began while a reporter at the *Province* newspaper, also in Vancouver, where then city editor Don MacLaughlin ruled with the help of assistant city editor Bud Jorgenson.

Research for this book was facilitated and materially aided by academic research access grants from both Vu/Text Information Services, Inc., a Knight-Ridder Company, and Westlaw, the on-line division of West Publishing Company. Officials at both services proved extraordinarily patient with requests for information and tutelage on their respective systems. The luxury of having available without cost both of these electronic resources was of inestimable value.

Graphic designer John Carter of Vancouver, B.C., reviewed and assisted with the illustrations included in this text. Production editor Catherine Lyons offered able advice and assistance during the sometimes difficult task of transforming a complex manuscript into what I hope is a consistently legible book.

The manuscript was written while I was first a Kiplinger Fellow and then a Kiplinger Scholar in Public Affairs Journalism at Ohio State University. These positions liberated me from the working journalist's typical bane of newspaper, magazine and project deadlines, and allowed me to concentrate fully on the project at hand. Ohio State University's Joe McKerns and Hugh Carter Donahue both provided able criticism of this work's early drafts. University president Edward Jennings and the School of Geography's W. Randy Smith also offered support and encouragement.

Finally, I am indebted to my friend Denis Wood of North Carolina State University. For almost two decades he urged me to consider the implicit assumptions of my chosen profession. When I finally accepted the necessity of that challenge, he gave lavishly of his own time to advance the work's theoretical position. As the project progressed, he provided what every writer most desperately needs, a brilliant and critical reading of the work in progress. No author could ask for more.

# THE NEWS AS MYTH

# Introduction: The News as Story

On April 13, 1738, the British Parliament passed a law declaring it a "notorious breach of privilege" to report on the debates and actions of Parliament. That effectively made illegal the then relatively new phenomenon of public reportage of the legislature. "Periodicals," magazines whose publishing schedule was often erratic, were then the primary vehicle for what today we would call news. To circumvent the ban, *London Magazine* began publishing occasional articles under the heading of "Proceedings of the Political Club," in which fictitious, young noblemen and gentlemen supposedly debated the issues of the day and managed, in that debate, to touch upon the general outline of what in fact was going on in Parliament.

Edward Cave, publisher of *Gentlemen's Magazine*, skated a bit closer to the law. In June of 1738 he began to publish reports on the "Parliaments of Lilliput" in which debates between "Hurgoes" and "Clinabs" corresponded to actual proceedings in Britain's Parliament between members of the Tory and Whig parties.[1] These supposedly fictitious reports were published periodically until March of 1744, when the law prohibiting coverage of Parliament was repealed. Cave's ruse was a thin disguise for Parliament's actual debates, but it sufficed, in part because of the quality of writing and the perceptual reportage of its primary author, a young, ambitious, and impecunious hack named Sam Johnson.[2]

## SAMUEL JOHNSON

At first Johnson was researcher and assistant to William Guthrie[3], and it has become something of a scholar's game to search those early stories for examples of Johnson's prose. Scholars have debated the extent to which the original idea and early columns were Guthrie's work and the extent to which they were, in fact, Johnson's brainchild and craft from the beginning. What is known is that from

1741 on, Johnson was sole author of the Lilliput reports and that these were almost universally acknowledged as a cipher for the debates of Britain's legislature. In all he wrote approximately a half million words on parliamentary debates and in all that time never heard a debate in person or interviewed a parliamentary participant. As he later wrote:

> I never had been in the gallery of the House of Commons but once. Cave had interest with the doorkeepers. He and the persons employed under him gained him admittance; they brought away the subject of discussion, the names of the speakers, the side they took, and the order in which they rose, together with notes of arguments advocated in the course of the debate. The whole was afterwards communicated to me, and I composed the speeches in the form which they now have in the Parliamentary Debates.[4]

It was a remarkable feat pulled off under grueling conditions. When deadlines approached, Johnson, who usually put off writing until the last possible moment, would in Boswell's words, "shut himself up in a room assigned to him at St. John's gate, to which he would not suffer anyone to approach, except the compositor or Cave's boy for matter which, as fast as he composed it, he tumbled out the door."[5]

"Cave's boy," the equivalent of a copy runner in more modern times, would bring in snippets of remembered debate or, sometimes, just a list of the names of debating speakers.[6] Based on these bare, disjointed facts, Johnson would then, when writing his report, fashion whole speeches out of his own knowledge of British political policy, personalities, and issues. Indeed, most of the *Parliament of Lilliput* copy was, by modern journalistic standards, pure fabrication. It carried the sense of the events in Parliament but almost never the actual words or actions of its members.

Despite the rush to deadline, there was no rush to print. These stories were never published while Parliament was sitting, and often not for at least a year after that session had ended. Neither immediacy nor absolute verbatim accuracy were, however, journalistic necessities in those days. Even with the long delay between session and publication, these reports were enormously successful. Sales of the magazine increased 50 percent on the strength of Johnson's reports, and Cave, to "demonstrate his good fortune," bought himself a coach and team of horses with the additional profits.[7]

The success of these reports long outlasted Cave's horses. For at least a generation they were regarded by many in England as recordings of authentic speeches given in that country's Legislature by men of the day. Members of Parliament knew better, of course, but had no desire to set the record straight. Johnson said so well what lords and members had intended to state that most were delighted to claim his words as their own. His concise, forceful evocation of the issues eloquently caught the essence of both the topics under debate and the personalities who fought for or against   fixed political viewpoints.[8]

His impartiality was another boon. Although he generally disapproved of Whig political positions, Johnson put brilliance into the speeches of Whig and Tory partisans alike. One example is the moving but totally invented speech supposedly given by Sir Robert Walpole during impeachment proceedings brought against him in the House. It was entirely Johnson's creation and written well after the fact, for a *Gentlemen's Magazine* report. Although Johnson did not admire Walpole's politics, the columnist's own view of fair play and drama allowed him to craft a brilliant and moving defence.[9] It, along with other excerpts from these "reports," stood   for more than a century in English language texts as a true record of superb rhetoric by men of the  day, whose fame  far eclipsed the young Johnson's then relative anonymity.

## JANET COOKE

A bit more than two hundred years later, *Washington Post* newspaper reporter Janet Cooke received the Pulitzer prize in 1981  for an exercise whose topic was different but whose method bore a strong resemblance to Johnson's own. The story of drug addiction in a ghetto family, of a malaise that touched each individual member's life, won praise for its style, its content, its accuracy, and its evocative portrait of an issue—drug use—then under intense social scrutiny. Her award was revoked when later it was learned that the story was a composite, a portrait drawn in words—Johnson-style—from readings and observations and real events that she pulled together into a single, forceful composite.[10]

Nobody doubted the essential truth of her story or that it was an accurate reflection of aspects of ghetto life described through the life of a single, young black surrounded by an  adult community  steeped in the culture of addiction. Her shame was in passing off a generally acknowledged but unattributed composite truth as a narrow, descriptively attributed fact. Like Johnson, who collapsed the processes of Parliament and a complex of then contemporary issues into a single, thematic whole, Cooke put all she knew and had learned into a single composite of families and addicts she had known and knew. By some definitions she did the work brilliantly, perhaps too well.

Paul Johnson, a British journalist and historian, defines as the task of both historians and newsmen "to communicate an understanding of events to the reader."[11] Certainly Cooke did that, providing a living portrait of drug use in a deeply alienated, racial community. Her article, which deserved its award, made of addiction a compelling, human story.  If Paul Johnson is correct, and Samuel Johnson would have agreed that he is, "both [historians and journalists] are involved in the discovery and elucidation of truth—that is, the search for the facts which matter, and their arrangement in significant form."

Cooke's exposition was clearly involved in the search for the "facts" of the matter, and that they were arranged in a "significant" and compelling form was acknowledged by the Pulitzer award.

Why then, has Sam Johnson's work stood the test of time with pride, while Cooke's was immediately reviled? Certainly Johnson was a pioneer, a man who helped create the form that today we call news. This was true both socially and stylistically. Johnson was a self-proclaimed drudge, a hack who wrote at speed and for pay; a man who, unlike Pope, Boswell—who had family monies to subsidize his early work—and others, needed to exchange his written work for money to pay the bills.  Thus he helped to create not only the "periodical's" form, but as well the role of a journalist working for hire in his society.[12] Cooke worked in the midst of a modern context in which the ideas of appropriate coverage and form are built upon an American as well as an English language tradition. But to dismiss the question with a shrug of "these are different times," is to beg the crucial questions of what it is, precisely, that contemporary journalism does and what its goal should be. Cooke's critics (she had no defenders) said that a story must describe a single event whose sources, like a scientist's experiment, can be independently verified, and her prize-winning piece did not fall within that modern definition of journalism. But many agreed that if only she had called the story "fiction," or a "composite" portrait"—anything else but news—it might have won an award and she could perhaps have stayed at the *Washington Post*.

The possible validity and acknowledged power of her portrait were, to these critics, utterly beside the point. But to men like Cave, Boswell, and Johnson, those objections would have seemed irrelevant and immaterial. Acknowledging the context of her portrait, one suspects they would have applauded the method by which she made an issue live through her subjects. Johnson, in tune with his times, went on to bigger if, perhaps, not better pieces of reportage and literary work. His dictionary, essays, and religious writings, all informed by techniques of craft honed in his "fictitious" reportage of Parliament, stand as models of prose for any and all ages. Cooke is out of the journalism business and remains a cautionary footnote to the ambitious journeyman who may be tempted to stretch the boundaries of journalistic definition too far.

The problem is that unlike most professions, there is no single perspective or substantive body of knowledge related to "the news". "Journalism has no widely agreed upon objective standards regarding proper practices."[13] Physicians profess a standard of care for their patients and lawyers profess, when called to the bar, to be servants of the court and its laws. But news professionals have no such code or body, no systematic viewpoint similar to that of, for example, geography[14] or a body of analytic theory like physics. At best newsmen can claim allegiance to a standard of truth and a concern for the public weal.  But there is nothing special in that  insistence on an exposition of fact in the public forum. It is part of the democratic ideal and a duty of all citizens. Newspeople, in fact,  have no public voice. They quote  and thus rely on the standards of truth and public concerns of others, from Presidents to "whistle blowers." The standard of truth that some would espouse as unique for the industry is, in fact, the standard of those whom newsmen quote, a borrowed position and not one of the industry's own.

When physicians err they are faced with malpractice charges whose strength is determined with reference to clear standards. Did the physician do the things which are considered reasonable and prudent? Was the anesthetic machine on, the dosage of halothane correct, the blood pressure monitored adequately?

There is no comparable standard of appropriate action or care in journalism. In a 1989 United States appeals court decision, for example, a charge of libel against *New Yorker* writer Janet Malcolm by psychoanalyst Jeffrey Masson was dismissed even though Ms. Malcolm may have "made up" some quotes used in her piece and attributed to Masson. The court ruled that even if Masson did not use the attributed words that the "substantive content" had not been changed and that her rendition was a "rational interpretation" of her subject's comments.[15] Slander and libel cases usually turn on the issue of "willful malice" in the journalist's mind. It is a question of nuance and interpretation, not of established procedure, clear standards, iron clad purpose and unalterable fact.

The story of Cooke's Pulitzer, won and lost, thus becomes ever more bizarre because there was no law, no absolute regulation, or even a clear body of historically defined procedure that she can be said to have violated. The recent ruling's standard of "substantive content" may, in Cooke's case, have supported her interpretive reportage which colleagues so heatedly condemned.

What, then, are the "facts of the matter" in a news story and what is, in Paul Johnson's phrase, the "significant form" in which those "facts" are to be arranged? To what degree does the form of a story's presentation affect its perceived, historical truth? Cooke's critics argued implicitly that there is an inviolate form whose limits cannot be transgressed. Is that form a consistent, journalistic pattern or merely a convenient chimera in the historian or journalist's mind? These are the issues this book addresses and it is the question of journalism's narrative form that it will grapple with again and again. To see how wide a gap there may be between fact and truth, however, consider one more series of stories, one more published description of a complex of events.

## HAROLD Y. SHINTAKU

On the morning of October 7, 1981, Hawaii Circuit Court Judge Harold Y. Shintaku was rushed into emergency surgery in Honolulu, Hawaii, to have pieces of bone shattered from his caved-in skull picked out of his brain. The events preceding that surgery and the days immediately following, were covered extensively by two local newspapers and three island TV stations.[16] Sam Johnson and Janet their work describes. The Honolulu newspaper and TV stations, however, wrote and aired stories daily on the Shintaku case. In its November 9, 1981, issue, *Time* magazine reported as fact, in a national story on physical attacks against members of the judiciary, that the Hawaiian judge had been beaten. By that time, however, the origin of Shintaku's injuries was a hotly debated issue in Honolulu.

Here is a summary of the events, as reported at that time:

On September 28, 1981, Shintaku infuriated the local district attorney's staff, with which he was not on good terms, by reversing a jury decision convicting Charles Stevens of two grisly murders that occurred in 1978. Stevens was convicted largely on the basis of testimony by Cedric Sookie Ah Sing, a less than model citizen whose testimony at times contradicted itself and, at other times, that of other prosecution witnesses. Shintaku said he reversed the jury's decision, an unusual action for a judge to take, because, legally, "reasonable doubt had been demonstrated. To allow a conviction to stand when that crucial standard had been demonstrated would, the judge argued, have been a miscarriage of justice

Shintaku's decision was widely reported, as was the angry response first of city prosecutor, Charles Marsland, followed by that of his superior, Governor George Ariyoshi, who called for an official review of Shintaku's action. Condemnation of Shintaku's decision continued until Hawaii Chief Justice William Richardson issued a public statement defending Shintaku's decision and castigating Marsland and Ariyoshi for making political points on legal issues. They were, in his words, "political animals . . . looking for votes."

Shintaku was then arrested, outside a bar appropriately named The Jury Box, for driving under the influence of alcohol, and after being booked and released on bail, left the police station for his beach house. That is where his brother, Graf, found him the next morning, dazed and bleeding from his ear. The judge's skull was fractured and an ambulance was called to take him to the hospital and into surgery. Almost immediately, the police were calling it an attempted suicide.

Police closed the case the next week after the consulting pathologist, John Hardman,— who had neither talked to Shintaku's doctors, seen X rays of the damage to Shintaku, or interviewed the patient—told a press conference that the judge's skull had been crushed in an attempted suicide by hanging. As Police Chief Francis Keala told reporters:

> It's thought that possibly he had in fact stood on a table and had tried to put a ligature around his neck and jumped and the ligature either fell or broke and he fell to the floor from a distance of anywhere from six to nine feet, hitting his head on the way down and toppling over onto his head.[17]

This was the story reported by local newsmen and remains, today, the official explanation of Shintaku's injuries. He retired, soon after, from the bench.

But as Shintaku's neurosurgeon, Dr. William Won, was at pains to point out, the official conclusion was also a medical impossibility.[18] X rays of Shintaku's injuries clearly showed not one but two blows to the skull, a pattern was hardly consistent with that of a "single fall". Following Keala's press conference, Won criticized the police conclusion and challenged Hardman to at least review the X rays with him. The next day Hardman admitted there were, in fact, two points of fracture shown on the X ray and that his report had been in error.

Even stranger, Shintaku suffered none of the usual secondary injuries commonly associated with hanging. There was, for example, no apparent damage to his voice box, a rather fragile piece of tissue normally damaged when the body's weight is dangled from the neck and throat. Further, Shintaku had none of the high, spinal injuries which typically accompany a hanging. In classic deaths of this type it is the weight of the body that snaps the neck, causing death. Shintaku also suffered a broken clavicle which is decidedly not common in hanging incidents and whose etiology was never explained.

Dr. Hideo Oshio, who treated the judge after the incident for hearing impairment, said that in his opinion Shintaku's injuries suggested not failed suicide by hanging but, instead, a "tremendous external force not sustained through a single fall." Added to this is the fact that police found no traces of blood in the beach house and no rope—frayed, broken or otherwise—that could have been used in an attempted suicide. Their explanation was that perhaps Shintaku's family members, who found the judge and called the ambulance, had cleaned it all up themselves. The judge's relatives categorically denied the suggestion. In a hospital bed interview given a local newspaper reporter after his surgery, Shintaku said in a clear voice that he had been attacked, presumably because of his decision in the Stevens case, but remembered nothing of the incident. Amnesia is not an uncommon result in head traumas of this magnitude.

Despite these glaring inconsistencies, the story died almost immediately after Keala's pronouncement of attempted suicide. Reporters throughout the life of the story had grabbed every interview possible and had written, faithfully, what each contestant in the public battle said from the day Judge Shintaku reversed the decision of Stevens's jury to the day the chief of police closed the book on his department's investigation. Weeks later, Harry Shintaku, the judge who became a victim, quietly left the hospital with a steel plate in his head.

The official police version, and thus the news stories that are now the public record, thus assert the following somewhat improbable sequence of events: The judge must have tried to hang himself—

twice—falling once from the perpendicular onto his temple and then, failing in that first attempt, immediately trying again. The first time he fell at an angle of perhaps forty degrees, striking his temple on the sharp edge of a conveniently located table with enough velocity to create the impression of a "tremendous external force" to his temple. Then, to create the second point of impact shown on the X ray, he must have dangled upside down from a ceiling beam by his heels before falling on his head. He committed this tortuously athletic feat, presumably in a state of depression or despair, while somehow avoiding all the usual secondary physical effects common to hangings (successful or otherwise): clear rope burns on the neck, laryngitic damage, and high spinal injury. Even could so bizarre a scenario be sustained, it would not explain the broken clavicle or the hearing loss which did not resemble a hanging injury but did suggest the aftereffects of an external "blow of tremendous force." Then the badly injured judge— or someone else—would have had to have cleaned up the beach house and taken all evidence away.

Although Honolulu reporters won no rewards for their coverage of these events, none were drummed from the profession either. Like the victims of Korsakov's syndrome, news folk were locked, day by day, into the isolated moments of each press conference revelation or attributable statement.[19] None looked beyond the context of a day's specific, attributed events or considered seeking the assistance of independent experts,[20] forensic textbooks, or plain common sense to try and string these disparate "facts" together.[21] The reports, read again after the fact, are devoid of any context—medical, political, or social—which could have given meaning to the isolated events (injury, investigation, and charges) or put the medically impossible lie of "suicide" into its proper frame.

Cooke's portrait was acknowledged as true. The Honolulu reporters' coverage was demonstrably incomplete and misleading. Yet she was cross-examined like a prisoner of war and then banished from the field while reporters for Honolulu newspapers and television stations remain on the job and their work, such as it was, stands today as a record of those 1981 events. Cooke's portrayal was all context, a concentrate of knowledge poured into the "fictional" persons who peopled the story. The work of Honolulu reporters covering the Shintaku case was all "fact," attributions that marched day by day through the news and yet failed to describe a scenario bearing the faintest resemblance to any theory that could account for the physical evidence.

Cooke, like Sam Johnson, was concerned with the context, the general picture of issues as they affected individuals. Honolulu's reporters were concerned with "facts," the attributable statements that make up the bulk of contemporary "news" or "journalism." Where do the lines lie between Cooke's true fiction and the "factual," if false, portrait of Shintaku's trials presented by the Honolulu media?

Honolulu's reportage of the Shintaku case was based on the generally accepted journalistic assumption that attributed fact is sufficient. Editorial judgement is for the op-ed page, while reporters need not and should not judge the statements of those they are sent to cover. For Samuel Johnson, however, it was precisely here that the hack showed his or her skill, probing on the basis of prior experience the limits of a single event's description. At least one of Cooke's transgressions was in the assumption that acknowledged truth and contextual description would outweigh accepted journalistic form. To deal contextually, as did Cooke and Johnson, is to describe an issue or complex occurrence through synoptic compression or summary description, compressing statements and cases into a single portrait. It is to choose a means of organizing data into a specific perspective rather than to assume, as did the reporters in Hawaii, that events would be self-ordering.

Honolulu reporters treated daily statements as facts whose presentation assumed a self-evident order. It was as if these discrete statements by individuals were in themselves sufficient for an understanding of the complex of events which, perhaps, began with the Stevens verdict and ended with Judge Shintaku in a hospital bed accused of an impossible suicide.

## FALSE TRUTHS

Cooke's true fiction and Honolulu's false truth—that is the problem of contemporary news. It would be too easy to charge the Honolulu reporters with being lazy and inept. If Cooke violated industry standards, as many have argued, the Hawaiian reporters adhered religiously to the form and standards of daily news. The issue these cases raise is the efficacy of an institutionalized set of journalistic practices which presumably guarantees veracity but ultimately leads, as in the Shintaku case, to the reportage of incomplete, misleading "false truths." The specific mechanism by which this process commonly occurs is the subject of this work. It argues that the bias is structural and rooted in the narrative form itself. The result is that news typically is constrained to present "false truths" through a consistent, structural transformation based in the journalistic form.

Others have argued a bias in the news, but their arguments have been from the posture of sociologic reflection, psychological introspection, economic rationalization, and political posture. This work does not deny the social and interpersonal arguments of others, but suggests instead that, to the extent that a structural bias can be demonstrated, the positions based on social and political theory may be symptoms and not the disease itself. News at heart is copy, words on the page written in a specific way, and the analysis of its form is central to understanding the content of the news.

Before examining what news "is," however, it will be useful first to consider what news defines itself to be and the clear limits of that definition. Then the narrative form of the news will be studied. Three separate descriptive languages are used in this exercise. The first is the "Five W's"—who, what, when, where and why—common to journalism schools and newspaper lore. The second is the language of semiology, which describes the relation between image and meaning in texts in general. The third language, used primarily in tracing the development of serial stories, is derived from information theory. These are complementary analytic postures, and their conjunction in this work provides a relatively complete system by which the form and content of news stories can be analyzed.

## NOTES

1. *Gulliver's Travels*, the political satire by Swift, enjoyed enormous popularity at the time. The use of that fictitious country's name, Lilliput, and the use of its denizens to stand for the houses of parliament was an open signal to all that this was, in fact, reportage of British legislative actions.

2. Details of this early journalistic experiment can be found in John Wain, *Samuel Johnson, A Biography* (New York: Viking Press, 1974); W. Jackson Bate, *Samuel Johnson* (New York: Harcourt Brace Jovanovich, 1975) and George Birkbeck Hill, *Boswell's Life of Johnson.* 6 vol. (New York: Harper and Brothers, 1891), 134-137. This volume of the often reprinted "Life" comes with a valuable index.

3. Guthrie was, according to Boswell, one of the first to designate himself an "author by profession" and a man "who deserved to be respectably recorded in the literary annals of this country." The contemporary distinction between author (books or plays) and journalist (periodical) was foreign to the age. "Author" inevitably described those who wrote in all forms—magazine, books, and poetry and criticism.

4. Wain, *Samuel Johnson*, 90.

5. Bate, *Samuel Johnson*, 206. Quoted from Hill, *Boswell's Life of Johnson*, and a passage cited by most who write on Johnson's life.

6. Boswell suggested that Guthrie listened to some of the debates and wrote up notes which were passed to Johnson for rewrite, but his report was partisan and written well after the fact. It seems clear that, session to session and debate to debate, the amount of information brought to Johnson on any specific day varied greatly. Sometimes there were quotes and synopses, but often he received no more than a list of speakers and statement of their broad topics.

7. Johnson did not prosper to the same extent. For him neither immediate fame nor fortune accrued. The economic disparity between publishers and writers was already clear in this nascent period of journalistic development. Johnson did acknowledge, however, payment for work completed and was satisfied with the money, which he badly needed.

8. Remember that parliamentary debate then was an often violent exercise in which insults and abuse were normal between members of majority and minority parties. The lines once drawn to separate the benches of opposing parties in the House were carefully measured to assure each was outside the sword range of the other.

9. Wain describes in the importance and power of Johnson's defence of Walpole while placing it within the context of both the writer's life work and the times. Wain, *Samuel Johnson*, 90-91.

10. She was further castigated for including in her job resume a college degree which was, in fact, fictitious. Her specific, central crime, however, was the story itself.

11. Paul Johnson, *A History of the English People*, 1972. Quoted in Paul Lihandis, "Room for a View," *The Buffalo Rocket*, Aug. 17,1988, 2.

12. On this point see Alvin Kernan, *Printing Technology, Letters and Samuel Johnson*, (Princeton, N.J.: Princeton University Press, 1988).

13. Ron Lovell, "Triumph of the Chi-Squares," *The Quill*, October, 1988, 22.

14. Geography professes to describe elements of man's relation with the spatial environment.

15. For a brief report of that decision see "The Right to Fake Quotes," *Time*, August 21, 1989, 49. In its reportage, *Time* condemns Malcolm's alleged use of interpretive quotes by itself quoting out of context a phrase from one of her previous articles to make it appear as if she new her actions were wrong.

16. Between October 7 and November 14, 1981, the *Honolulu Star-Bulletin* and *Honolulu Advertiser*, published almost daily stories and editorials on the Shintaku affair. Both papers are published under a joint operating agreement in which they maintain separate editorial but joint operating services. Stories from this period are listed separately for each paper in the newspapers' shared index, published annually. This overview of the case is drawn from the newspapers' files and from notes made by the author at the time of Shintaku's injuries. Honolulu's three major TV stations, each affiliated with one of the national networks (CBS, ABC, NBC) also covered the story extensively. The case is returned to in chapter 3 where the mechanisms by which the journalistic narrative form creates "false truths" are examined in detail.

17. Keala's quote was reported in both local newspapers and televised

by all local television stations.

18. Dr. Won was so angry at the official version that he would explain to people at cocktail parties how impossible it was for an individual to crush his skull in two places in an attempted suicide by hanging. One of those he talked to was then Gannett Fellow at the University of Hawaii Ron Ishoy. Ron Ishoy, *personal communication*, December, 1981.

19. Korsakov's syndrome is a fairly rare malady in which an individual loses all short-term memory. For a definition and case history see Oliver Sacks, *The Man Who Mistook His Wife for a Hat* (New York: Summit Books, 1985), 22-42.

20. For example: none asked Dr. Won or the patient for X rays of the skull that could have been sent to an impartial forensic pathologist for examination.

21. Common sense, for example, would dictate a reporter check on the characteristics of suicide by hanging in a forensic pathology textbook. Slightly more innovative would have been to try to simulate Shintaku's injuries by hanging a small doll and watching it fall. I tried it while researching this story in 1981. It was impossible.

# 1

# The News as Social Context

It is the form of news as it is currently reported—its definition of an event and its use of "attribution" by officials—that this work examines in an attempt to understand the effect and limits of its rules. The central argument will be that contemporary journalism has at its base one or more innate, institutionalized biases or structural flaws. These flaws may result in political or informational biases, but they are primarily rooted in the textual structure of the generally accepted narrative style that reporters use to describe specific events. To be more explicit, the hypothesis states that even when all the facts of a story can be shown to be correctly reported,[1] it may still be so slanted, so incomplete in its choice of fact or inaccurate in its manner of presentation as to be propaganda and not objective news.[2]

Indeed, it is through this "facticity," the accumulation of officially sanctioned, partial quotes about events whose boundaries are narrowly and arbitrarily prescribed, that contemporary news daily and consistently abdicates its promise. The question is not one of the competence or ability of a specific reporter or editor at any one newspaper or in any one situation, but rather the issue of an institutionalized bias at the heart of the concept of news today. Others who in the past have criticized the news as an information system have focused their analysis on the composition of a television news program or a newspaper's bureaucratic structure.[3] Rather than attempting an analysis at that level, this work focuses its attention at the level of the narrative, the news text itself.

Others have argued that bias enters news as a result of organizational socialization,[4] as a function of capitalist hegemony,[5] through "gatekeepers" within each organization,[6] or what Gaye Tuchman calls "rituals" of objectivity and performance. Failures of objectivity in journalism have been blamed on the physical limitations of print media, the economic considerations that bind industry managers, and even the fantasies that professionals bring to their work. Each of these views has its defenders and detractors. It is not the intention of this work to enter directly into debates on the sociology of the newsroom, the psychology of the journalist, or the issues of newsroom economics. But to the extent that a structural bias or flaw can be described as occurring within the narrative form of the news, the argument will be that these other factors may be the result of and are certainly dependent on the nature of that textual pattern.

This work  examines the narrative form itself, the generative rules of news writing as they are used in mundane stories. It is believed that to the extent that a narrative bias exists, its description may embrace the mechanisms of hegemony and the form in which those who believe they are performing an objective function present, instead, biased and incomplete reports. These result from the text, outgrowths of what is at base a narrative practice that has not been adequately studied. The argument is that the problem of facticity and false truths exists first and foremost at the level of the structure of the text itself. This study focuses its efforts at that level and only later attempts to integrate its findings into the political, sociological, and psychological debates.

Thus there is no attempt to interview or investigate the actors in the Hawaiian drama centering on Judge Shintaku's injuries. Issues of responsibility among the news directors, editors, and reporters who covered the Oahu story are  irrelevant, at this remove, to the stories themselves. They are the traces remaining of that complex of a 1981 event bundle. The value of the Hawaiian case is, in fact, precisely in its narrative reliance on the accurately reported  individual "facts"— the attributed statements by police, prosecutors, physicians, and other officials. The impression and conclusion, however, was either demonstrably false or, at the very least, suspect from any but the officially sanctioned perspective. The inaccuracies, which should have been evident to a first-year medical student, were never addressed by reporters or questioned by editors. What was said, the "facts" of the story, are what stood and stand as a record that lives in our present.

To the extent that this can be shown to be a typical result of the narrative form used by contemporary reporters, the result is that North American journalism appears, because of its flaws,  to become what it purports to most despise: a powerful propaganda  tool for the maintenance of the status quo and an organ of the literate and elite.[7] Because of its structural flaws it is too rarely a vehicle for the dissemination of  balanced, unprejudiced information or a force for social change.

Thus this work takes the political, sociological, and economic criticisms of the press and reformulates them at the level of the narrative mechanism. It  seeks a position in the dialogue on the nature of journalism that begins with the technique of the narrative irrespective of its subject.  This will  require, first, the search for and description of a  consistent, narrative pattern in contemporary journalism. That, in turn, requires the analysis of specific news stories  as if they were exotic artifacts from a distant culture and not items of such familiarity as to have a form whose rules appear self-evident or natural. The form in which news is written has such consistency and ubiquity as to be part of what phenomenologists have described as the "taken-for-granted world." To be so accepted means, often, not to be seen, and if news is to be studied for potential structural deficits, it must be taken from the assumed world and placed within that of the exotic. Just as Roland Barthes used his semiologic system to examine the content of French cultural artifacts ranging from movies to magazine text, so must news be seen as a systemic artifact in which the assumptions inherent in the form can be made overt.[8]

## NEWS AS FACT

Contemporary journalism presents itself as offering a record of reality that is as unbiased and as complete as possible.[9] Individual newspaper, newsmagazine, and broadcast stations each maintain a formidable system of editors, reporters, artists, and technicians whose job it is to gather, prepare and present periodic collections of nonfictional stories that mirror as closely as possible the unbiased—if editorially selected—facts of existence within their circulation worlds.[10] Daily and weekly news organs promise, in North America at least, the description of discrete and discontinuous events of presumed relevance to the lives of their auditors, those readers or viewers who choose to read a newspaper or magazine report, listen to a radio broadcast, or view a television news hour and accept it as a representation of shared reality.

Daily journalism, to put it another way, is supposed to be an unreflective exercise in which facts are presented in a specialized form without overt interpretation in as tightly written, legible and cohesive a manner as possible.[11] Were it reflective it would be not news but "commentary" or "opinion." This is what Graham Murdock calls the "canon of objectivity":

> The canon of objectivity requires that news should offer as complete a capture of events in the world as possible, and that the presentation of those accounts should not be shaped by the personal values or commitments of the journalists involved. The ideal of objectivity, then, rests on the claim that the news is accurate, comprehensive and neutral, and consists of independently verifiable facts that are clearly separated from expression of opinions or values.[12]

### Fact and Propaganda

In theory the news story—the objective description of an event in the world—should be easy to describe, analyze, and distinguish from its cousins, advertising and propaganda. Advertising is the presentation of facts or perspectives with the express purpose of selling or promoting an article, position or belief. Propaganda refers to the selective presentation of possibly spurious facts to advocate a political position or point of view. In reality, however, these are enormously plastic concepts whose boundaries shift from generation to generation and from writer to writer. It was once common in the British press, for example, to pay reviewers to cover new theatrical productions. Today, however, the payment to publications or reporters for information on a new show is advertising and the acceptance of money for a review would be viewed as immoral and grounds for the writer's dismissal. It remains common, however, for newsmen to use information distributed by a corporation's paid public relations functionaries whose job is the selective presentation of information ("news releases") favorable to their employers.

The relation between contemporary journalism and propaganda is at least as equivocal. Propaganda is both "the systematic propagation of a given doctrine" and "material disseminated by the proselytizers of a doctrine".[13] It can be argued that American news broadcasts and periodicals, despite pretensions to value-free reportage, regularly fulfill the first and almost certainly the second definition. Todd Gitlin, for example, describes the "dominion and continuance of an ideology through the news" as an unspoken, unacknowledged, persistent process by which large amounts of information are daily sifted into a single, journalistic perspective that adopts a single, official point of view.[14] The "frame of the news," the context in which stories are chosen and presented, is dominated by the quotes and observations of officials and accepts, usually without question, the official perspective of moderation as opposed to extremism, individualism as opposed to collectivism, gradual reform as opposed to radical change.[15] The result is a news context that "precludes a full explanation of dissenting views."[16]

The domination of the news by official policy makers has been described frequently, but it is so crucial an element in our argument that it deserves one more exposition. One survey of 2,850 stories in the *N.Y. Times* and *Washington Post* found that almost 80 percent of the stories in both publications were based on the official pronouncements of public officials.[17] Another study of 2,500 stories in those papers found that 78 percent of the articles were based on statements by public officials.[18] These stories, an overwhelming majority, typically present as fact and without critical examination the statements of officials with a vested interest in a single position or policy. The poor, the black, the disenfranchised, and the unemployed, on the other hand, tend to make the news only when they appear to threaten or confound the known values and established order. As Chomsky has shown, the result, at least in terms of United States reportage of foreign affairs, leads to a consistent exclusion of facts unacceptable to U.S. officials and a consistent bias supporting official U.S. positions.[19] As Lewis H. Lapham notes succinctly:

The American press is, and always has been, a booster press, its editorial pages characteristically advancing the same arguments as the paid advertising copy. Together with the teaching in the schools, the national media preserve the myths that the society deems precious, reassuring their matrons . . . that all is well, that the American truths remain securely in place, that the banks are safe, our generals competent, our presidents interested in the common welfare, our artists capable of masterpieces, our weapons invincible and our democratic institutions the wonder of an admiring world.[20]

In short, American newspapers can be seen as presenting "the systematic propagation of a given doctrine"; the dictionary's primary definition of propaganda. It is precisely for this reason that critics, like Chomsky, argue that "the media's purpose in a free society is to manufacture consent among the governed, rallying the population to endorse elite decisions. Propaganda, in effect, is for a free society what force is to dictatorships."[21]

*Pravda.* This is the way news has come to be. It is not a necessary pattern. The Soviet news system, to take one contemporary example, is characterized by a very different balance between official and civilian views. Despite a near-universal North American assumption that the "free press" is unbiased and populist in comparison with the presumably elitist and propaganda-laden Soviet news, a 1988 report in *Editor and Publisher* (a newspaper trade magazine) revealed that over 79 percent of the official Russian newspaper's content originated not from press conferences or official statements but with citizen complaints, queries, revelations, and observations. *Pravda's* staff devoted the majority of its time to investigation of these reader tips and not to slavish coverage of Kremlin views. Finally, one presumes, although the story did not report, that the degree of *Pravda's* copy that is official in origin is overtly so and therefore easy for a skeptical reader to discount. It is at least theoretically possible to argue that the form and pattern of news in *Pravda* (*Isvestia*, etc.) is more responsive to Soviet readers' concerns than the *New York Times* or the *Washington Post* is to those of their respective clientele.

*Sports.* For sports "news" reportage, the lines between news, advertising and propaganda are even more blurred. Television networks bid, for example, for the exclusive right to televise Olympic games and present them, at least in the United States, as news. Both broadcast and print journalists create, every four years, through supposedly unbiased reportage of an international event, a dramatic contest between U.S athletes—heroes—and "foreign" competitors who were "challengers."[22] Advertisers queued for the right to pay to be "Olympic sponsors" in Los Angeles in 1984, using the game's logo and prestige (with contestants sometimes wearing their corporate symbol) in return. The name of a gold medalist may be news, but the format and thrust of Olympic television coverage is demonstrably advertising and nationalistic propaganda.

At the 1984 Summer Olympics in Los Angeles, California, Canadian broadcasters protested the degree to which American television coverage focused on U.S. athletes to the virtual exclusion of non-U.S. participants.[23] U.S. news coverage was seen by the Canadian broadcasters (who shared broadcast markets in trans-border regions) as so slanted and biased as to prejudice their attempts to report shared events.[24] Reportage of actual sports events, commercial advertising by official sponsors of the Olympics, and nationalistic propaganda—the assertion of U.S. supremacy and the superiority of the U.S. socio-economic system—all were hopelessly confused in the television coverage of those games.

## FACT AND BIAS

Despite these inconsistences, daily journalism purports to present "real facts." At least in theory, the essence of the news as it is both taught and practiced today is the presentation of objective, unbiased information free from the taint of slander or libel: somebody died, somebody was jailed, the speech of an official was heard and is presented to the readers or viewers as news. Daily stories are defined, as they were in the Shintaku reports, by the ability of a reporter or news organization to prove, if questioned, that the journalistic narrative offered without malice an accurate if selected trace of single event. This is the basic conceptual framework with which sometimes complex processes are distilled and aspects of them isolated to fashion distinct news stories measured, professionally, in column inches or, in a broadcast format, seconds of time.[25] Modern news folk, at least in North America, stand by the "'journalistic method,' i.e. the modern reportorial stance—probing, fact-obsessed, "objective"—which evolved through the 19th century" and has become, in the later part of the Twentieth century, an unexamined given.[26]

One problem with this perspective is that the general public does not, in the United States at least, appear to hold the success of that exercise in great esteem. Polls since the 1970s have consistently shown public confidence in journalism on a par with confidence in politicians and significantly behind that accorded school officials.[27] More than 70 percent of those surveyed did not trust either the politicians who were a newspaper's primary source of information or, not surprisingly, the periodical itself, which provided a primary arena for the politicians' views. It is with some chagrin that news people find that viewers and readers do not maintain a high estimation of either the daily content or the general perspective of most contemporary news organs. Public opinion surveyors periodically check and recheck the degree to which Americans believe or trust their domestic news sources. The logical conclusion, that most readers and viewers assume news is not an unbiased, accurate, germane representation of the world, is a continuing source of concern to many professionals.

Nor is this distrust solely the property of the uneducated reader.

Articulate and educated individuals, including some journalists, argue generally or anecdotally that news is persistently slanted, inaccurate, or incomplete. For example, playwright Arthur Miller, who had extensive experience as the subject of many news stories, suggested that the problem was systemic, rising from the necessity of newspapers and magazines to publish consistently and rapidly. Summing up press coverage of Marilyn Monroe, Miller said:

> You know, journalists usually come around with an angle. They have to. They simply never get the time or the opportunity to hang around long enough to decide anything. Over the years, that angle becomes the easiest [if prejudicial] thing to do, and its gotten, in Marilyn's case, to be very fruitful in terms of copy. And they keep pounding on her all the time until the thing becomes reality.[28]

Poet Robert Frost was even more succinct in his view of journalists. It was the paraphrase, the attempt to summarize what for Frost could not be condensed, that infuriated him. As he said of one reporter: "My grounds for wanting to let him have both fists in succession in the middle of the face are chiefly that he stated me so much worse than I know I state myself."[29] Such condemnation by poets and writers may, perhaps, be expected and yet remain worrisome in light of generally declining public esteem. But veteran reporter Mark Harris admits to urging his friends not to read newspapers and to spurn television news as limited, ephemeral and unreliable. He thus echoes Thomas Jefferson who was, I believe, the first to argue that a man who did not read might be better informed than one who did because the potential for less information also meant the certainty of a decreased amount of disinformation.[30]

Reaction by contemporary news professionals to such attacks typically has been to investigate individual incidents of alleged bias but not to question the general framework or organization of the news story as a form of information itself. When a CBS documentary[31] charging that U.S. Army Gen. William C. Westmoreland falsified accounts of enemy troop strength in Vietnam resulted in a $120 million libel action, for example, intense and involved studies—by CBS and by others—were begun into that specific story's generation.[32] Unquestioned, however, was the general narrative structure of the story itself, the format of its copy, and the wisdom of its editorial reliance on disparate "facts" to organize the information that was the framework of that show.

## NEWS AS A SOCIAL CONSTRUCT

News is a social construct empowered by a cultural history and a tradition of institutional practice based on material and cognitive realities. As such it has, in Western's words, the "power of definition."[33] While it may not mirror reality—the omniscient eye—it becomes a record of and the accepted version of past events. As Tuchman puts it, "the act of making news is the act of constructing reality itself rather than [simply] a picture of reality."[34] Thus any report, whatever its inherent bias or failings, confirms an occurrence and simultaneously changes it into an event by placing it in a specific context:

> News is a window on the world . . . but like any frame that
> delineates the world, the news frame may be considered
> problematic. The view through the window depends upon
> whether the window is large or small, has many panes or
> few, whether the glass is opaque or clear.[35]

### Objectivity

Others have commented on the degree to which a social context defines, politically and socially, the information that will be presented. The frame offers an encoded "preferred reading." Given possible multiple readings of mass media, the power of the news lies in its ability to ensure that readers or other active users are presented with the same or similar bureaucratically created and ideologically embedded accounts. Hence the frame may be more important than the specific details it organizes.[36]

The assertion that all news functions as the frame or context of an event, thus distorting by the act of selective description, affirms the proposition that real objectivity is a chimera, a false Grail that all observers may seek but which remains unobtainable. In physical science this has become a central truth of physical reality,[37] and in social science it is an equally accepted, if more bitter truth.[38] By being involved in an event—even as recorder—we influence it. As Max Weber argued and David R. Caploe restates, it is manifest "that even the most apparently simple 'description' is, in reality, highly dependent on a whole series of major and fundamental analytic assumptions that are usually implicit."[39] "The facts"—or any fact—cannot and do not stand alone but are mediated through a complex of bias and assumption that can and must be made overt before information can be assessed. Journalism is not unique in this regard, although it is unusual, perhaps, in its members' resistance to the self-reflective analysis of its prejudices and preconceptions.

If news is not and, indeed, cannot be objective (free from bias and individual perspective) what can be said about it? First, it can be shown to be consistent, following a general pattern of presentation accepted, usually without question, by journalists and readers alike. From its grammatical structure to its choice of topics, the news follows a specific pattern that can be examined and discussed. The use of the English language, choice of paragraph styles and definition, techniques of opposing paragraphs for balance are, for example, all aspects of a reportorial style currently accepted by television, radio, newspaper, and magazine reporters writing for local, regional, or national presentation.[40]

Further, mainstream journalism in all its forms is highly predictable in the way it organizes information. News professionals (radio, newspaper, newsmagazine or television) can be expected to cover most classes of occurrence—murder, courts, and natural disasters—in set ways. As Joseph T. Scanlon and Suzanne Alldred noted:

> The mass media behave roughly the same way when responding to all major events whether these are natural or man-made disasters, criminal occasions such as assassination attempts, hijackings, hostage takings or other acts of terrorism or simply major, unexpected events.[41]

This is not a new or radical view, although it may be an uncomfortable one for those who wish published or televised reports to mirror precisely the apparent uniqueness of the events they choose or are assigned to cover. But for coverage to occur, consistency and predictability are both a virtue and necessity. The world must be "tamed to meet the needs of a production system in many respects bureaucratically organized."[42]

Structural analysis provides one method by which one can attempt to understand the way the world is ordered. It assumes a series of principles that can be made overt and whose description makes clear elements of the whole. It is therefore integrative and hierarchic. As Roland Barthes stated: "In order to conduct a structural analysis, it is thus first of all necessary to distinguish several levels or instances of description and to place these instances within a hierarchic, integrationary perspective."[43]

Structurally, one is interested in the form as well as the specific datum of any story. To the degree that the structure is both consistent and predictable, one should be able to analyze specific stories as examples of broader, narrative classes and say: What is true of A is true of $A_1.....A_n$. This is to say that an examination of the news for inherent bias and systematic exclusion must be structural and can be carried from one to another level of journalistic output at stages of story generation, research, and production.

But any such analysis must begin at the basic level of the grammar of news, the structural characteristics of its text. The concept of a frame in journalism typically refers to social and political perspectives or constraints that reporters, editors, and producers bring to or have imposed upon their work. Here the "frame" will be taken to mean the narrative form itself, the pattern of words that create the copy that becomes the news. Issues of information, bias, and social content raised by others result from the text, and it is in the domain of the text that the mechanisms of embedded meaning must be found.

## NEWS AS MYTH

Practitioners insist that news reportage is neither propaganda nor advertising. It is, most argue, as objective as possible a description of discrete and discontinuous events. Reporters, from this perspective, are not writers or thinkers participating in the event itself but recorders whose function it is to capture the speech and actions of a specific time and place so they can be disseminated to a wider audience. Like Lévi-Strauss's anthropology, reportage becomes at its best a *technique de dépaysement* and the best reporter, like the consummate anthropologist, is not simply a neutral observer but a man distanced from his subject and in control of that alienation.[44]

Clearly this is the exception rather than the rule, in news reportage at least as much as anthropology. Reporters are not impartial observers, and their stories do not necessarily define accurately or completely the discrete events they purport to cover dispassionately. While Johnsonian techniques of editorial involvement were used to paint a portrait that all agree is true, the reporter/writer was castigated for transgressing assumed bounds and rules. The lines between news as a *technique de dépaysement* and as a *technique de politique* are, as Chomsky, Gitlin, and others have pointed out, continually blurred or blurry.

"If you can't put the news in perspective," argues one journalism instructor, "you're not a journalist—you're a tape recorder."[45] The baggage of personal history, individual or cultural perspective, and professional background all newspeople bring to the coverage of any event mediates their reports. Tape recorders, for example, have a clear function, and while tapes can be modified and edited, at least their function and limitations are clear. Sounds of a specific range and intensity when emitted within the range of an activated microphone are picked up indiscriminately and held on tape until altered or erased.

The reporter's role is more equivocal. A two-hour speech is condensed to perhaps a forty-five second radio report or twelve inches of newspaper copy. He or she cannot tell the proverbial "truth, whole truth and nothing but the truth." There is not time enough on television or space enough in the newspaper for even a tithe of that complex truth. Nor can any newspaper or broadcast station deliver what the *New York Times* promises: "All the News that's Fit to Print." Even if one could describe what is and is not "fit to print" by some objective standard, there is no room for so much data and there are not enough writers to fashion it. If the reporter's job is to selectively describe an event, the questions multiply immediately—what event, based on what subjects, and for whom? Is the report fashioned for some amorphous public at large or to satisfy the editor who sent the person out? Who judges the story—the reporter, members of the public, or one of a pantheon of editors whose job is to assure that appropriate stories march through a television news hour or across a newspaper page?[46]

The ultimate purpose of a recording machine is clear— to capture sounds indiscriminately within a certain decibel level issued issued within the range of its microphone—but the ultimate service of a newsperson is more equivocal. Newspapers and television and radio stations serve first and foremost an economic function. They exist to create profits and make money for the owners through the sale of individual copies and of space within the publication or news broadcast to advertisers. The latter are not primarily interested in public service but rather in advertising products to increase profit margins. Thus the newsperson works for a corporation whose primary purpose is the return of capital to the corporation owners. The corporation's critical clients are a group of other corporate entities who buy space or time slots abutting the news in the hopes of selling more of a specific product and thus of increasing their profits as well.

The extent to which these realities limit or define the news reporter's job and the degree to which they shape editorial perspective is unclear. At one end of the debate is Mark Crispin Miller, who said of television reporters simply that they "serve commercial television. Their aim is to boost ratings: They always tell the people what they think the people are already thinking."[47] At the other end of the spectrum is the news professional's insistence, taught in schools of journalism, that news is absolutely separate from economic consideration, that issues of advertising and economics never affect a story's content. Between them, perhaps, lies the measure of truth. News is a mediated, synthetic product, and the best indication of its warring factions may be the story itself. There in the narrative of specific stories are the traces of decisions, judgments, selections, and battles. There is where we will soon have to begin.

### Semiology and Myth
To understand this problem at the level of the text it may be helpful to consider a specific vocabulary with which reportage can be analyzed anew. The French structuralist Roland Barthes offers a paradigm called semiology.[48] It promises one way out of the maze, allowing the narrative form of news reportage to be described as a category of myth. Myth does not, here, mean a fairy story or ancient tale told long ago around camp fires in early or preliterate worlds. Myth describes, in Barthes's language, a consistent system of narrative representation in which symbols (words) have cultural and contextual relevance. Myth is an attempt to describe the cultural context of specific human events, actions, or artifacts using a structuralist perspective that is linguistic in origin.

To say that news reports present a mythic, narrative system is to say that it describes signs (actions or events) that are presented through a series of cultural filters which include values of the reporting and reading culture. News reportage thus takes the raw events of our world and places them in a unifying context, a translation that renders them comprehensible and safe to readers or viewers, who can disregard that system of presentation just as readers of this passage do not stop to think of the degree to which the language (English) and style (academic-narrative) that order these words as I write also define and limit my mode of presentation.

An example Barthes uses to make overt how this mythic system functions as a frame  is the cover photograph of a *Paris Match* magazine showing a young black soldier in a French uniform saluting, with his eyes uplifted, the French tricolor flag. The photographic image is sign (a man stood for an instant at a time and place and his image was captured on film using an indelible chemical process). What he signifies—the meaning carried by the image itself and the source of its power—is France as empire with all its citizens (of all colors and in any location, even, perhaps, Algiers) faithfully serving the fatherland. At a second level of meaning this signifier, a black soldier giving the French salute, brings together ideas of race, nationality, colonialism, and imperialism simultaneously. Finally, what is signified, the underlying imperative, is hidden by the sign itself. Here it is, the photo says, the French empire with the ideals of liberty, equality, and fraternity turned out in imperialistic or at least military splendor.

Barthes's system of meaning thus describes an information system imbedded in the narrative. In this case the sign was a photograph that pictured an individual saluting. The photograph captured and emphasized details of an "objective event" that signified simultaneously  certain social and political messages. The photograph was placed in a magazine (or run in the newspaper or used on television) where its political message resonated from but may have been obscured in the sign—a photographic image presented in a national paper whose reproductive screen is perhaps 350 dots per inch. The editor's selection of the  photo, one of presumably hundreds he had to choose from, was based not merely on aesthetic value or abstract composition, but ultimately on its mythic value: the interplay of sign, signifer, and signified which together loaded the original signifer with meaning. It is myth precisely to the degree that this interplay occurs and seemingly isolated signs are taken over by cultural meaning and messages. Thus it is not a harmless and value-free record of a moment in time at a single place, but an encoded statement of politics, empire, race, and allegiance.

### Sign, Signifier and Signified

While the language is specific in Barthes's analysis, others have commented on the three legs that must inform all opinion. More than sixty years ago, Lippmann noted that "the analyst of public opinion must begin, then, by recognizing the triangular relationship between the scene of action, the human picture of that scene and the human response to that picture working itself out upon the scene of action."[49] His observations, prescient and penetrating for the time, dealt with the general problem of the objectivity of the observer and not the issue of the way in which meaning was imbedded into the narrative form. In the intervening sixty years, techniques of linguistic analysis, structuralist theory (in social science and well as linguistics), and content analysis have been devised to allow one to see the specific datum as a part of the whole and the individual, apparently banal rule as part of a larger social structure.

"*Joe Died.*" Seeing news as a structural system of representation provides a certain distance and a perspective of its own which Barthes's semiology can analyze. His system, ultimately, allows the reconciliation of the traditional view of reportage—"the description of discrete events"—and the criticism of individuals such as Chomsky that "news is propaganda." This becomes clear in the general structure of the attributed newspaper sentence. Consider, for example, the information for a story describing the death from heroin overdose of an individual whom the police suspected of trafficking in drugs. It begins with an event (Joe died), which is placed in official context (Joe died, the police said) and given import by the police suspicions (Joe, a suspected drug dealer, was shot Thursday, police said). The death, the event of Joe's demise, can become a sign to be treated by the reporter. But what is to be signified by that death (Joe represents an illegal, antisocial activity requiring police intervention) comes not from the event itself but rather from the officials' involvement (he died unnaturally, else why would they be involved?). Finally, the implicit message (drugs are evil and police fight evil drugs) is far removed from the sign and subsumed in the political war against the use of controlled substances, which may have, in the end, little to do with this specific death.

"Myth hides nothing and flaunts nothing: it distorts: myth is neither a lie nor a confession: it is an inflection," Barthes argues.[50] Thus news as myth distorts not consciously or dramatically—as many presume overt propaganda must—but by "inflection," by choice of sign and level of attention. Do we quote Joe's grief-stricken mother who says he was a good boy accidently addicted to drugs while being treated at a Veteran's Hospital where the standard of care was abysmal?[51] Does the reporter credit Joe's girlfriend who says Joe was in fact no longer using drugs (and thus his death was related to some other complex of events)? Or do we accept the police report and base the narrative on its official view moralizing, at least by inference, that drugs always lead to an untimely end?

Normally we simply quote the police, who signify authority, professionalism, social consensus and investigatory prowess. To a newspaper of record they *are* the record, signifying the judicial system that is America's guarantee of fair treatment, equal protection under the law and so on.. News's relation to myth is, as Barthes argues, not one of truth but of use. The truth of Joe's death is not necessarily informed by the police official's statement. It tells us less than nothing about the man, the degree of his drug use, or the reasons for it. It is useful for contemporary politicians to say that cocaine (or heroin or marijuana or crack) is a scourge but that does not mean, necessarily, that it is true. Pharmacological literature has consistently described cocaine, for example, as neither physically addictive or biologically harmful except when used in massive amounts. Cocaine is far less physically damaging to humans than state-subsidized drugs— tobacco or alcohol[52]— but promulgation of this fact is not politically or

**Illustration 1**
**Barthes's Soldier: Levels of Meaning**

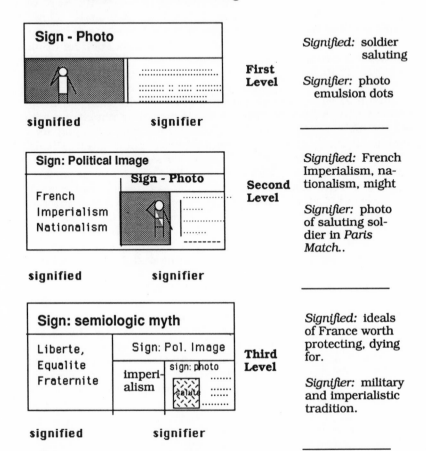

**LEVEL 1.**
The sign is a combination of the pattern of dots and the recognition of the image as that of a French Soldier, Black, saluting the French Flag.

**LEVEL 2.**
This combination of signified (photo image) and signifier ( photo dots) become, together, a signifier alone. They are a political sign meaning French Imperialism, active French, nationalism.

**LEVEL 3.**
At another level the *political sign*, which in turn is based on the *photo sign*, means the highest French ideals worth defending, fighting for or dying for.

culturally useful at present and thus generally ignored in all but the most technical of biochemical literatures.[53]

In Barthes's language, myth is "depoliticized speech" that reflects a bourgeois ideology born in the Nineteenth century. It "records facts or perceives values, but refuses explanations; the order of the world can be seen as sufficient or ineffable, it is never seen as significant."[54] This is precisely why the police investigators and not Joe's mother would be quoted. The police's and therefore the reporter's interest and perspective is bounded by the judicial system, which does not seek the context of the event or the significance of an individual life. Rather, it allocates an event's place within proscribed rules of socially sanctioned right or wrong. Reasons and explanations, antecedent contexts, and mitigating circumstances do not require, in this model of myth, interpretation or assessment. The apparently simple, declarative statement that Joe died, according to the police, can be passed off as sufficient. It says nothing, in the end, about Joe—his life, his possible habituation or the context of his demise. It is sufficient and insignificant, part of the daily dross of a police reporter's beat. Overtly it says nothing about drug use, drug abuse, the specific causes, or social effects of chemical habituation. It says a great deal, however, by inference and exclusion. Like Dragnet's Sergeant Friday, reporters can insist on "just the facts, Ma'am," and deny their brief reaches beyond the role of record and into the complex of inference and social order.

### Unary Transformations

The levels of imbedded meaning, the progression from the original sign to the affirmation of the final myth is clear. There is little ambiguity in its message and little room for a reader to ponder its meanings or nuances. It is, borrowing from the language of generative grammar, unary in the progression from original signifier (Joe in physical extremis) to final signifier to final sign:

> A transformation is unary if, through it, a single series is generated by the base: such are the passive, negative, interrogative and emphatic transformations. The Photograph is unary when it emphatically transforms "reality" without doubling it, without making it vacillate (emphasis is a power of cohesion): no duality, no indirection, no disturbance. The unary Photograph has every reason to be banal . . . ."The subject," says one handbook for amateur photographers, "must be simple, free of useless accessories; this is called the search for unity."[55]

This, Barthes argues, is a typical quality of the news photo and, I will argue later, equally typical in journalism's written form. The photo of the French soldier saluting was effective precisely because it lacked resonance. Its emphatic refusal to describe events outside a series of socially accepted precepts led the viewer (or reader) to a political position and statement. It insisted on a specific meaning while it trumpeted what appeared to be a picture or story filled with content. In photography, one is reminded of *Life* magazine's decision in 1937 not to use photographs by Andre Kertész because his images "spoke too much" and opened the doors to shifting references, which its editors did not want.

In the story of Joe's death, a similar series of transformations occurs, leading without question to a specific cultural message. The signifier in this generic story depends not on the events of Joe's death but on what police say are the circumstances. The reporter quotes the police officer, who says Joe was being investigated for drug dealing, perhaps adding with a sigh that Joe was "another victim of cocaine." Had the investigation continued perhaps it would have been shown that Joe was in fact neither selling nor using drugs at all. The headline reads "Another Victim of Cocaine" and the meaning, whatever the facts of Joe's life may have been, is set in the story—by "fact" and in narrative context—forever.

### Myth and Reality

Thus the news as myth gives a "natural image of this [culturally defined] reality," forming an umbrella and overview that can shelter both Chomsky and other critics from the rain of complaint by those who argue as an article of faith that news is truth. This inherent value system—the mythic language—describes a reportorial perspective in which events consistently are mediated through a single complex of cultural values. Two examples used by Chomsky and Accuracy in Media, a watchdog group, will suffice to show how structurally similar events are described differently when mediated through this mythic lens.[56]

The 1986 Russian downing of an off course, Korean passenger airplane near its coast was editorially condemned in the United States as an "unforgivable act."[57] In 1988, however, the U.S. military's destruction of a nonmilitary passenger airplane on its appointed course in the Persian Gulf was generally described in the U.S. news media as a tragic but understandable accident resulting from then current hostilities in that geographic region. Similarly, Russian involvement in an Afghanistan civil war was decried as adventurism by U.S. news organs, which in the 1960s and early 1970's, had supported an equivalent American involvement in the Vietnamese civil war.

Structurally, both sets of events were separately consistent. Both countries claimed, in their respective incursions, to be present at the legitimate request of a recognized and sympathetic government fighting rebel forces in a civil war. In each case an unarmed, civilian airplane was shot down by the respective super power. But the structural similarities between these events—East and West—were largely ignored or denied by American journalists because they were not in accord with the prevailing sociopolitical perspective that pits American virtue against Soviet evil. After all, as then President Ronald Reagan was fond of pointing out, the U.S.A. was a light to the world while the

U.S.S.R. was an "Evil Empire". Thus in their reportage of these two structurally similar but politically different events, U.S. media followed the prejudices of their national leaders. The similarities and responsibility for lives lost was not, really, the point because, as Barthes noted, "men do not have with myth a relationship based on truth, but on use."[58] Use is defined in news by the sources a newsman chooses and, as we have seen, these are largely official. Truth is who reporters quote—"President Bush said," "Police Chief Keala said," "Governor Ariyoshi said." Thus news reports become, as Chomsky suggests, propaganda. It is not the work of a perfidious cabal, however, but a banal and unconscious reflex, the sum of assumptions that pour through at the level of the sign.

If news is myth, however, it cannot operate simply in the domain of political reportage. That would be too limited and would set apart reporters, editors, and readers of international affairs from the general newsroom group. In most city newsrooms the same editor who lays out a page of local copy also handles international reports. The style of news runs seamlessly across the page from political to economic to city beats at the scales of international, national, regional, and local reports. If news is myth, then its bias must pervade the form of mundane reportage as well as international stories. One can postulate generative and "taken-for-granted" rules, by which the social bias is inserted into mundane descriptions of real-time reports, "depoliticizing" as it transforms complex events into a publishable form. The means by which this occurs is explored in the third chapter, which analyzes a category of apoliticized reports of real-time events.

Thus to the extent news can be described as myth, it presents as objective "truth" a specific and proscribed reality that is based on a cultural inflection. The question is how one can study this "inflection" in contemporary news. If it exists as a structural pattern it must be pervasive in not only political and international reportage but mundane stories as well. Thus, the next chapters will examine examples of police stories, obituaries and newspaper reports based on coroner inquests in an attempt both to define the narrative form and to describe the way in which that form systematically transforms specific signifiers into socially potent symbols.

## NOTES

1. That definition of accuracy is, fundamentally, a legal one that judges the degree to which statements are fair and accurate and protect both the writer and his employer from charges of libel and slander.

2. It would be interesting to correlate the results of this project with opinion surveys describing public dissatisfaction with the news. That, however, will be beyond the scope of this project, which focuses on forms of narrative production and not on values as perceived by gen-

eral readership. That public dissatisfaction with or distrust of news reports is based on a perceived and consistent bias is an argument which could be both made and tested.

3. See, for one example, Av Westin, "Inside the Evening News," *New York*, October 18, 1982, pp. 48-56; Herbert T. Gans, *Deciding What's News* (New York: Pantheon,1979); Guy Tuchman, *Making News: A Study in the Construction of Reality*, (New York: Free Press, 1978), 12.

4. Walter Breed, "Social Control in the Newsroom," *Social Forces* no. 33 (1955), 326-35.

5. For a summary of this argument and a review of all these positions see Allan Rachlin, *News as Hegemonic Reality*, (New York: Praeger, 1988).

6. Rachlin cites White as the first to present the idea of gatekeepers in David M. White, "'The 'Gatekeepers': A Case Study in Selection of News," *Journalism Quarterly*, no. 27 vol.1 (1950), 383-90.

7. This project confines itself to Canadian and U.S. media. To the degree that the form is a function of culture, the assumptions underlying news may and indeed do change. The cross-cultural study of news remains an untouched mine of information for the communications researcher.

8. See, for example, Susan Sontag, ed., *A Barthes Reader* (New York: Hill and Wang, 1982); Roland Barthes,*The Eiffel Tower and other Mythologies* (New York: Hill and Wang, 1979); Roland Barthes,*The Pleasure of the Text* (New York: Hill and Wang, 1975).

9. This is axiomatic. William Morris, ed., *The American Heritage Dictionary of the American Language* (New York: American Heritage Publishing Co., 1969), 884-885, defines "news" as "recent events and happenings, especially those that are unusual or notable." Secondary definitions include: "Information about recent events of general interest, especially as reported by newspapers, periodicals, radio, or television."

10. Thus we have the *New York Times*'s promise of "all the news that's fit to print." Media advertising promises increasingly, in the words of one newspaper's television campaign, to "bring the world to you."

11. Magazine journalism promises, in some cases, an interpretive power. *Time*, for instance, promises to interpret events for its readers while *Readers' Digest* condenses events.

12. Graham Murdock,"Misrepresenting Media Sociology: A reply to Anderson and Sharrock," *Sociology*, 12, (1980), 457-68. Quoted in

Rachlin, *News as Hegemonic Reality*, 126.

13. Morris, ed., *The American Heritage Dictionary*, 1048.

14. Todd Gitlin, *The Whole World is Watching: Mass Media in the Making an Unmaking of the New Left*, (Berkeley: University of California Press, 1980). Quoted in Edward Diamond, *The Last Days of Television* (Cambridge: M.I.T. Press, 1982), 241-2.

15. Edwin Diamond, *The Last Days of Television*, 148. Diamond summarizes Gitlin, who in turn relies on the perspective of Irving Goffman. The point is widely recognized. The problem, of course, is that nobody knows what to do with it.

16. Martin Mittelstaedt, "Is It Really All the News that's Fit To Print?" The (Toronto) *Globe and Mail*, October 8, 1988, p. D. 3. Chomsky's analysis of American media, especially its coverage of foreign affairs, has been exhaustive, intellectually rigorous, and damning. See, for example, Noam Chomsky, *Necessary Illusions: Thought Control in Democratic Societies* (Toronto, Canada: CBC Enterprises, 1989).

17. Diamond, *The Last Days of Television*. He in turn extensively quotes Gans, *Deciding What's News* whose source was content studies of these papers.

18. *Editor and Publisher*, May 9, 1981, 116. From an interview with *Mother Jones* magazine editor Adam Hochschild.

19. Chomsky, *Necessary Illusions*. The body of this study is a painstaking demonstration of the degree to which information was systematically excluded from U.S. newspapers but published in other countries or alternate sources.

20. Lewis H. Lapham, *Money and Class in America* (New York: Ballintine Books,1988), 50.

21. Martin Mittelstaedt, "Is it really All the News that's Fit to Print?" For the full argument by Chomsky see: Samuel Herman and Noam Chomsky, *Manufacturing Consent* (New York: Pantheon Books, 1988).

22. This occurs, of course across North America at the local level as "home" teams are touted and supported by local newsmen and broadcasters who trumpet wins and bemoan losses for those regionally supported groups. This becomes spectacularly overt, for example, in the coverage given each season to Ohio State University's "Buckeye" football team and its individual members who personify, in the language of area advertisers, "Buckeye Country" which covers at least a four county area.

23. At the 1984 Olympic Games in Los Angeles, for example, Canadian

Broadcasters objected to both the commentary of American broadcasters like Howard Cossell and the choice of activities for broadcast. The former was seen as biased against non-American athletes, and scheduling decisions ignored Canadian needs and athletes to focus on American necessities. The protest did effect some change.

24. Indeed, it is precisely this issue of inherent bias that has caused Canadian governments to support a national broadcasting network as a counterweight to the U.S. perspective. It was also the rationale behind Bill C-85 which in 1975 effectively barred Time from publishing a Canadian edition and opened the market for McLean's magazine, a wholly Canadian publication.

25. Others have studied the organization of the news and the means by which events are chosen and changed from real events to media portrayal. Gans, Deciding What's News, is one example. For balance, the story of Time-Life, Inc., and its avowedly "interpretive" approach is well worth reading. See David Cort, The Sin of Henry R. Luce: An Anatomy of Journalism (Secaucus, N.J.: Lyle Stuart, 1974). The degree to which information is, in fact, a function of technology was examined eloquently by Marshall McLuhan, The Gutenberg Galaxy (Toronto, Canada: University of Toronto Press, 1962). Other treatments of all these topics abound.

26. Origins of this perspective are viewed by some as being primarily Nineteenth century, growing from the then emerging U.S. popular press. Others see it as more appropriately assigned to the present century's growing sense of professionalism in all fields and, simultaneously, of journalism as a distinct profession. Dan Schiller, Objectivity and the News, (Pittsburg: University of Pennsylvania Press, 1981) is an exponent of the first view, and Michael Shudson, Discovering the News (New York: Basic Books, 1978) of the second. Important to that argument is Walter Lippmann, Public Opinion (New York: MacMillan, 1926). What seems most likely is that Nineteenth century scientism lead to a growing, Twentieth century emphasis on ideals of objectivity, acceptance of the "scientific method" as a general means of knowing, and the emphasis on professional as opposed to trade associations.

27. A summary of Gallup polls first published in Editor and Publisher from 1973-1980, were collected by Thomas A. Schwartz in "A Proposal for a Research Project Measuring Freedom of the Press Ideology" (unpublished manuscript, Ohio State University, 1980), 13.

28. Quoted by Mark Harris in "The Last Article," Short Work of It: Selected Writings by Mark Harris (Pittsburgh: University of Pittsburgh Press, 1970), 41. Harris is best known as an author but was, for a number of years, a journalist who wrote for, among other publications, Life magazine.

29. Ibid., 43.

30. Ibid., 28. "I seldom read a newspaper, and you shouldn't read one, either."

31. The documentary was called "The Uncounted Enemy: A Vietnam Deception" and aired in January, 1982.

32. For a study of the Westmoreland case see Burton Benjamin, *Fair Play: CBS, General Westmoreland, and How a Television Documentary Went Wrong* (New York: Harper & Row, 1988). Benjamin was a former CBS vice president and director who, after Westmoreland filed suit, conducted an in-house investigation into the case for CBS.

33. He was speaking not of journalism but of the power social elites have to define the worlds of the disenfranchised. See J. Western, *Outcast Capetown* (University of Minnesota Press, 1981.) quoted in Kay J. Anderson, "The Idea of Chinatown: The Power of Place and Institutional Practice in the Making of a Racial Category," *Annals of the American Geographer* Vol. 77 No. 4 (1987), 581.

34. Gaye Tuchman, *Making News*, 12.

35. Ibid., 1.

36. Gaye Tuchman, "Consciousness Industries and the Production of Culture," *Journal of Communication* 33, 330-341. Also quoted in Rachlin, *News as Hegemonic Reality*, 13.

37. In science the principle of uncertainty was first stated by Werner Heisenberg in about 1927. Godel's proof, which deals with the mathematical limits of knowledge, was enunciated in 1931. For a brilliant discussion of the first—and the degree to which it has been over extended into a popular cliche see Douglas Hofstadter, "Heisenberg's Uncertainty Principle and the Many-Worlds Interpretation of Quantum Mechanics," *Metamagical Themas: Questing for the Essence of Mind and Pattern* (New York: Basic Books, 1985), 455-477. For a discussion of Godel's proof see Ernest Nagel and James R. Newman, *Godel's Proof* (New York: New York University Press, 1958).

38. Curiously, news seems to be the last bastion in which recorders or reporters presume even a potential for objectivity. Claude Lévi Strauss's reflections on the effect of his presence on his subjects is one of the more moving passages in his memoir *Triste Tropique*. Scholarly treatments on the impossibility of objectivity also can be found in the works of Sigmund Freud, who argued that perception of events was variable to the subject; Max Weber, Karl Marx etc.

39. David R. Caploe, "Max Weber and a Dialectical Theory of Objectiv-

ity" (unpublished manuscript, Duke University, 1988), 7. Caploe's work applies Weber's dialectical theory of objectivity to journalism.

40. This ignores the North American, non-English, ethnic press. Here we are limited, by space as well as by expertise, to English language media. It is worthwhile noting, however, that the presence of Spanish, German, Chinese and Japanese publications presents a rare opportunity for comparative content, style and subject studies of simultaneously published reports.

41. Joseph T. Scanlon and Suzanne Alldred, "Media Coverage of Disasters: The Same Old Story," *Emergency Planning Digest*, (October/December, 1982), 13.

42. Phillip Schlesinger, *Putting 'Reality' Together*, (London: Constable and Company, Ltd., 1978). Quoted in Scanlon and Aldred, ibid.

43. Sontag, *A Barthes Reader*, 258.

44. For a brilliant discussion of the issue  of participation and distance from a cultural subject see Susan Sontag, "The Anthropologist as Hero," in E. Nelson Hayes and Tanya Hayes, eds., *Claude Lévi-Strauss: The Anthropologist as Hero* (Cambridge, Mass.: MIT Press, 1970), 184-196.

45. Anthony Mancini, professor of journalism at Brooklyn College, quoted in Lindsay Van Gelder, "Can the Chatter, Sweetheart," *Business Month*, February, 1989, 52. Mancini was critical of Gannett Corporation chairman Al Neuharth's reportage of foreign leaders.

46. The editors who define a newspaper story's suitability include, at any time, the following: city editor, assistant city editor, assignment editor, copy editor, and news editor.

47. Mark Crispin Miller, "TV's Anti-Liberal Bias," *New York Times*, November 17, 1988.

48. Three essays by Barthes, Myth Today," "The Imagination of the Sign," and "Introduction to the Structural Analysis of Narratives" are especially critical to this perspective. All have been translated into English and are included in Susan Sontag, ed., *A Barthes Reader*.

49. Lippmann, *Public Opinion*, 17.

50. Sontag, *A Barthes Reader*, 116.

51. Nor is this an unlikely event. A federal VA hospital audit completed in the 1980s and reported in various newspapers showed a widespread laxness in VA hospital pharmacies and inconsistencies in the

dispensing of medication to veterans.

52. Tobacco is carcinogenic and leads to a wide range of respiratory and cardiovascular disorders. Alcohol's sustained use can cause liver damage and, if use is heavy, other adverse physiologic reactions. This issue is discussed in greater detail in chapter 4.

53. Cocaine is considered by many experts as not chemically addictive but habituative. That is, it is used for reasons not related to a physical dependency or need. I am indebted to Bruce Alexander of Simon Fraser University, a leader in addiction and habituation research, for information on this topic.

54. Sontag, *A Barthes Reader*, 130.

55. Roland Barthes, *Camera Lucida*, Richard Howard, trans. (New York: Hill and Wang, 1981), 40-42.

56. Martin Mittelstaedt, "Is It Really All the News that's Fit to Print?" These are simply two of the more recent examples. Newsmen and propagandists for politically distant countries typically draw different conclusions from identical incidents.

57. For a good analysis of news coverage of this incident by U.S. periodicals see Rachlin, *News As Hegemonic Reality*, Chapter 3.

58. Sontag, *A Barthes Reader*, 133.

# 2

# The News as Rule

As John Ullmann notes wryly in his introduction to *The Reporter's Handbook*: "If the truth will out, we in journalism don't know as much about reporting as we think we do"[1] Journalism today remains a largely intuited craft in which fully articulated and generally accepted rules stand like occasional direction markers on a largely untraveled country road. The rest of this chapter explores some of the profession's rarely articulated but nevertheless observable rules.

The essence of North American reportorial technique stands today with Rudyard Kipling's "six honest serving-men:" who, what, when, where, why, and how.[2] These are the basics of what a reporter is told to find out and the essence of the craft. It is all he or she is supposed to know about any event to be covered. As Ullmann wrote:

> If you are a typical journalist, like those with whom I come in contact on a daily basis. . . you never have had an economics course that explains how a local business can affect the outcome of a bidding procedure, influence the growth patterns of a city, or even cheat its stockholders or consumers.
>
> Nor have you ever taken an education course that explains how to evaluate the local school system, how to probe the wisdom of the ways in which it spends its millions of dollars, or even how to evaluate the (now annual) bond issue. . . . Instead you spent a great deal of time during your journalism education practicing how to ask questions and learning how to arrange the answers in an understandable format. Then, as now, your touchstones were Rudyard Kipling's "six honest serving-men." You need not be a specialist, you were told, you need not be well versed: You need only to ask *who, what, where, when, how* and *why*, and accurately report what you've heard.[3]

That, in essence, is the operative, basic assumption of modern daily journalism. The criticism that journalists are not adequately trained in the subjects they cover is an old one, although the ramifications of it are rarely explored. In 1967, for example, Irving Kristol lamented the general lack of reportorial expertise in the subjects newsmen covered, using the *New York Times* as his example. A managing editor for that newspaper replied, attempting to refute Kristol and the printed exchange between both men merely served to underlined the accuracy of Kristol's views.[4] Even were experts generally employed by North American news organizations to cover current events, however, they would still be required to report and not to comment, to follow the form of the news and work within its generally accepted, narrative parameters. Acceptable reportage, even the work of experts, is based on a form describing what has been said or seen at a time and place. It is this in great part this form, proponents say, that guarantees the ideal of objectivity. This was neither the rule nor the ideal in Sam Johnson's day, first appearing as a specific, narrative form perhaps a century after his death.[5] Indeed, Johnson argued strongly that a writer's task included the imposition of an individual perspective beyond the merely observable or descriptive:

> To abstract the mind from all local emotion would be impossible, if it were endeavored, and would be foolish, if it were possible. Whatever withdraws us from the power of our senses; whatever makes the past, the distant or the future predominate over the present, advances us in the dignity of thinking beings. Far from me and from my friends, be such frigid philosophy as may conduct us indifferent and unmoved over any ground which has been dignified by wisdom, bravery or virtue.[6]

Johnson was not required to write only what he actually saw at a specific instant but had the leisure—and the grueling work—of successfully capturing a complex of events, issues, and postures in a single composite portrait.[7] His serving men had a latitude their descendents no longer enjoy. Since perhaps the days of Kipling, those "six honest serving-men" can only march, undignified by the journalist's own "wisdom, bravery or virtue," behind "real" individuals whose speech or actions is recorded.

As symbols of the school of "scientific" reportage in which observable "facts" are the central fact of news copy, Kipling's servants do suggest that reporters extract themselves from all emotion and subject involvement. They insist upon the chimera of uninvolved, dispassionate observation in which a reporter can and in theory should simply record what is seen, thought or heard by other individuals to create a basic, narrative record. Indeed, as Ullmann points out, journalists need no prior topical background or interest in a subject to fulfill an assignment. They need only know whom to interview and what the story is supposed to be before "filling in the blanks" (of who, what, when, where, why, how) to do a story. Ullmann would argue, perhaps, that "investigative" or "enterprise" journalism goes beyond this limited definition. That, however, is an open question that will be returned to in a later chapter. First it is necessary to understand the basic form and the rules that describe it.

If news stories have become uninformed, "factual" descriptions of specific occurrences they have remained cultural events nonetheless. Each carries the baggage of a country's history, a culture's perception, an individual publication's position and a single newsman's point of view. Kipling's "honest men" are the essence of that baggage and the structure of its form. Together and fully articulated they become what Barthes calls the "studium,"[8] a pervasive atmosphere and frame in which stories are written and edited. If there is a familiarity to the daily news report, a feeling of continuity and constancy of style and subject, it is the result of this studium, a narrative conformity that informs the  the interplay between sign, signifier, and signified. By understanding those elements, we will perhaps be better able to see the elements of cultural importance that Barthes argues must be there in "myth." So before returning to an analysis of the myth of the news,  it is first necessary to examine the form of contemporary, mundane news stories. This begins with the  most basic of journalistic forms: the obituary.

## THE OBITUARY

For daily journalists it was once and, for many, still is the first assignment, the place all started on the road to the various beats of police, political, foreign, or financial reportage.[9] "Knowing how to report and write an obit is important to you," a current journalism textbook cautions fledgling newsman "because you may make your first impression on a city editor by the way you handle the assignment."[10] In magazines like *Time* and *Newsweek*, obituaries today are typically subsumed under headings like "Milestones," but they remain in essence the simple, direct, declarative record of the event of an individual's death. They share with editorials the unique distinction of requiring no attribution.[11] Obituaries are, like editorials, the community's voice, and thus inhabit a peculiar and unique place in the published sector of the public sphere. Their function is to announce the death of one of the community's own, and thus they need no verification, no "he said" or "she said," to convey that finality. Lacking attribution, obituaries offer the simplest point from which our analysis can begin.

This is not to say that obituaries are "simple." They are not. Even a mundane, three-paragraph newspaper notice contains the rules and relations—sign, signifier, and signified—that structure all other "hard" news pieces. "You begin," a current journalism textbook explains, "by answering the same questions you would in any news story."[12] Most death reports are very brief, a matter of between one and three paragraphs, although in the case of the death of suitably famous people the story can run for many column inches of newspaper length, minutes of air time, or pages of magazine text. In its most developed form the obituary becomes a virtual biography not unlike Janet Cooke's ghetto story, although one whose characters are usually better known.[13] More commonly, however, the typical "obit" is a small, staff-written piece announcing the death of an individual and placed at the back of a newspaper or periodical.

As the following examples of newspaper and magazine text are dissected, the immediate reaction of a skeptical reader may be that its assertion of rules seem trite, self-evident and mundane. The results, however, are greater than the sum of the parts, and the power of these rules is not lessened by their mundanity. The degree to which these apparently self-evident rules inform and form the news will be shown in subsequent chapters. Thus I can counsel only patience to the skeptical and offer the following obituary as an example. It is from *Editor and Publisher*, a trade journal for American print news managers.[14] The analysis is not intended to be exhaustive, encompassing all rules which generate this one story, but rather to describe the principal rules and corollaries which can then be examined and applied to other news forms:

> THEODORE F. KOOP, 81, a former vice president of CBS, died July 7 of complications following surgery at Georgetown University Hospital in Washington.
>
> Koop, a 1928 graduate of the University of Iowa, worked as a reporter and editor for the Associated Press and director of the *National Geographic* magazine's news service before joining CBS in 1948 as director of news and public affairs in Washington.
>
> He conceived the "Face the Nation" program and took part in the expansion of the network's news programming. Koop was named vice president in 1961 and retired in 1971.[15]

### Overview

What can we say about this story in general? What, more importantly, does it say about and to us? It is clear that the subject is American as, presumably, is the publication in which his obituary appeared. We know this not simply because of the United States-specific place and corporate names but because of other clues, especially what the story leaves out. For example, it records no military career or extended service for Koop and thus can be the product of no country where universal conscription for adults is a necessity. It is thus not, for example, possible that this could be an obituary from the English-language *Jerusalem Post*, where obituaries include pro forma a man's military career. Were it, say, the obituary of a Swiss journalist of similar stature it also would of necessity note the man's military service record. In Switzerland, a career as successful as Koop's would be unthinkable without a parallel ascending career in the civilian military.[16] Further, we know this is not a British obituary, because in Great Britain a man of Koop's stature surely would have received official recognition in the form of an honor from the royal family—if not a knighthood, some less grand honor that would append initials after the man's name.

Were this a Chinese or Soviet record of the death of an eminent citizen, party rank and affiliation necessarily would have been included. In those countries it would be unthinkable for an individual to rise to Koop's level without holding a position, and probably a fairly high position, in his or her nation's ruling party. No, this is a North American man. Finally, the style is spare, lean, and businesslike, a bit more efficient, perhaps, than that used by Canadians describing the death of their own in, say, the (Toronto) *Globe and Mail*.

Because it is in English it naturally calls upon some of Rudyard Kipling's "honest men" to fashion sentences into its paragraphs of homage. The English language demands a subject, verb (with tense), and object—the "who," "what" and "when" of Kipling's basic form. Theodore F. Koop (who) died (what) July 7 (when) of complications following surgery (how) at Georgetown University Hospital in Washington (where).[17] Indeed, these five of Kipling's six serving men do greater service than as a simple mnemonic for reporters. They are present, virtually imbedded, in the structure of the language, and Kipling's doggerel simply makes them overt to newsmen pressed for time and short on column inches. These, the poem says, are what *has* to be gotten in. The rules we will begin with have, then, at least to some degree, a linguistic boundary that constrains their form. The question will be the degree to which these five "honest men" function to define the narrative rules of story generation.

## RULES

### Why

The existential "why" is the joker in Kipling's pack and the question typically unanswered by the obituary. "Why" always appears as the unanswerable, a question whose response (because of surgery) is usually followed by another question (Why did he need surgery? Because he had cancer. Why did he get cancer? Because he smoked. Why did he smoke? etc.). American journalism usually substitutes a general, locational response to the question "how"—"of complications during surgery"—to stand for the tricky "why." Perhaps Koop's surgeon was drunk and botched the job, or perhaps the patient received an inadvertent overdose of anesthetic gas. We do not know "why" Koop died at all and precious little, really, about "how." The problem of the sixth honest man—"why"— will be returned to later but an easier and more essential question can be asked first with Kipling's last guardian: Why report Mr. Koop's death at all? What purpose does it serve? What makes Koop's death certain news while that of, say, a copy editor from the *Springfield News*, a good, hard working news soldier who also retired in 1971—and died as well on July 7, 1988—may not be found in *Editor and Publisher*'s pages? What are the rules of this story and this choice?

### Who: the Social Context

This specific event is worthy of an extended note in *Editor and Publisher* because Mr. Koop was important in his profession. Most of the copy is dedicated to justifying the reportage of Koop's death through a description of his role in the growth of information-based American corporations. Reportage of Mr. Koop, alive or dead, was based on his status in the national news community and his place in its recent history. Presumably the unsung *Springfield News* editor's demise was reported by his former employer in that publication, but the importance of his work did not justify a notice at the national scale that *Editor and Publisher* obituaries usually mark.

We do not learn, here, about Mr. Koop's personal life, military service, hobbies, interests, or passions. There is no record of his marital status, service to the community or mention of those friends or relatives who survived to mourn him. Between his retirement in 1971 and his death in 1988, Mr. Koop's life was already ended, at least to the degree that it was of potential interest to *Editor and Publisher*'s obituary writer.

This short story is about one man, an individual defined by his career who worked for CBS and the once important *National Geographic* News Service. All else is secondary to that fact, to the single datum of a professional individual. More specifically, Mr. Koop is described and defined by his relative importance in his profession during a specific period of rapid growth and change. He was important enough to rate three paragraphs in a national trade magazine, and what is left out—almost everything about the man as a human being—is irrelevant to the facts of his position as a man of news.

This is a social definition, a specific context enjoined by the publication that happens in this case to be dominated by publishing news. Mr. Koop's death would not be noted in a magazine dedicated to hang gliders, for instance, or one dedicated to great model railroaders. Their obituaries, like this one, however, may share the narrow focus that sees the man in terms of business success or specific accomplishment, not as a complex individual but in terms of a narrow focus of professional achievement (or infamy).

The social rule, then, is that an obituary describes an individual who is defined by actions or accomplishments in a specific context or field. In more general news an individual's value (both as story focus and as attributive subject) also is defined, typically, by his or her professional position or a specific expertise. The degree to which an individual's statement is given weight is, as we will see, in direct proportion to his or her title.

Consider the following scenario to see how crucial the rule is: Two individuals, a Catholic bishop and an unemployed but highly educated, immigrant refugee, are present at a "Right to Life" protest at an abortion clinic. The former has a Catholic education and the latter a degree in philosophy from the University of Mexico. Most news reporters would seek to quote the Bishop while the immigrant, if quoted at all, would be given short shrift.

## What: the Cultural Context

The obituary—any obituary—describes a specific event, death, which is of importance to the culture. In all towns and cities with a newspaper, the most anonymous, marginal individual's death is usually noted—especially if it occurs in any but the most natural of ways. Even if it is only a single paragraph, something must be present to note that passing in a public form, to inform any who may once have known the person that he or she is no more. Thus the cultural context of the singular event—death of a specific individual within a group— is the obituary's (and news's) unspoken rule.[18] That Mr. Koop died is the reason for this story.

A corollary to this would be that certain types of death are of greater cultural import than others. Death of the professionally adept is more important than death of the mediocre and unknown journeymen. Means of death is another issue, with homicide, for example, increasing the news value of any demise. Death at the hands of a fellow human is of special import in our world, and if that death is not accidental then the news, like the courts, takes even greater note.[19]

As a bilingual reporter in Springfield, Massachusetts, I worked hard in the early 1970s to increase coverage to the resident Spanish-speaking community. Its members consisted largely of Cuban refugees and migrant workers brought from Puerto Rico to work for the local tobacco industry. The *Springfield Union's* editor, Joe Mooney, decreed that coverage was to be minimal because, he explained, few Spanish migrant workers bought the newspaper and thus were of little value to the newspaper and, as migrants, of less value as general subjects. The sole exception was when they became involved in illegal drugs, violent deaths, or homicide. All these were covered pro forma by the newspaper's resident police reporter. In the not infrequent violent fights that punctuated the community's life, the anonymity of the victim was outweighed by the fact of violent death or near death, and his name (complete, whenever possible, with middle initial) was reported in full along with any available details of the incident.[20]

Other cultural rules can be easily described, although many may be irrelevant to this obituary. Almost any story linking an individual to large sums of money, for example, makes that individual worthy of note. If a steelworker wins the lottery, that person's decisions on what to do with the money is immediately newsworthy. If a bank robber steals $500 it is a crime brief, but if someone steals $5 million it is major news. The greater the sum, the more important the event. Whether the person's professional or personal accomplishments are considered noteworthy or not, the fact of large amounts of money defines the degree to which that person's life, actions or death will be journalistically important.

Indeed, money and a subject's mews value are often synony-
mous. Former newsman Lewis Lapham suggests it was the fact when
he worked at the *San Francisco Examiner* and remains a constant of
news perceptions to this day:

> At the *San Francisco Examiner* the editorial staff observed
> the protocols of wealth by assigning prices to people as well
> as to objects and events. An executive known to earn
> $800,000 a year was entitled to more space in the paper
> than an executive earning $500,000 a year—unless, of
> course, the less opulent executive committed an especially
> atrocious crime. Actresses living in beach houses worth $2
> million outranked actresses living in bungalows worth $1
> million; aircraft carriers that cost $17 billion were more to
> be feared than aircraft carriers that cost $10 billion. The
> sums of money stood as surrogates for further efforts of
> imaginative definition.[21]

In November and December of 1988, as I wrote this section, news
media were filled with stories about the death of Christina Onassis. Excepting a few business stories that speculated on the future head of
the Onassis empire, the focus was exclusively on the deceased individual's fortune and her young daughter, the billionaire heiress apparent. In the vast sea of copy (from television's *Entertainment Tonight*
through the *New York Times* to supermarket tabloid "exposes") almost
nothing was said about the woman's professional accomplishments.[22]
Her vast wealth was the essential fact everyone reported again and
again.

As an editor put it succinctly in a truism common among traditional newsmen, a good story need only include two elements—death
and money: "Tell them how they're going to die and then tell them what
it's going to cost."[23]

Another cultural rule, one specific to contemporary North America, is the fetish with novelty or uniqueness. If it has not yet been
recorded, it is news at first completion. This *Guiness Book of Records*
syndrome which accords air time and column inches to the largest,
longest, fastest, grossest, smallest (and perhaps stupidest) is part of a
peculiarly modern pattern which sees immortality in a statistical
niche. Finally, violence in all its forms is worthy of attention. To maxi-
mize coverage it should be a situation in which more than one individual died at the hands of a spouse, bank robber, plane crash, thief,
stranger, or accident. No news tradition handles murder with more
panache than the traditional Chinese press but, from multiple car
crashes to serial murders, delight in a recurring pattern of death and
disaster is a contemporary cultural imperative of the American press.[24]

News, then, can be described as having both a cultural context
or rule that defines the specific class of events worthy of note and a
social rule that sifts between incidences of that event to determine

what or who will be described and, perhaps, to what extent.

The inverse of these cultural and social rules—the "what" and "who"—also describe what will be excluded from any report. The cultural context, at least in *Editor and Publisher*, acknowledges deaths and, in a separate section, professional promotions but not births, marriages, or demotions. To the extent that an individual is defined by professional association, births and marriage are extraneous events. Demotion's exclusion suggests a unidirectional theme to the cultural rule: one seeks the highest point of individual accomplishment and does not report the failure.

Even where such personal announcements are common, their degree of coverage is usually based on a family's wealth or professional standing. Wedding notices are the cultural rule in local newspapers, which publish, usually for a fee, announcements of marital engagements (usually with pictures). The weddings of a community's better-known children, however, are typically covered lavishly, slavishly and at no charge to the happy couple-to-be. The cultural context accepts marriage as an event worthy of advertisement and perhaps reportage, while the social context determines the degree of coverage for any single wedding.[26] Other, lesser known individuals may have to pay for their nuptial stories. Birth notices are a matter of official notice and common items in the records section of local newspapers. When the child is born to someone of real prominence, however—a president, crown prince or Henry Kissinger—then the parent's professional prominence raises even the newborn to newsworthy status.

Divorce, the inverse of marriage, is rarely reported, although it is in some jurisdictions announced in a one-line statement on a newspaper's paid legal items page. Again, to the extent the news is unidirectional and progressive, reportage of a divorce would be like reporting a demotion. It is a step back, a reversal, and North Americans tend wherever possible to ignore retreat. An exception is made in the case of very famous people (the divorce of actress Joan Collins was a recent example). The social rule changes for the famous, especially when the event in which a person with "name recognition" becomes a public spectacle played out in a public courtroom with lovers and mutual allegations. Then it is not the divorce at all that is at issue but, more clearly, the public icon defined by "who" that is dominant.

### When: the Temporal Context

Two other rules assist in defining degree and extent of coverage. They are those which define temporality and locational boundary. Although they are linked, as are all issues of time and space, the attempt has been made to separate them, here, for the purpose of discussion.

Koop's death was reported in a specific issue of *Editor and Publisher* because it was recent. Had he in fact died in 1968 (with his obituary forgotten for a generation), it would now be too late to rectify the error by publishing it. Similarly, it would be ludicrous for *Editor and Publisher* to publish a death notice this year for either Sam Johnson or James Boswell (although both were arguably more crucial to journalism's development than Koop) even though obituaries were not published for either men by *Editor and Publisher* at the time of their demise.[27] It is not simply that both men were British (and thus active outside the weekly's circulation region) but that their deaths occurred just too long ago. They lived and died outside not only the publication's geographic context (which can be stretched, on occasion; Boswell was after all a defender of the American cause) but its temporal context of modern news as well.

There is a widespread recognition of this temporal rule, if little analysis of its effect. Speaking of vice-president elect Dan Quayle in early 1989, Republican consultant Eddie Mahe, Jr., for example, insisted that Quayle's numerous problems during the 1988 presidential campaign would require him to undergo a six-month period of hiding until he could reappear as vice president, free of the earlier associations and questions:

> If he asked me for advice, I'd say, "Danny, just get down into the woodwork." He's got to let all the campaign stuff written about him die down so when he bubbles up in six months as the new vice president, all that will be old news and the focus will be on him [as vice president].[28]

The obituary, however, is distinguished from other types of news by often including in the body of the story elements of distant occurrence. If six months is a period sufficient to cleanse Mr. Quayle of embarrassing campaign gaffs, obituaries often reach back years to frame the lives of their subjects. We learn in Mr. Koop's story, for example, that he graduated from university in 1928 and joined CBS during television's commercial infancy in 1948. If the first "lead" paragraph justifies publication through placing the man's death in the current time frame, the story's body does give pertinent professional details substantiating the story's inclusion in this publication and the one personal bit of information—his graduation from the University of Iowa.

A temporal rule exists, then, which defines the limits of a reportable event in at least two ways. First, it describes an immediate and present time boundary for the obituary itself and, by extension, for news in general. The death (and by extension, accident, robbery, wedding, promotion, or election) was today, this week, or this month. The signifier, the dead body, crumpled car, or couple-before-an-altar can only be included in the news narrative if its distance in time from the reportorial present is short. As that specific event fades into the past, the news value diminishes immediately. Secondarily, the temporal context also creates a longer-term frame that provides a social context for that immediate event. Thus Mr. Koop died July 7, 1988, but his importance began in 1948 when he joined CBS. Immediately after the cessation of his vital bodily functions in 1988, an obituary was written and published. But the events of 1948 describe a longer, temporal frame in which cultural importance is added.

It is in this second frame that what is signified becomes imbedded. The signifier—cessation of bodily function — signifies death at the level of normal language. Call that death the "boundary event" where an old man dies in hospital. It becomes a story worthy of eulogy (or at least recognition) because, within the broad temporal contextual rule, the dead man is identified with successful and active participation in the growth of both a specific medium, television, and activity within a powerful corporation, CBS. The sign at this second level of information is the death of a CBS official who was important in the recent history of American television. What is signified here, that the successful are recognized and eulogized, involves the simultaneous loss of a crucial human element.

### Where: the Geographic Rule
Geographic boundaries function in precisely the same way. Koop was American, not British or Canadian. *Editor and Publisher*'s brief is people, subjects, or events relevant to information managers in the United States. Their advertising base is U.S. newspaper and magazine suppliers and companies, while their "help wanted" classified columns are for that same geographic area of the continental United States, Alaska, Puerto Rico, and Hawaii. Further, despite his Iowa education, Koop was an easterner who worked for the *National Geographic* News Service, CBS, and "Face the Nation" in Washington, D.C. Koop's geography fits the American boundaries of the magazine's editorial bias, and his career (which is what the magazine was concerned with) was centered upon corporations in a city (Washington, D.C.) that is the seat of the nation's sociopolitical power.

It is unlikely that Koop's death, for example, was noted by most British or Canadian newspapers or journals despite his apparent importance in the growth of modern television news. Koop was an American (educated in Iowa) and a power in both Washington, D.C.*(National Geographic)* and New York (CBS). His death is thus an appropriate event to acknowledge in a publication whose purpose is the reportage of events occurring to and within the broad context of American print journalism. Our Springfield copy editor, however, lived on a smaller scale, and while that death was presumably reported by his former employer, the geographic specificity of that career does not argue for an *Editor and Publisher* obituary.

Koop's death is located not only in the present but also in a specific hospital in a specific city. So we have here, as in the temporal rule, two levels that operate jointly in association with time. The Cultural rule (death) is joined with an immediate, constricted time frame (present) and a precise location (Georgetown University Hospital in Washington). The social rule (Who) allows for a broader time frame (1928, 1948, 1971) and a wider geographic context (Iowa, Washington, D.C.)

Another way of stating this is to describe the geographic and temporal boundaries as joint corollaries of scale that may change from publication to publication but which must exist internally for each newspaper, magazine, or television story. Stations and periodicals choose stories that fit a vision of their audience, which can be defined in terms of physical boundaries. *Editor and Publisher's* obituaries, for example, will report the deaths of individuals whose professional careers were of importance to news organizations operating on a supra-regional scale. Officials of large organizations whose outlets span the continent (Knight-Ridder, Gannett, Newhouse, CBS, etc.) earn their obituaries in this way. Local newspapers publish obituaries on the lives of individuals whose lives were lived within a single urban or regional context.

The geographic component of the rule structure also assists in defining the perspective of a specific story. Even if the events occur elsewhere, they can be reported in *Editor and Publisher* if perceived to be of importance to the regionally defined advertiser or reader. Thus the eventual death of a foreign news magnate like Rupert Murdock, owning U.S. papers in a multinational empire based in, say, London or Australia, would be reported in *Editor and Publisher*, but with the body of the story given over to his relations with U.S. publications.

More generally, western U.S. news representatives have long argued that, in the words of *Los Angeles Times* media writer David Shaw, the national news in general is "largely shaped and driven and distorted" by an emphasis on the perspective of eastern regions.[29] He offers a number of examples of thematically identical stories occurring in both California and New York. Western events are reported only regionally, while the latter are transposed by wire services and magazines into national events.

While not necessarily critical to the obituary, the geographic rule thus includes a more general function of scale in which "national" may mean, in fact, "eastern United States" and distance from the Atlantic coast may create a barrier to the reportage of any specific event. Former CBS president Van Gordon Sauter called this the "attitudinal incestuousness" of the "Cambridge-Manhattan-Georgetown axis."[30] Interestingly, that is clearly an easterner's definition. Anyone who lived and worked outside that region would have substituted Boston for the suburb of Cambridge, New York for the borough of Manhattan, and Washington, D.C., for the district of Georgetown.

One element of this complex dialogue is the relation of event to geographic boundary and the insistence on addressing issues from a fixed, physical perspective centered on the United States. This point will be returned to when the effects of the combined rules are examined as a whole. But it is worth noting at this juncture that it is precisely this type of perspective, albeit at a very different scale, that Chomsky criticizes when arguing that similar events involving the U.S. and Russia are reported differently (brave U.S. soldiers in Vietnam, Russian intruders in Afghanistan) by the U.S. press. Statements by officials in or near Washington, D.C. are given greater weight than those speaking from distant capitals.

"Where" as a rule can be described as defining the importance of an event through its relation to a specific, arbitrary region. Its corollary defines the parameters of the event through reference, in conjunction with the temporal rule, to other locations within a broader geographic context. The scale of the event as defined by this rule changes from publication to publication.

### How: the active rule

In obituaries, the "how" is severely truncated and, in this case, barely annunciated. Koop died of "complications following surgery" but whether these were complications linked to the medical problem that required surgery or, perhaps, a result of the surgery itself, is something the obituary does not state. Does "complications following surgery" mean his heart stopped because of incorrect medication? Perhaps surgeons left a scalpel in Mr. Koop's abdomen, and it caused complications by severing an artery when he was moved. Were the complications following surgery related, in fact, to the surgery at all, or rather a result of the stress of a surgical procedure on a body whose cardiovascular system's powers were previously diminished?

Actually, "complications following surgery" is more temporal and geographic (when and where), modifying the location of the hospital, than it is descriptive (did he die from cardiac arrest, an overdose of drugs? a surgical mistake?).

### Why: the Existential rule

Within the narrow and immediate temporal context we do not know "why" Mr. Koop died any more than we know "how." If his operation was for lung cancer, then perhaps, "why" he died is a function of the voluntary inhalation of carcinogens over a period of fifty years. Was his surgery, whose resulting complications appear to be related somehow to the death, from an automobile accident? If he was driving while impaired (physically or chemically) then "why" he died is because of a foolish act—driving an automobile while being physically unable to complete that act safely. But these questions are not addressed by the obituary, and indeed "why" something happened (the specific signifier) and specifically "how" it occurred are untreated in this story.

"Why" this obituary was written at all—the justification of the broad temporal frame—is implied by the broad temporal frame. Because Mr. Koop was a media doyen his death is recognized and his life given value after the fact. Thus at the level of myth and in the interplay of symbol one learns that the death of a retired man was important because he had been important during a long tenure in corporate media growth. The death of that formerly important man ("why" he died is not important) becomes a sign in itself which signifies the value placed upon those who succeed as media administrators at CBS.

## FOUR RULES FOR THE NARRATIVE FORM

In describing the narrative rules that define the content of this story there are, therefore, four components that can immediately be identified. These represent both means of proscribing the event itself (cessation of an individual's bodily functions at a specific time and place) and an assigning of importance to that boundary event so that it can become a reportorial event worthy of publication :

1. A cultural rule or context defining the event, death in this case, as worthy of note.
2. The social rule or context, which determines the degree of coverage of any specific, discrete event. The social context assigns a perceived social weight to specific event types, determining which will be given reportorial time (in broadcast) or space (in print).
3. The geographic rule: the spatial boundaries which define the location of a specific news outlet. If an event, even one of significance, occurs beyond those boundaries—outside the accepted scale of news—then the chances of publication are diminished and the potential social value of a story will be considered diminished as well. Corollary to this is a boundary function that defines the parameters of an event's antecedent through the description of distanced locations in which prior events relevant to the specific story may have occurred.
4. A temporal rule: the time frame within which an event occurs. Usually, the more recent the event, the greater its potential social value. This rule modifies both cultural and social contexts. Corollary to this rule is a boundary function in which the parameter of prior events is included. This historical level justifies coverage of the immediate event.

### Rules in Consort

These rules do not exist independently of each other but function instead as a seamless whole. The death of a sitting president or prime minister, for example, will be reported widely despite the lack of interest or familiarity with that individual's policies or geographic background by distant readers. Thus the assassination of a Pakistani national leader will be described in a U.S. newspaper that previously carried little information on his policies or his nation's problems.

Not only is it Death but it is the immediate, sudden death of A Leader. The social importance we place on the leadership of a country (and on sudden death) overrides Pakistan's geographic distance.

Some individuals become so important that they are news icons even long after their death, transcending temporal and geographic contextual boundaries. Thus in 1988 there was an orgy of reminiscence on the twenty-fifth anniversary of the death of John F. Kennedy. The sudden, violent nature of that death, the importance of the man (a U.S. president), and the singular myths that have grown up concerning his life  and death overrode all normal temporal boundaries and geographic rules regarding the reliving of his life and death. It was as important in Miami, Florida, (where long features were written in the respective newspapers) as it was in Dallas, Texas, where Kennedy died, and in the nation's capital, where memorial services were held for him.

**Sign and Signifier**

How then, can we interpret Mr. Koop's obituary? What, in Barthes's language, is the meaning of the myth encoded in the form? The rules express the studium, the sense of familiarity and consistency that make this an unremarkable, mundane example of the form. What, then, is the result?

The signifier is the death of one man, which is acknowledged by a publication serving, in this case, what had been the deceased's professional community. Through the exclusion of virtually all personal details about Koop or his death, this is made to signify the definition of success (publication) as a function of professional accomplishment or notoriety. News is business, in short, and the perhaps endearing but private quirks of a person are extraneous to the issue of his or her contribution to corporate growth. At the level of myth, the signified is that individuals are what they do, remembered not for honesty, morality, humanity or courage. Those are intangibles and not who, what, when, where, and how. One is instead remembered for contributions to business, politics, or science because of an action or event in which the subject is perceived to have been instrumental. The final sign (where signifier and signified meet) is America as successful business, the famous dictum that "The business of the nation *is* business."

One could argue pragmatically that in a country as large as the United States it is merely efficiency that defines these values. If *Editor and Publisher* made note of every dead newsman, then it would be not a periodical for industry managers but a compilation of the lives of those who worked in the industry at one time or another. That, too, would be a choice, but there are many ways in which such things could be handled without sacrificing other stories.

*Editor and Publisher*'s obituaries could be on a special page, like the crime beat section of many newspapers, which included all relevant stories just as the "crime beat" section of a newspaper lists all break-ins, reported robberies and assaults. Thus the magazine's page would include a section, perhaps called People, in which changes affecting the professional and personal changes of its readers' lives were listed by category in small type. Any reader could send in a notice and have it published. Were *Editor and Publisher* to adopt this procedure, under "Deaths" one would find a series of one-line or two-line announcements including KOOP, THEODORE P.—July 7, 1988, in Washington, D.C. Formerly of CBS and National Geographic News Service. CINI, PHIL, July 7, 1988, Springfield, Mass. Former *Springfield News* copy editor. Similar short entries could be used for promotions, demotions, marriages, retirements, and so forth—all in the same, truncated fashion. But that is not the form and these other areas of interest (births, marriages, etc.) are not part of the publication's rules. Choices, in short, have been made, and they are editorially consistent with the generative rules of obituaries in other magazines or newspapers. Certainly the form, even within the constraints of English, could have been far different.

The argument that these are merely practical conveniences dictated by space and time will not wash. The form is too consistent, too arbitrary to allow for one to wish away the significance on the plea of efficient form. The central fact, politically and socially, is that individuals are defined by what they do to make a living, that their inclusion or exclusion is based on financial and professional considerations within a clearly defined hierarchy. Politically, one can argue that this is part of a larger, social definition of capitalistic worth criticized by thinkers ranging from Kierkeggard to Marx: "The bourgeoisie has resolved all personal honor and dignity into exchange-value; and in place of all the freedoms that men have fought for, it has put one unprincipled freedom - free trade."[31]

Free trade means, in this context, commercial position. It is the social definition that gives meaning to Koop's life and thus to his death. Mr. Koop's definition in death as in life was who he worked for, and his life's work is summed by the tract of his career. The "who" of this obituary is the individual, Mr. Koop, as defined by his career. The "why" of publication is similarly answered by his professional associations, but the manner of his death—the "why" and "how" of his demise—is not. We know "where" and "when" he died, but "how" and "why is unspoken. Complications during surgery conveys, really, very little information. Did his heart suddenly stop? Was the a problem with anesthesia? Did the surgeon's knife perhaps slip? We do not know. Nor, to be fair, are we usually given the answers to these questions in newspaper stories, even those which supposedly cover surgery-related mishaps.

These are the basic rules for the obituary, at least for obituaries in a single magazine. To what degree are they operative in other classes of story or publication?

## A SIMPLE WIRE STORY

If these general rules are of wider importance than a single category of news in a single publication, they also should be applicable to more general publications and copy. Obituaries, after, all, fulfill a specific function describing a single event (death) occurring to one individual whose importance can be easily defined. Further, since they do not require attribution, they lack a whole level of information commonly required by general news stories.

An extremely short wire service story is examined next Published in the *Province* newspaper, it contains no personal names—unusual for all but wire "briefs"—and was part of a round-up of national news published on February 3, 1987, in that daily newspaper.[32] The story's attribution, "news services" signals that it was condensed from one or more pieces moved by the newspaper's wire services, which include Canadian Press, United Press International, and Associated Press. Following this analysis, a locally generated story on the same subject—

deaths during anesthesia resulting from dislodged or defective inhalator tubes used —is reviewed.

In 1983 the *Province* switched from its traditional broadsheet to a tabloid format. Its editorial emphasis simultaneously changed from that of a traditional, "serious" newspaper to a "breezy," informative "morning read"with shorter stories and an upbeat style resembling a regionalized, Canadian version of USA TODAY.[33] Its television advertising campaign currently emphasizes the tabloid's ability to inform readers quickly and promises the "busy professional" a summary of important stories. "Briefs" are common devices used in many North American newspapers and magazines to condense a story or report published in one area for readership in another, more distant location. They are fashioned from longer reports by news or copy desk personnel who cut them to fit a specific page's hole. Following the *Province*'s style change, this form of shortened, condensed story became the rule and has been used in recent years with real frequency by the editorial staff. This brief, attributed to the newspaper's wire services, thus represents a polished, highly edited piece that attempts to present the essential facts of a specific situation to provincial readers. Its analysis illustrates some of the ways in which the rules described above can proscribe even a very short newspaper story:

# DEATHS SET
# OFF ALARM

*News Services*
WINNIPEG—Health-care authorities across Canada have been alerted to a problem with oxygen inhalator tubes which is being blamed for the deaths of at least three women.

The tubes are prone to buckling, which starves patients of oxygen.

Federal authorities issued the alert after two Winnipeg women died. Then it was discovered that an Ontario woman had also died because of a similar problem.[34]

There is a comforting anonymity to this short piece. No family or personal names are used. Federal authorities are not named, even by agency, and identification of the deceased is only in the grossest geographic terms of city or province. It is a surprisingly generic piece of work for a story describing an apparently systemic health problem worthy of nationwide, federal concern. In Mr. Koop's obituary he was first named and then justified in terms of his professional career. Here the individual actors are described only in the most general, professional terms—"federal authorities," "health-care authorities,"—or as geographic ciphers ('two Winnipeg women," "an Ontario woman"). "Who" is both anonymous and official. Federal authorities have issued an alert to Canadian health-care authorities about (what?) a problem that is currently being blamed for the death of at least three individuals. We do not know the name of the official who issued the alert, the authorities who received it or even the precise date of its release. The story is further distanced from Vancouver readers by the Winnipeg dateline and a by-line which credits neither a wire service reporter nor a specific news agency but instead the more general and generic "News Services." The story has all the appearance of a filler included in the newspaper where there was an empty three inches that required a small, boxed story to complete the page.

Alerts are, in fact, official bulletins disseminated by Health and Welfare Canada's Health Protection Branch to warn hospital administrators and medical professionals when a specific product or piece of equipment has been determined to kill or injure individuals in hospital. Typically, they are issued after product tests or provincial coroner inquests have determined that a specific piece of medical equipment has directly contributed to one or more deaths. Federal Alerts are sent to hospital administrators, provincial ministries of health and concerned professional organizations (the College of Physicians and Surgeons of British Columbia, for example) for dissemination to appropriate members.

By changing the noun "Alert" to the lead paragraph's verb, "alerted," the official and declarative statement of deaths resulting from buckled inhalator tubes is downgraded to a warning of problems currently "being blamed" for deaths elsewhere in Canada. It is all very tenuous. While they are now—at this moment—being blamed, the present tense's construction suggests it is a tentative attribution of fault. If the story read that health professionals were warned that "deaths have resulted and continue to occur from," it would have been conclusive, but as written it is implied that in the future these deaths may, indeed, be blamed on something else. A reader reasonably can assume that since Canadian health care officials have been alerted, the problem—if one does in fact still exist—is under control. What a reader can be assured of, however, is that federal authorities are alert to a situation (even one so unusual) that might affect the health of citizens in hospital.

Everything in this short story is understated. The dateline, a geographic locater, is Winnipeg rather than Ottawa where the Health Protection Branch is located. All Alerts are in fact issued from the nation's capital, but it was presumably a Winnipeg wire service reporter who, interested in the subject because of two deaths in that city, read the Alert and wrote the first story from which this brief was constructed. The names of the deceased have been omitted, subsumed under the general status of patients starved for oxygen by the failure of inhalator tubes used during surgery. Authorities issuing the warning are not named or quoted, and local officials who have received the bulletin also are neither identified nor, presumably, interviewed.

On the surface this is a story published as much for its novelty and uniqueness as for its reportage of the death of citizens outside the newspaper's circulation area but within the wire service's national boundaries. We do not know if this type of death has occurred in Vancouver but assume not. Federal authorities say only three cases have been reported.Why assume otherwise? Omission of the specific names of authorities issuing or receiving the Alert, and even the city in Ontario where one woman died, assures that this story will receive little attention. It is simply another piece of Ottawa-speak, of official paper that filled, this story says, a hole in the local newspaper.

These lacks will not bother the average reader because the story's subject, it's "what," is not the death of three individuals but instead an official Alert sent to health care officials by federal authorities concerned about those deaths. Were this a story whose purpose was the description of a pattern of recurring, surgical deaths, then its anonymity and brevity would be a glaring deficit. But since instead it is a story whose subject is the federal Alert, the issue of the deaths ("who," "where," "when," "why," etc.) is secondary. The fact of attribution creates a second level of meaning on which each rule will operate simultaneously. Call the focus of an attributed story the *specific* or *reportorial* event and the antecedent, background occurrence, in this case the death of three women, the *boundary* event or events. The latter concerns the prior occurrences informing the recent, specific action being described. Just as Mr. Koop's death was framed by the geographic and temporal boundaries of his Iowa past, so too, in an attributed story, must all factors relate to one of two levels.

"Who," for example, here describes not the deceased but rather the officials issuing the official Alert. Its authors are anonymous functionaries subsumed under the official rubric of "federal authorities." If Mr. Koop's obituary was confined to issues of his professional history, the brief's authors have likewise shed human detail and confined the story to official ciphers. There is no Dr. X or Health Protection Branch Director Y for a reporter or reader to question. Federal authority has alerted (regional) health officials. Individuals, people who can be questioned or interviewed, are not involved. The subject of this report—it's "what"—is information from those official, federal authorities *as a class* about a possible medical problem. Again, we do not know who, specifically, received this alert in British Columbia (what "health-care officials?" nurses? physicians? dentists? osteopaths? chiropracters? who?). Nor do we care. The scale is national—universal—and the assumption is that a report by federal authorities is itself worthy of note. Multiple deaths, the cultural rule that should make this story important, become the boundary context of the specific, reported event that is the alerting of health care professionals. Temporally, the story itself is bounded by the unspecified times of the three, disparate, anonymous (again no names) deaths and the recent alerting of health authorities. Geographically, the specific reportorial event is located nationally (federal authorities) with separate boundary locations in a city (Winnipeg) and a province (Ontario). The national context is emphasized because both places are distant from Vancouver readers but within the Canadian fabric. The method of death, the "how" is starvation of oxygen through the "buckling" of inhalator tubes, but the reasons this occurs ("why") or even the factors that make it occur in one situation and not, perhaps, in another are left to the reader's imagination.

Were there questions to be asked of this story, it would not be about the peripheral, boundary events—the death of two women in Winnipeg and one in Ontario—but about the Alert itself. Reading Mr. Koop's obituary, one did not ask if he was a good student in university because an answer to that question would have required greater emphasis on a different geo-temporal boundary which was peripheral to the story's subject—his death. Similarly one does not ask here if more than three women have died in this curious circumstance or if men may have died as well. The Alert said that three women died, and to question that fact is to go from the specific, reportorial to the boundary elements of the story, a transition the form urges the reporter, and hence the reader, not to undertake. Kipling's institutionalized form asks who said what to whom at a specific time and place. That is what is expected, and it is the newsperson's job to cover public events, to describe what is said (the "facts") by whom at an inquest or in the Alert. This is the studium, the feel of constancy in which one assumes veracity in reportage and editing. This brief is, after all, a typical story, one of hundreds of similar size and type that fill the paper every day. Cross-examination of those attributed statements is not what the reader or, Ullmann says, the reporter, is trained or expected to do.

Thus in this news story Kipling's honest men serve at two separate but related contextual levels: that of the specific, reportorial event, and simultaneously that of a secondary, boundary occurrence. This is caused by the inclusion of attribution as a narrative technique assigning statements to a specific individual or agency. The primary focus is, in an attributed story, not on the boundary event itself—in this case multiple deaths—but the secondary event, which in this story is an official, federal warning to the nation's health-care officials. Even though attribution is generic here, using titles and generalities without specific names, the very fact of attribution itself irremediably changes and redefines the story from boundary focus to that of reportorial event.

## A SINGLE DEATH

As this wire story moved, an official coroner's inquest into a very similar death was about to begin in greater Vancouver. On Sept. 20, 1985, Cloverdale music teacher Robert Graham died during surgery at Peace Arch Hospital in the Vancouver suburb of White Rock. His death was attributed to hypoxia, oxygen starvation, caused by the undiscovered and untreated dislodging of an inhalator tube during surgery. The death was one of a number of anesthesia-related deaths receiving attention in British Columbia in the mid-1980s. Several of these deaths occurred at Peace Arch hospital.

Under British Columbian law, the provincial coroner's service has the mandate to examine all unusual or questionable deaths and to hold a public inquiry if, in the presiding coroner's judgment, that will serve a public function. Coroner inquest juries do not have the power to assign blame for a specific death but are charged with assuring that all the facts of a situation are made public. Inquest procedures in this province thus differ from those in some U.S. jurisdictions where findings of fault are allowed. A further difference between the two locations is that private hospitals are a rarity in Canada. Peace Arch, like most regional hospitals, is under the legal jurisdiction of the provincial ministry of health. Thus an official, provincial inquest into a hospital death sets one arm of government (the British Columbia Coroners Service) to investigate, through a juried hearing, the events that occurred under the jurisdiction of another governmental branch (the Ministry of Health).

A full report, published in the *Province*, of the crucial testimony from the official inquest into the death of Mr. Graham offers an excellent example of the means by which boundary and specific, reportorial events are handled in a single news story:

# Fatal slip
# unnoticed

**By Holly Horwood**
**Staff Reporter**

The life-giving oxygen tube accidently "came out."
But it wasn't until 15 minutes later that hospital staff discovered the mishap, which cost a retired Cloverdale music teacher his life.

A coroner's jury was given that evidence yesterday at an inquest in the death of Robert Graham,64, at Peace Arch Hospital in White Rock.

Graham died two weeks after undergoing a routine operation for varicose veins last Sept. 20.

Anesthetist Dr. Robert Barnbrook said that, by the time it was discovered that the tube had come out, Graham was already brain dead.

Barnbrook told the inquest that, "in 20/20 hindsight. . . .it's my belief that the patient extricated the tube when we turned him over."

He said the oxygen tube slipped out between Graham's vocal cords and became lodged in the esophagus which leads to the stomach.

The mishap occurred when the overweight, anesthetized Graham was turned over on to his stomach in preparation for the operation.

Barnbrook said there was no indication of any problem.

He said the congested, bluish hue of Graham's skin resulted from the face-down position of the patient.

Witness Dr. Rinz Dykstra said he first pointed out a
bluish color in Graham's complexion to Barnbrook when
the tube was first inserted.

Barnbrook replied that the color was normal under the
circumstances.

When Graham's leg was cut open, and the blood was a
purplish color, doctors realized they had a crisis.

Two minutes later, Graham's heart rate dropped to
zero and he went into full cardiac arrest.[35]

Like the wire brief, this story works on two levels simultaneously. It describes a specific, reportorial event, an official British
Columbian inquest whose boundary occurrence was the ultimately
fatal operation on Mr. Graham's varicose veins. Published on February
11, 1986, and describing testimony given the previous day, its geographic and temporal locaters are bounded by the place and date of the
original operation, Peace Arch Hospital in 1985, but focused reportorially by events occurring in the February, 1986, inquest courtroom.
The subject of the story, it's "who," includes both the event-specific
physician(s) testifying at the inquest and, as boundary subject, the
deceased music teacher Mr. Graham.

### The Official Version
Because this is reportage of an inquest, the body of the copy focused exclusively on what was said in testimony. The "how" of Mr. Graham's death, which Ms. Horwood calls a "mishap," is attributed by Dr.
Barnbrook to Mr. Graham himself: "In 20/20 hindsight . . . it's my
belief that the patient extricated the tube when we turned him over."
The point is not questioned and, indeed, is elaborated on by the reporter who offers that the fatal "slip" occurred when the "overweight,
anesthetized Graham was turned over on to his stomach in preparation
for the operation." There is a subtle suggestion that, if only he had
not been overweight, perhaps the tube would not have become dislodged. In his obesity Mr. Graham contributed, somehow, to his own
demise. If his weight were not important and the sheer mass of his bulk
irrelevant to the patient's extrication of the tube, why include the ad-
jective "overweight" when describing the unconscious patient?

Dr. Dykstra suggested in his testimony (specific event) that a
cyanotic color typical of incorrect intubation was evident early in the
operation,[36] but Barnbrook's testimony assured the inquest that a
bluish hue to the patient's skin was "normal under the circumstances." It is difficult, especially in retrospect when we know there
was oxygen starvation, to credit this, but the story marches on too
quickly and is itself too brief for any but the most critical to pause
and query this point. There is an implied difference of opinion between
the two doctors on the importance of this coloration, but the story, our
only trace of that event, does not make it an issue. One is left with a

medical physician's informed and unchallenged statement that the overweight patient somehow extricated the life-giving oxygen tube himself.

### Attribution as Information

This is an interesting example of the force of attribution and the means by which it excludes information. An experienced physician is *who* is speaking. It is, further, the crucial doctor in this case who is making this statement. *Where* and *when* is he speaking? Nowhere but at a formal inquest presided over by government officials. Further, this man is explaining *how* his patient died, not *why* he died or *how* it could have been prevented. The newsperson's job, as Ullmann notes, is to accurately report what is said, heard, or seen by an individual at a place and time (the Five W's). That the physician's explanation may make no sense is irrelevant to the fact that it is *what was said by the doctor* and thus to be reported without question.

Inclusion of other information readily available from the newspaper's files would have severely compromised Barnbrook's statement. White Rock Hospital suspended Dr. Barnbrook's hospital privileges following Mr. Graham's death, for example.[37] In addition, he was under investigation by the British Columbia College of Physicians and Surgeons because of this case.[38] In light of this one can argue that Ms. Horwood should have been suspicious of Dr. Barnbrook's testimony, especially when it conflicted with that of another physician not reported to be under suspension or investigation. But Dr. Barnbrook was the physician of record, and unless the coroner's personnel made an issue of his credibility (and they did not), it was not, under current journalistic conventions, Ms. Horwood's job to do so. Like the Honolulu journalists who reported on Judge Shintaku's attack, Ms. Horwood reported what was said without reference to its plausibility or completeness.

### Omissions

The result is a story that minimized or ignored virtually any element that could be expected to contribute to reader understanding of the causes of and responsibilities for Mr. Graham's death. Dislodgement of an inhalator tube leading to a patient's death is more serious than a "slip." It is a life-threatening problem whose prevention, through proper placement and proper monitoring, is an anesthesiologist's job.[39] Failure to notice an unconscious patient's inability to breath after he or she has been moved—especially when another doctor warns of cyanotic skin coloration—is not a random "mishap" but incompetence that would be actionable in many jurisdictions.[40] None of this is in the *Province*'s story because, however pertinent to Mr. Graham's death, it was not accessible to attributable quotes from actors at the inquest.

The question to a forensic pathologist would not only be "What caused the tube to slip?" but, just as importantly, "Why was that problem not immediately noticed?"[41] There is available and in widespread use a vast array of anesthetic equipment armed with warning alarms and designed to alert a physician in surgery to precisely this type of situation.[42] Anesthesiology texts and the current professional literature argue strongly that life-threatening problems with oxygen transfer and anesthetic administration can be almost entirely eliminated through proper patient monitoring and through the use of this appropriate monitoring equipment.[43] From the traditional stethoscope to the pulse oximeter, technology and traditional medical technique should assure performance of the life support system as long as the patient's pulse, blood pressure, heart rate, and other vital signs are constantly checked. Should a problem like Mr. Graham's occur, available equipment and standard medical procedure are supposed to warn operating room personnel before a situation becomes critical. The story does not mention whether equipment was in place or monitoring procedures were followed.

### Brief and Inquest

The headlines in both stories are misleading and inaccurate. Dr. Dykstra did notice and warn Dr. Barnbrook of a cyanotic color to Mr. Graham's complexion. As every physician, nurse, and ambulance attendant knows, a bluish tinge to the skin is usually an early and clear warning of lack of oxygen in a patient.[44] But despite this sign of oxygen deficit, it was fifteen minutes before the problem was investigated, a delay that, in Ms. Horwood's words, "cost a retired Cloverdale music teacher his life." One must conclude, then, that signs of the "fatal slip" were not so much "unnoticed" as ignored. If the tube became dislodged when health professionals moved the patient prior to active surgery but after anesthesia had been induced, it was not a "fatal slip" on the part of the unconscious patient but a fatal error by the medical personnel who moved him.

The wire story does not say what equipment was used to monitor the operations on the Winnipeg and Ontario women, although that information would be critical to an understanding of their deaths. But if appropriate monitoring equipment was in place, the warning mechanisms apparently were not triggered. It is thus highly likely that it is precisely because the tube failures and resulting problems did not set off alarms, despite the brief's headline, that these deaths occurred.

## THE REPORTORIAL FUNCTION

The headline was not the work of Ms. Horwood but of an editor on the *Province's* staff. She cannot be blamed if it is misleading. But it is tempting to lay at the door of reportorial incompetence her story's inconsistencies and lack of information concerning the context and causes of Mr. Graham's death. If that boundary event were her focus, there is much more that should have been done to describe how Mr. Graham died in White Rock Hospital on September 20, 1985. For example the reporter could have:

- searched newspaper files for other, similar deaths.
- interviewed biomedical engineers about the buckling tubes.
- sought reports on the White Rock Hospital's suspension of Dr. Barnbrook. Was he fighting it? Did he agree with it?
- sought reports from the British Columbia College of Physicians and Surgeons who had begun an investigation of the incident.
- interviewed biomedical engineers about the tubes and other operating room equipment.
- interviewed or questioned coroner or anesthesiology authorities about these things.

Were her subject the death of the Cloverdale music teacher, she should have questioned the fifteen minutes between Dr. Dykstra's warning of the onset of a cyanotic complexion and the official recognition of a medical crisis. If the issue were Mr. Graham's demise, her failure to question Dr. Barnbrook's actions as an actor in the operating room drama was unforgivable. *But the death of Mr. Graham was not Ms. Horwood's subject.* Her assignment was the February inquest and dealt only peripherally with the events of the previous September. She was assigned to cover an official, reportorial event in which the statements of participants could be accepted at face value. Like other reporters covering the inquest, Ms Horwood's job was to focus on inquest testimony and not to investigate aspects of the prior, boundary event.[45]

Finally, there is no mention in this story of the fact, also reported in the *Province*, that at least three other Canadians had died of oxygen tube problems or that federal authorities were concerned enough about these deaths to "alert" provincial health authorities. We do not know if the "buckling" in those cases is similar to Mr. Graham's "fatal slip," but the similarities in all three cases—lack of oxygen during surgery from problems with a "life-giving" tube—strongly suggest congruence. But the Alert was from federal authorities, it was datelined Winnipeg, and it referred to distant deaths. The *Province*'s reportorial focus is a British Columbian inquiry into the prior death of a single White Rock man. The two events, Alert and Inquest, are sundered despite the structural similarities of their boundary events.

There is a splendid isolation of the individual components occurring at all levels of this story. The inquest is, by definition, into Mr. Graham's death. It is by law limited to the elements of that one event, and, were Mr. Graham's the fourth death of its kind in B.C. in that year, information on the previous deaths (and assigning of responsibility for them) would not be admissible. If each death is by definition unique to the coroner, it must be unique also to the reporter for whom each inquest also is an isolated and distinct event. Thus to prepare for the inquest Ms. Horwood did not go to the newspaper files and look for any and all newspaper stories on similar deaths. It was not her job to report on the cause of a death or of a pattern of deaths, but rather to write about the inquest itself. Ms. Horwood reports on what was said under oath in the inquest room and is as isolated from its actors as Mr. Graham was from the women in Winnipeg and Ontario. She is equally distanced from the final mediation of editors, who may, without asking her permission, change her copy and attach a headline to her story which may have no relation to the story at all. Lost in it all is the biomedical cause of Mr. Graham's demise.

In the same vein, the brief describing a Health and Welfare Canada Alert had as its subject not the deaths in Winnipeg and Ottawa but, instead, the attributed statement of federal authorities to health officials across the country. There was neither reason nor mandate for wire reporters or the *Province*'s editors to delve more deeply because the story's subject was an official announcement and not three or four separate Canadian deaths. This is an institutionalized, crafted confusion of levels. One thinks these stories are about specific deaths but, in fact, they are about what authorities said at a time and place clearly removed from issues of responsibility.

This is once again the studium, the feel of the format and style whose rules are to report events one by one, to quote only involved individuals in the reportorial context, so that readers will know what, precisely, was heard and said. In each story, short and direct, facts are similarly isolated each from the other. The headline "Fatal Slip Unnoticed" is not really what the story says, but the distance between it and the paragraphs of copy that explain the incident assure the error will not be noticed. Anesthetist Dr. Robert Barnbrook said that Graham was already brain dead by the time it was discovered that the tube had come out. But six paragraphs later, Dr. Dykstra noticed a cyanotic tinge to the patient, which is common to oxygen starvation. We do not notice this because each attribution ends a thought and each statement is attributed. The relation between statements, paragraph to paragraph, is tenuous. Each statement within the description is isolated from its neighbor, and inconsistencies are, because of this stylistic isolation, difficult to notice. That none truly address the boundary issue—what killed Mr. Graham—is hidden by the application of the form itself as each level of information is isolated from its fellows.

## SIGNIFIED AND SIGNIFIER

Thus there are two or more levels of narrative simultaneously active in both the wire brief and the coroner's story. The lowest, thematic stage of the story appears to explain boundary events, while the other, dominant theme presents the immediate, official version of those antecedent events. The issues of time and subject as boundaries to the story become descriptors of these respective narrative levels. The signifier in the wire service piece is not the death of three anonymous individuals but rather the alerting of health-care authorities by federal officials. That is the event that is attributed and the subject of the piece.

What this wire brief signifies, the underlying message of the story, is underlined by the highly inaccurate but superbly political headline: *Death Sets Off Alarm.* This says that officials watch out for the citizen's health and if anyone dies, authority (health-care authorities, federal officials) will find out why. The official, institutional nature of it all is underlined by the substitution of bureaucratic titles for given names. Thus national vigilance for the well-being of the citizen is signified. It is a reassuring statement: both federal and regional health- care authorities are even concerned about "slips": alert officials and professionals protect the citizen. Three anonymous deaths occur in far-flung parts of the country, and federal officials, working with health authorities, are on the job to protect each of us. It won't happen again, you can be sure. Everyone is "alerted."

Like the wire brief, the inquest story assures readers that while "slips" may occur, the regional government through its attendant services (in this case the British Columbia Coroners Service) will leave no stone unturned in its search for the cause of that "mishap." From the headline on, the story plays down any cause for reader concern over the boundary event. "Fatal Slip Unnoticed," implies a rare error, a minor "glitch" inadvertently overlooked. Physicians are called to explain the death of a retired music teacher—everyone is important and all involved can be called, the whole signified, to public account. But at the same time, the boundary event is isolated systematically from other, similar occurrences (three deaths in Winnipeg, one death in Ontario), and the conflict between official witnesses' statements, those of Dr. Dykstra and Dr. Barnbrook, are made to disappear through paragraph separation so that differences dissolve into an official and unanimous presentation.

What has occurred in both cases is translation of boundary into reportorial event such that the resulting sign is reassuring, hopeful, something each reader can take pride in. The story's sign is official concern and assurance that whatever has happened, the government will make sure that the truth will out. Signification is the official statement "Officials and professionals care for and will protect you." In Barthes's discussion of the black soldier saluting the French flag the signification was based on his uniform and color. Here it is the officialdom of the inquest and the white coats of the doctors that bring about the unconscious inflection.

The newspaper's institutionalized system of copy production is an active partner in this transformation. Its headlines, written by an individual who did not attend the inquest, minimize the seriousness of both stories'—reportorial event *and* boundary occurrence. Ms. Horwood's copy (like that of the brief) has been polished by various editors who are distant in time, geography, and interest from these deaths.[46] All is presented in an atmosphere of professionalism and breezy expertise with assuring, official attribution ("Dr. Barnbrook said," "Federal authorities issued the alert") should a nervous reader be inclined to skepticism. The two-paragraph brief is condensed from Province Wire Services, the inquest story is the work of a local reporter who listened to the physician's testimony. The studium, which is based in turn on the rules of reportage, says that competent professionals prepared these reports based on the work of experts (doctors) and acknowledged officials (coroners): here is what there is to know.

It is not that the stories are empty. They clearly contain a great deal of information. Rather it is that they are, in Barthes's phrase, unary and thus incomplete. They lead nowhere, least of all to an examination of why these individuals died and who is responsible. There is no transformation possible between levels of event discourse —journalistic to boundary—because there is no way for information to flow between them. The newsmen report on the Alert or the inquest and have no direction connection with the boundary deaths that appear to a casual reader to be their subject. Thus the culturally crucial questions —Why did Mr. Graham or these women die? How precisely did the deaths occur? What exactly happened? Who is responsible?—are buried in the apparently complete, officially based news form.

One thinks they are dealt with but, upon examination, they are not. In Marx's phrase, "all that is solid melts into air," and explanations offered by Dr. Barnbrook and federal authorities in the end explain nothing at all. Further, there is little in these news reports to suggest to even the most careful reader that something is wrong. Because the rules are well known by all —reporters quote what was said by third persons—reader, reporter, and editor alike are lulled into accepting a narrative whose social message is clear and consistent even if the information presented regarding the boundary occurrences is at best of questionable value.

It is the narrative rules of news, those limiting story context by time, place, and actor's role, that create a consistent narrative definition resulting in journalists largely confining themselves to specific events in which a limited number of actors are involved in a narrowly bounded, sanctioned event. To the extent that those are officially defined —federal alerts, provincial inquests, official investigations, and professional conclusions—information that is included in a newsman's story will, not surprisingly, reflect the perceptions and positions of the officials whose public statements are transformed into attributed quotes. That the result is perhaps less than many would want is a result of the confusion between boundary and reportorial event. There is no transformation, and the final, reportorial product promises information (on the deaths) that it cannot deliver. What has happened is simply illustrated in the accompanying graph (Illustration 2) in which the various components of each story are illustrated.

Information flows in one direction from the boundary events of a specific death through the mediating levels of multiple investigation, official inquest, reportorial treatment, and finally the editing process to the final product. Information is not bidirectional, and the critical treatment of the boundary event by a reporter is virtually absolute. Ms. Horwood does not participate in the autopsy, interview the doctor, talk to the coroner's pathologist, read medical articles on anesthesia, or seek independent authorities in the area of anesthetic mishap. Nor is that her job. Her assignment is to report on the actors' statements at the final, public forum following the investigatory pro-

**Illustration 2**
**Boundary to Journalistic Event Distances**

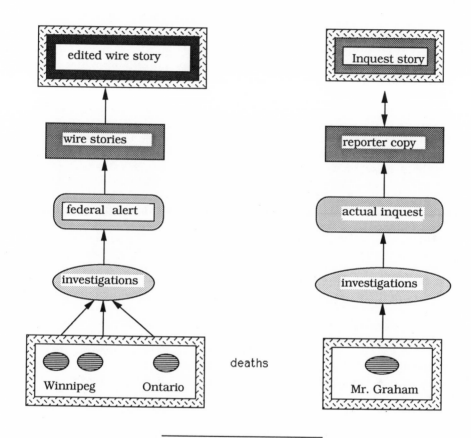

cess. There is no independent, journalistic treatment of Mr. Graham's demise, here, because it is the inquest that is Horwood's story, not the death. Her final story begins at far remove from the official boundary event, and the rules of her form encourage that isolation. After the inquest, her raw copy is reworked by news, copy, and rewrite desk employees even more distant than Ms. Horwood from the events—reportorial and boundary.

It is through this whole process that the reader, like the news professional, is distanced from the real, legitimate and often scary issues raised by the boundary event. Four of the most general and, for me, most critical come to mind:

- Why didn't Dr. Dykstra make Dr. Barnbrook pay attention to the patient's coloration?

- Why wasn't appropriate monitoring equipment used to assure that problems would in fact set off alarms?
- If the hospital and the College of Physicians and Surgeons began investigations into this death, shouldn't that information be in this story?
- How many people have died in this way and will more die from similar "slips" in the future?

There is the appearance of information on Mr. Graham's death here, but what the piece really is, however, is a story on an inquest whose data is abstracted from official investigations occurring well after the fact. We know only what Dr. Barnbrook said but not, really, anything about how or why the death occurred. Dr. Dykstra demurred, but the focus of the copy (and the inquest) is the drama's critical actor, the physician of record, Dr. Barnbrook. He is the crucial witness and, not incidentally, the person whose reputation would be most damaged were it shown that he were in any way at fault. Because information is largely unidirectional, individuals like Ms. Horwood have little opportunity to question him, determine the degree to which this isolated event was in fact part of a series of deaths (Winnipeg, Toronto), or assess responsibility for it. Her participation is at the level of an observer, not at the level of investigation where crucial questions (degree of monitoring, for example) could be raised. The boundaries for information exchange become absolute, while the form of the narrative gives the impression of questions asked and answered.

In the Alert, the distance is even greater. Three separate deaths in two provinces were investigated by provincial coroners, and the results of of those studies were passed to Ottawa, where further study resulted in a synthesis, the official Alert. Either the Alert itself or a press release from the Health Protection Branch describing it, we do not know which was then read by one or more wire service reporters in Winnipeg, who wrote not on any specific death but instead about the federal Alert that is the reportorial event. This wire story was then read by a *Province* editor, who ordered it fashioned by a reporter or rewrite-desk person into the final story, "Death Sets Off Alarm".

The barrier between events—boundary and reportorial—is absolute. This can be graphically described with a simple set theory diagram in which each level is assigned a specific and distinct designation. Each level may include descriptions or information from the preceding level, but the situation does not reverse. Thus the boundary event will inform, perhaps, the official investigations into its parts, but the official investigation cannot change or alter the complex that is the specific death or occurrence.

### Set Theory
These levels of information can be represented graphically, using

**Illustration 3**

**Levels: Boundary Event to Journalistic Event**

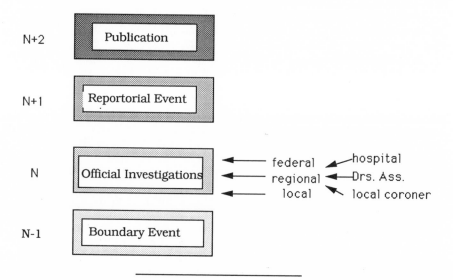

set theory designations for each level. The intent of set theory is to describe a "well-defined collection of objects or elements"[47] which, in this case, allows for a clearer description of the levels of event that occur. It is necessary in the distinction of set elements to assure that the higher order, abstracted groups are not confused with members of the lower, more specific groups. Thus house, street, neighborhood and city are all different levels in which individual houses make up a street that is part of one of many neighborhoods in a specific city. The intent, in terms of news, is to distinguish the sets that are subordinate and those which are superordinate such that the breaks between them can be clearly identified.

Since the basis of these reports is the boundary event, it can be designated, as we have in Illustration 3, "N-1". Deaths are the original occurrence. Mr. Graham died. A woman in Ontario died. A woman in Winnipeg died. These are the bedrock events described with a minimum of interpretation. The initial investigations leading up to inquest or Health protection branch Alert will be labeled "N." The preliminary studies by hospital or pathologist, perhaps at the request of a family member, occur at this level. They may include a number of different tests of tissue samples, toxicology screens, autopsy, and direct interviews with participants. News personnel normally become involved only at the level of N+1, when a final, official statement of finding is issued (the Alert) or an inquest is scheduled. The reporter's story—already highly distanced from the event it promises to cover—is then further mediated through a series of news channels (news desk, copy desk, city editor, etc.) until the final product is published or, for television, presented on air.

Each level is an abstraction directly related only to its antecedent. The investigations do not directly inform the report's story and that story (N+1) has no direct effect on the investigation (N). Each level, further, includes progressive abstraction and the exclusion of perhaps pertinent details, facts, issues, or perspectives. There are expectations at each level that form a sieve to eliminate elements that seem inappropriate. For example, an inquest witness may say, "Fuck no," but it is unlikely the reporter will include that quote in his or her story, knowing that it would be excised by a vigilant rewrite or news desk editor. While a coroner preparing for the inquest may query the hospital about its suspension of Dr. Barnbrook, that information will not necessarily be included in the inquest itself. Perhaps the issue of monitoring equipment is raised but then rejected at the hospital's request as damaging to its reputation and not necessarily germane to the case.

The issue, ultimately, is "who" is the subject and "what" happened at a place and time. The questions of "why" and "how" are, in this process of abstraction, truncated and lost, although the appearance of their treatment remains strong. That is because officials are quoted about their opinions based on investigations of prior, boundary events. It is the facticity of the attributed quote that signals the emphasis of the story and assists in creating barriers between the levels of action "N-1" and journalism, at least "N+1."

### Combined Rules

This returns us full circle to the rules formulated earlier, those defining the obituary. Who and what is investigated may not be so different from who and what is reported when the reporter's and the official's job seem so clearly interrelated. But those rules now require restatement and division into at least two levels, one describing the boundary occurrence and a second set for the journalistic or reportorial event. Sometimes, and the obituary is a good example, these two levels coincide but more often, as we will see in the next two chapters, the distance between reportorial and boundary events is vast:

1. **Who—cultural**

   a) *Journalistic:* Individual, usually an official, quoted for attribution in an official context. The title of the official tends to give standing and import because this is information from the official context of statement ("federal officials said today") and events ("at the inquest, Dr. Dykstra said").

   b) *Boundary:* Subject of secondary, boundary event. Of secondary importance to the story as a whole.

2. **What—social**

   a) *Journalistic:* Public statement or public forum where attributed statements are made. Coroners inquest in this case is "what" has been covered, with the importance of that forum defined to the degree that the individuals in 1.(a) are prominent.

b) *Boundary:*   Secondary and antecedent event. Justifies interest in the 2.(a), the specific, journalistic occurrence, but may have different social weight. In the Canadian cases reviewed, the boundary occurrence is multiple death, for example.

### 3. Geographic

a) *Journalistic:* Defines proximity of reportorial event to be covered. Locater for 1 (a) Journalistic event must be in or bear directly on the immediate circulation district of the publication or audience range of the broadcast station.

b) *Boundary:* Defines physical proximity of secondary, substantiating event. Geographic context may be broader, especially to the degree that it includes multiple, antecedent occurrences.

### 4. Temporal

a) *Journalistic:* Time frame is by definition extraordinarily short, usually within twenty-four hours ("Dr. X said at an inquest today").

b) *Boundary:* Substantiating event can be more distant in time.

These rules are the form of the news, which defines the extent of its coverage and therefor the information a story can contain. These narrative boundaries are not, however, necessary and inevitable. In a later chapter precisely this type of medical story will be reexamined and manipulated through the use of alternate assumptions. First, however, it will be necessary to apply the perspective of boundary and scale to another type of story to see if it remains a consistent pattern in longer-form and multiple-event reportage.

## NOTES

1. John Ullmann and Steve Honeyman, eds,*The Reporter's Handbook: An Investigator's Guide to Documents and Techniques* (New York: St. Martin's Press, 1983),1. The introduction to this volume was written by Ullmann alone.

2. Ullmann gives the original stanza from Kipling as: "I keep six honest serving-men/(They taught me all I knew):/Their names are What and Why and When/And How and Where and Who." Ullmann and Honeyman, *The Reporters Handbook*, 1.

3. Ullmann and Honeymann, *The Reporter's Handbook*, 3.

4. Clifton Daniel and Irving Kristol,"The Times: An Exchange," *The Public Interest*, 7 (1967), 119-23. The original article by Kristol appeared in The *Public Interest* 6, (1966) but is recapitulated by both Daniel of the *New York Times* and Kristol in this exchange.

5. This view of journalism as reportage was just beginning in Johnson's day. Compare, for example, Boswell's and Johnson's respective treatments of joint trip they took to the Hebrides, for an understanding of the two styles. Boswell was far more "modern" in his use of description than the elder Johnson.

6. J. A. Pottle and C.H. Bennett, eds., *Boswell's Journal of a Tour to the Hebrides* (New York: McGraw-Hill,1936). quoted in W. Jackson Bate, *Samuel Johnson* (New York: Harcourt, Brace Jovanovich, 1975), 473.

7. Cooke did not "abstract the mind from all local emotion," and obeyed, to her shame, Johnson's injunction to advance the "dignity of thinking being." That, in the end, may have been her greatest crime.

8. Roland Barthes, *Camera Lucida* (New York: Hill and Wang,1981), 26. Barthes defines studium as "application to a thing, for someone, a kind of general, enthusiastic commitment, of course, but without special acuity." My use of this originally Latin word differs slightly, drawing from both his definition and the argument he later develops around it.

9. This was, until very recently, the common means of inculcating new reporters into the form and general outline of a news story. At least as late as 1972, new members of the *Springfield Union* staff would be given a seat at the obituary desk and enjoined, by then city editor Jane Muroney, to learn the form and the nature of news through death announcements brought in each day by funeral directors and local undertakers.

10. Brian S. Brooks, et. al. *News Reporting and Writing*, Third Ed. (New York: St. Martin's Press, 1988), 155. Brooks laments that some reporters view obituary writing as a "tedious exercise in formula writing, an attitude fostered by editors who assign the obits only to new writers". He then goes on to teach that formula which is its major lesson.

11. Editorials are commonly written by members of a newspaper's editorial board who meet and discuss issues as a group. While one writer is assigned to each topic, the final product is reviewed by others and the result is not signed but taken as the "newspaper's" position. Some newspapers do now allow board members' names to be apended to their statements but this remains the relatively rare

exception.

12. Brooks, *News Reporting and Writing,* 155.

13. Alden Whitman, for years the chief obituary writer for the *New York Times,* has been credited with raising the obituary from apprentice work to a master's craft. He had the rare honor of writing his own obituary, which was published in that paper upon his death. Examples of Whitman's work have been collected and published as Alden Whitman, *The Obituary Book* (New York: Stein and Day, 1964).

14. By chosing an obituary from this magazine rather than, say, the *New York Times* or *Washington Post,* the intent is to describe a publication whose rules and focus are clear. In obituaries as in all forms of news, information chosen for inclusion will vary somewhat from publication to publication, but the rules of story generation, it is argued here, will remain consistent.

15. *Editor and Publisher,* Aug. 6, 1988, 24.

16. John McPhee, *La Place de la Concorde Suisse* (New York: Farrar, Straus & Giroux, 1983), 58. In Switzerland, where universal military service is accepted, even notices of professional promotion usually indicate a man's military rank and division.

17. Brooks describes the obituary's lead paragraph as "who (Michael Kelly, 57, of 1234 West St.), what (died) where (at Regional Hospital), when (Tuesday night), why (heart atack) and how (suffered while jogging)." see Brooks, *News Reporting and Writing,* 155.

18. Nor is this necessarily universal. Chinese language newspapers do not publish death notices to the same degree or in the same style (see *Ren Ming Er Bao,* currently published daily in Beijing for an example). Navajo peoples do not make of death the communal event that Judeo-Christian peoples do. This is a cultural artifact and not a universal, human given.

19. Traditional Chinese reporters had a bewildering array of words to describe with some precision the type of strike from sword or knife used to kill another. There is also a technical vocabulary for strikes from hands and feet that was once used widely in Chinese-language newspapers and, certainly, which live on in Chinese literature. Alas, the gun has replaced the hoary blade in many areas and the vocabulary for projectile deaths is rather mundane.

20. I worked at the *Springfield Union* and *Springfield Republican* from 1972-1974. The same rules apply, in general, at other papers

where I've worked and in wire reportage.

21. Lewis H. Lapham, *Money and Class in America* (New York: Ballintine Books,1988), 51.

22. Onassis took over the company from her father, Aristotle Onassis, and ran it with acumen and vision. Had she been less wealthy and perceived more as a business person, perhaps the stories would have focused on her accomplishments rather than on her vast inherited wealth and its eventual effect on her daughter.

23. Don Maclachlan, city editor, the *Province*, Vancouver, Canada. *personal communication*, 1981. This is so hoary a phrase that it probably needs no attribution; every news editor I've worked with has quoted it—or a variation on it— at some point.

24. See footnote 20. It is interesting to note that while Hong Kong and Taiwan newspapers preserve, to at least some degree, this specialized language of mayhem that it is, at this writing, virtually absent from the mainland Chinese newspapers.

25. This is an old culture rule. Consider the line in Shakespeare from Mark Anthony's speach in which he announces he has comes to praise Ceasar, not bury him, because the man's good will live after.

26. These rules become exceeding complex. Wealth, political position, and professional statue all are crucial elements in the degree to which an individual is quoted. But the relation between the Who and the What, the context of a reported event varies greatly depending on location, circulation, politics and custom. It is, quite literally, a dissertation topic on its own.

27. Their deaths rather drastically precede the publication's birth.

28. Michael Kell, "Quayle Likely to Stay in Bush's Shadow," *Baltimore Sun*; reprinted in *Columbus Dispatch*, January 3, 1988, 5A.

29. M.L. Stein, "Who Sets the News Agenda?" *Editor and Publisher*, December 31, 1988, 7.

30. Quoted in Stein, " Who Sets the News Agenda?"

31. Karl Marx, *Marx-Engels Reader*: quoted in Marshall Berman, *All That Is Solid Melts Into Air* ( New York: Viking Penguin, Inc., 1982), 111. Berman argues eloquently and at length on the relation between Nineteenth century nihilism and Twentieth century modernity. I recommend without reservation his analysis of the social effects of this view in modern society.

32.The *Province* 's story library was made available to me through the kind offices of its former city and now its managing editor Don Maclachlan. Vancouver BCTV television reporter John Daley also assisted by checking both his station's and the Vancouver Public library's story index for stories I needed but did not have in my files. I am grateful to them both.

33. During the early transition under then managing editor Donna Harvey it was to become, in her words to a staff meeting, a "bright morning read."

34. "Death Sets Off Alarm, the *Province*, February 3, 1987, 9.

35. Holly Horwood, "Fatal slip unnoticed," the *Province*, February 11, 1986, 4.

36. Roy G. Soper, et al., *EMT Manual*, (Philadelphia: W. B. Saunders Co.,1984). It is worth noting in passing the value of this type of simple manual to the lay person attempting to understand complex procedures in a specialty like emergency medicine.

37. This was reported at the time by the *Province*, however.

38. Larry Still, "Patient Death Sparks Probe," the *Sun*, October 24, 1985. In its official announcement the hospital did not call the patient's death a "mishap." Rather, the official statement said that "a surgical patient suffered an incident." A separate story in the *Province* said the investigation was dropped by the B.C. College of Physicians and Surgeons after Dr. Barnbrook decided to retire following Mr. Graham's death.

39. "Ultimately, prevention and correction of equipment malfunction depends on the anesthesiologist, who must understand the function of each piece of equipment." F. K. Orkin and L. H. Cooperman, eds., *Complications in Anesthesiology*, (Philadephia: Lippincott,1983), 639-645.

40. There are a number of U.S. cases in which failure to appropriately monitor a patient has resulted in large malpractice awards. For a discussion of one case, see "Medical Negligence: Damages: Loss of Adult Consortium," *American Trial Lawyers Association Reporter* (November 29, 1986), 388-90.

41. This type of differential diagnosis is precisely what pathologists do in iatogenic briefs. For an example of a thorough analysis of a surgical death in which the failure of a physician to monitor a patient contributed to death, see Dianne Y. Messier, "Judgement of Inquiry into the Death of Ronald James Mason," *Coroner's Court of British Columbia*, November 1988.

42. A critical article in this area is H. Eichorn, et. al., "Standards for Patient Monitoring during Anesthesia at Harvard Medical School." *Journal of the American Medical Association* (JAMA) 256 (1986), 1017-1020. It has been widely quoted since its publication. For a popular treatment, UPI, "Move to Save Lives in Operating Room/Researchers urge Anesthesia Standards," *Sacramento Bee*, August 22, 1986, A.24. For a description of the equipment that, when used, provides sufficiently prompt warning to eliminate or severely reduce deaths like this, see C. Whicher, et.al., "Anesthetic Mishaps and the cost of monitoring: a proposed standard for monitoring equipment," *Journal of Clinical Monitoring*, 4 (January, 1988), 15.

43. F. K. Orkin and L. H. Cooperman, eds. *Complications in Anesthesiology*, (Philadelphia: Lippincott, 1983) 639-645. Also see John L. Sun, *Manual of Anesthesia*, 2d. ed. (Boston: Little, Brown, and Co., 1982).

44. Roy Soper et. al., *EMT Manual*, 43. Blue skin (cyanosis) is caused by "inadequate oxygenation" and requires immediate oxygen, airway control, and ventilation assistance.

45. The Vancouver Public Library maintains a clipping file that collects stories from local newspapers on specific issues. Neither that file nor the newspaper library at Pacific Press reveal stories diverging significantly from Ms Horwood's.

46. Wire stories are edited by members of the news desk, while reporters copy is typically filtered first through the city desk, and then a rewrite desk. Finally it may again be cut by the news desk when final page placement is decided.

47. Anthony Gatrell, *Distance and Space: A Geographical Perspective*, (Oxford: Clarendon Press, 1983), 9.

**3**

# The News as Attribution

One might argue that the analysis so far is suspect because its examples include either a single obituary from a trade magazine or short, not necessarily typical stories excerpted from a tabloid where space for copy is by definition at a premium. With more room in which to craft a piece, one might hope that reporters could complete a story in which these criticisms were invalid. The question, then, is the degree to which this studium differs in full length newspapers. If the barrier between specific and reportorial events is institutionalized, it should be as evident in, say, the *New York Times* as it is was in the *Province* stories. If the argument is that a structural barrier exists between information supposedly conveyed and information actually presented, then it should be everywhere valid in the world of daily journalism.

Further one could argue, at least in Ms. Horwood's case, that even if the studium is consistent, the example of the inquest was unfair. Perhaps Ms. Horwood was constrained by her bosses to write only about the inquest itself and cannot be blamed for failing to report on a wider context. Maybe she just is not a good reporter and didn't know what quotes to check or how to ask questions afterward. Since we worked together at the *Province* in the early 1980s, I am convinced that this is not the case but, my testimonial regarding Ms. Horwood's abilities will not necessarily convince others. Certainly the inquest story offered little to invite reader confidence.

## A POLICE STORY

To ascertain the degree to which patterns of specific and reportorial events affect the content of the final story in other contexts, this chapter examines two different examples of police reportage. One is a full, column length story from the *New York Times,* and the second is drawn from Honolulu newspaper coverage of the Shintaku case introduced earlier. The former represents a story of sufficient length in which brevity alone cannot account for the type of information presented. The Shintaku stories apply the argument to a series of reports on a complex of events over time. If the studium is pervasive and institutionalized, it should be isorythmic, a constant across the map of daily journalism. If the studium defines the content of a story, its effects should be evident equally in these examples.

The first story in this chapter is included in its entirety, despite its length, because of the wealth of information it appears to convey:

# 2-Year-Old Dies After Operation In Dental Office

**by Robert O. Boorstin**

A two-year old Queens boy died yesterday afternoon hours after a routine dental operation went awry, the police said. Transportation of the child from the dentist's office to a hospital was apparently delayed by a dispute between the dentist and paramedics who were summoned by police officers, they added.

The child, Rifa Setiyono, of 36 Slocum Crescent in Forest Hills, was pronounced dead at Elmhurst General Hospital about six hours after the end of the operation to repair and extract some of his teeth, according to a police spokesman, Sgt. John Venetucci.

Authorities said they were awaiting the results of an autopsy by the medical examiner's office, which is scheduled for today. No charges were filed.

The child was removed by emergency personnel from the office of the dentist, Dr. Philip Howard, at 10036 67th Avenue in Forest Hills after a confusing series of incidents in which two police officers and four paramedics went to the office and apparently failed to persuade the dentist and associates to let them remove the child, according to police accounts. The police did not know how many dentists in addition to Dr. Howard were in the treatment room.

**Declined to Comment**

Reached early this morning through his answering service, Dr. Howard declined comment.

Efforts to reach the child's father, identified as Bambang Setiyono, were unsuccessful.

According to an account provided by the police, the child was taken by his father to Dr. Howard's office, which he shares with at least four other dentists, at about 8:30 a.m.

During the operation, the child received unspecified doses of a combination of anesthetics and pain killers including pentathol, ketamine, nitrous oxide and Valium, Sergeant Venetucci said.

The dental work was completed at about 11 a.m. and the child was placed in another room to recover from the anesthetic. At about 3:30 p.m., Mr. Setiyono noticed that his son, who was not fully awake, was having difficulty breathing.

The boy was then brought into a treatment room, where Dr. Howard—later joined by associates—used suction to remove an obstruction, gave the child oxygen and performed cardiopulmonary resuscitation, Sergeant Venetucci said.

A pediatric dental expert said early this morning that there was an "incredible range of possibilities" to explain what might have gone wrong. The factors include the combination and dosage of anesthetics, the procedures followed and the state of the child's health, Dr. Stephen J. Moss, past president of the American Academy of Pediatric Dentistry, said after being informed of the details provided by police.

As emergency efforts continued, a dental assistant identified by the police as Lisa L. Klein called for the police and an ambulance. It was not clear whether Miss Klein took the initiative to make the call or was responding to requests from others.

Just after 4:20 p.m., two police officers from the 112th Precinct arrived at the office, which is in the basement of an eight-story brick apartment building. They went into the front room of the office, but when they entered the small treatment room they were told by Dr. Howard and other dentists to leave, according to Detective Jerry Friedman, the investigator in charge of the case.

Minutes later two teams of paramedics arrived, entered the treatment room but failed to convince the dentists to allow them to remove the child, Detective Friedman said.

A police sergeant arrived minutes later and took control of the situation and convinced the dentists to let the paramedics remove the child.

A team of six trauma experts at Elmhurst General Hospital attempted to revive the boy, but he was pronounced dead at 5:25 p.m.[1]

## Observations

The *New York Times* story appears different on first reading from the previous examples. It is, for one thing, far longer than the three stories discussed in the last chapter. Another difference is that this reporter did make independent calls and garnered information from various sources on his own. Ms. Horwood, on the other hand, merely quoted elements of inquest testimony in her piece.This *New York Times* piece also used proper names (with middle initials) instead of the titles which made the wire brief so generic. Finally, this example of police reportage has a lot of names or, at least actors in its drama: five dentists (Dr. Howard and his associates), an unknown number of paramedics, two police officers, the dental technician, at least one police sergeant, a detective, the deceased, his father, and the reporter's outside expert, Dr. Moss.

Unlike  the last chapter's examples, this story appears to describe neither an overt institutional event or  a simple, official report. It is a piece of police reportage describing what investigators said about a recent and apparently isolated event. Finally, it is distinguished from the previous examples by the short distance between boundary and reportorial occurrences. This report was published less than twenty-four hours after Rifa Setiyono's death. Months separated the death of Mr. Graham and the inquest Ms. Horwood covered for the *Province,* and the time between deaths and the Alert in its wire service story is unknown but presumably substantial. The tight temporal parameters of this story thus further distinguish it from the other stories. Like the previous examples it does, however, deal with death.

### Event Definitions

The boundary event that justifies this story appears to be clearly stated in the first and second paragraphs. A two-year-old boy, Rifa Setiyono, died after a "routine dental operation went awry, the police said." Sergeant  John Venetucci is quoted in the next paragraph, affirming that the boy  was pronounced dead at Elmhurst General Hospital about six hours after a dental procedure was performed to "repair and extract some . . . teeth." Police answer hundreds of distress calls each night, and children die in hospital as a result of a variety of occurrences all the time. Few of those deaths are considered sufficiently noteworthy to command a column of copy in the *New York Times,* however.

What distinguishes this story from others is not the notoriety of the child or the fame of his family. There is no suggestion of either money nor extraordinary social prestige attached to the Setiyono name. The story earned its space not as a social marker of the demise of a professionally important person as did Mr. Koop's obituary, but instead because it describes a *reportorial* event directly involving the following professionals: police officers, police detectives, city paramedics, private dentists, and a dental technician. Further, it involves them in a specific, if not unique, human drama. The story's focus is clearly stated in the opening paragraph: "Transportation of the child from the dentist's office was apparently delayed by a dispute between the dentist and paramedics who were summoned by police officers, they [the police] added" to the reporter. Rifa Setiyono's death—its causes and its fact—are secondary to that dispute and its subsequent, official involvement.

From the beginning it is made clear that this story is based on police information concerning a disagreement between one or more dentist(s) and officialdom—paramedics summoned by police—over an apparent emergency involving the two-year-old Queens child. The story's actual focus, then, is the "confusing series of incidents in which two police officers and four paramedics went to the office" of Dr. Philip Howard at 10036 67th Avenue in Forest Hills, "and apparently failed to persuade the dentist and associates to let them remove the child." That's what the police told Mr. Boorstin and what Mr. Boorstin is writing about.

### Attributive Event

There are already three separate stages to this story. One is that of the specific, boundary event—the untimely and apparently unnatural death of Rifa Setiyono. The second is the reportorial event in which police officers and later paramedics were called to Dr. Howard's office and denied entry. Third and most important is what we can call the *attributive* event. This is the basis of Mr. Boorstin's story and includes the complex of police inquiries attributed to Detective Jerry Friedman and Sergeant John Venetucci. What is being offered is a summary of police statements mediated, apparently, through two officers of moderate rank who are or were in charge of the official investigation. Remember that Ms. Horwood listened to testimony at the inquest and wrote on what she heard. The wire reporter in Winnipeg read Ottawa's *Alert* (or a press release describing it) and perhaps even talked to someone involved in its crafting. Here we have Mr. Boorstin's summation of police and expert (Dr. Moss's) testimony. This is not a story about what the reporter saw firsthand or heard from principal actors.

That the real subject of the story—expert testimony— is distinct from the apparent subject—a boy's death—is a simple but crucial point which demands amplification before its ramifications are made clear. What, exactly, does this attributive event level say? According to an account provided to newsmen by the police officials, Rifa Setiyono was taken by his father to an office shared by Dr. Howard and at least four other dentists about 8:30 a.m. on the morning of June 3. We do not know who provided which police officer with this information. Both Sergeant Venetucci and Detective Jerry Friedman, the investigator in charge of the investigation, are quoted by name. But they were not on the scene or personally involved in these events. Direct actors who presumably provided this information to them included an unknown number of paramedics and two police officers from the 112th Precinct as well as an unnamed police sergeant who may or may not be Mr. Venetucci himself. The information related by the sergeant to Mr. Boorstin also could have come from any or all of the following: Mr. Setiyono, Dr. Howard, his associates, or the dental assistant, Ms. Lisa L. Klein.

The information is thus at least third hand and therefore really unattributed. We do not know with any precision where this information comes from and thus cannot judge with any certainty its validity and, therefore, its importance. Perhaps Miss Klein told a police officer who reported to Sergeant  Venetucci who cleared it with Detective Friedman who condensed it for Mr. Boorstin. But then again, maybe one of Dr. Howard's associates talked directly to Sergeant  Friedman who had an as yet unnamed, subordinate officer take down the associate's statement about what Dr. Howard did or did not do before or after Miss Klein called for help. Mr. Boorstin's information, and thus ours, is based on the statements  by individuals to police officers to other police officers, and is thus in some serious doubt.

### What Is Known

Applying Kipling's reportorial mnemonic  to the boy's death tells us very little. The who, what, when, where of the story's boundary incident is clear: Rifa Setiyono, 2, of 36 Slocum Crescent in Forest Hills, Queens, New York, died yesterday, June 3, 1986, at Elmhurst General Hospital. Further, he died after  undergoing dental surgery. That is all that is known, based on police testimony. The relationship between the boy's death, the dental surgery and the reportorial event—an "apparent dispute" between the dentist and, at first, police but also later paramedics —is strongly implied but unproven. We do not know, despite the overwhelming number of "facts"  included in this story, anything about how or why the boy died. Someone said that four and a half hours after Rifa Setiyono's surgery the boy's father noticed he was having trouble breathing. We do not know if the boy was alone or attended for all that period . Nor do we know why he was still in the office four hours or more after the operation. In a "treatment room," Dr. Howard then removed an unnamed obstruction and began emergency procedures. Whether the "obstruction" removed was related either to the dental surgery or the boy's respiratory difficulties is likewise uncertain. Perhaps Rifa, bored with his four-and-a-half-hour wait in the dentist's office, picked up something from the office floor and swallowed it.

Other actors in this drama were unavailable for comment and one can perhaps sympathize with Mr. Boorstin's problem. The father and the dentist declined any comment to the press. Ms. Klein's conversation with policemen is reported secondhand but apparently she too was unavailable to the *New York Times*. Whether the reporter tried to locate the paramedics or the specific officers involved is unstated. What is included in the story is a summary of the police description, presumably based on participant statements, which was then summarized and placed into a news form by Mr. Boorstin.

What gives this story its sense of informative veracity is the attributive, abstracted level. The police department's official investigator, Detective Jerry Friedman, summarized what he knew of the boundary event for Mr. Boorstin. Sergeant Venetucci, who may or may not be the sergeant who resolved the situation at the dentist's office, also gave the newsman information based on his participation or investigation. Kipling's rules, then, are clear in this case: Detective Jerry Friedman and Sergeant John Venetucci (who) informed *Times* reporter Robert O. Boorstin "What" they and other police officers had been told happened on the day (when) Rifa Setiyono died in Dr. Howard's dental office (where) following an operation (when). How and Why are perhaps suggested in this story but not really described.

Reasons and causes of Rifa's death, despite the length of the story and the reporter's clear ability to question police and experts, are not known. What the story provides is an abstract of what police officers reconstructed based on the statements of boundary actors. As with Ms. Horwood's story, the difference between levels—despite the initial assumption of a clear statement about the boundary subject's demise—remains. The story's focus is not how Rifa died, why he died, how that death could have been prevented, or the identification of agents responsible for his death. Mr. Boorstin's story describes an event of police and paramedic involvement following a medical emergency. The city's (police) officials are his subjects, the source of his quotes and the reason this copy was given a good column's space in the *Times*.

### Dr. Moss

Dr. Stephen J. Moss, past president of the American Academy of Pediatric Dentistry, told Mr. Boorstin there were an "incredible range of possibilities" which could explain the incident. Anesthetic drug overdose, incorrect anesthetic administration, and "general health" are mentioned based on information provided by police to Mr. Boorstin and related by him to Dr. Moss. Sergeant Venetucci is quoted, earlier, saying that Rifa received a virtual pharmacopeia of drugs including pentathol, ketamine, nitrous oxide, and Valium.[2]

The clear unattributed implication is that either the anesthetic drugs, the dental procedure, or more likely both together were responsible for the boy's death. The headline implied this by melding the death with the dental operation to suggest a temporal and thus perhaps casual relation: "2-Year-Old Dies After Operation In Dental Office." If the death were not drug-related, however, Mr. Boorstin's pharmacologic catalogue of tranquilizer (Valium) and anesthetics (nitrous oxide, ketamine, pentathol) would be extraneous. Were Rifa's death the result of some nonprocedural obstruction in the throat and not a result of the dental surgery, then the issue of dental surgery would be totally irrelevant. Further, it would be misleading. The weight of detail concerning drugs and Dr. Moss's comments suggesting their possible relevance to this case all suggest this was a drug-related dental death.

That Dr. Moss has no direct or secondhand information concerning the case and is commenting only on what Mr. Boorstin learned from police officials (and we *do not know* who they talked to) raises the critical issue of why he was consulted at all. Further, the degree to which his attributed quote seems, on first reading, to add both authoritative weight and depth to Mr. Boorstin's news story, is curious. The answer is based on the first of Mr. Kipling's six serving men and "who" Dr. Moss is to us. As past president of the American

Academy of Pediatric Dentistry, he is expertise and authority personified in a person whose views will be acknowledged and solicited no matter how tenuous his grasp of the facts of a specific event. Just as, in the discussion of an obituary, professional status determined the degree to which a death deserved special recognition, so, too, in life does professional accomplishment widen the grasp of an individual's omnipotence.

Call this, for want of a better term, the force of prior weight. To the degree a subject can be given a title of professional prominence, his or her perceptions will be awarded greater attention by reporters no matter how removed that individual may be from the specific event being discussed. Thus, for example, in a story on higher education in which a specific department is under investigation, the word of a university president will be given greater value (weight) than that of a graduate student or assistant professor—whatever the relative involvement of the actors may be in that context. Indeed, the less involved an actor is at the boundary the more "objective" his views and the more truthful he or she appears to be. The assistant professor and graduate student may be actual participants in the complex being reported, but the president (without any direct involvement) will, by stating an opinion, add a feel of authenticity and authority to the story and his conclusion must be featured prominently in such a report.

This has been described as a general news pattern by Lewis Lapham who remembers that:

> Over a number of years in the newspaper business, I dutifully took down notes of speeches delivered by people noteworthy for the titles and offices they held, not for their wit or intelligence. Most of what they had to say was bland or fatuous, but this didn't prevent their remarks from being prominently displayed on the front page of next day's editions.[3]

The prominence of such worthies in a specific story, Lapham suggests, was directly proportional to the titles held and not necessarily related to their knowledge of the subjects on which each was asked to speak.

### The Police Version

The implications of complications with drug administration suggested by Dr. Moss are inherent in the police summary of the boundary event, but their understanding is irrelevant to the reportorial event. An autopsy is scheduled, the story says, and that will determine the facts of Rifa's demise. In the meantime, the story's focus is the barring of police and paramedics from the dentists' office while the patient remained in distress and presumably in need of attention. On this level, there are few real details but a nicely drawn sketch whose atmosphere includes fear, desperation and confusion. Ms. Klein, either on orders from a superior or out of personal concern, called for police, who arrived at 4.20 p.m. They were barred, Detective Friedman said, by Dr.

Howard. Presumably that is what the participating officers told the detective, and it makes some sense. A dentist or surgeon trying to save a child's life would not want to pause to discuss details of the origin of that patient's distress with a layperson. Paramedics then arrived at the request of the 112th Precinct officers, and they were admitted to the treatment room but barred from transporting the child to hospital by the dentists, who allegedly were working to save the child's life. Finally, a police sergeant arrived and convinced the dentists to let paramedics remove the child to Elmhurst General Hospital, where Rifa was pronounced dead at 5:25 p.m.

### Unanswered Questions

A computer search of *New York Times* files finds no subsequent stories on this case.[4] A computer search of court records also finds no legal action by the Setiyono family against the dentist.[5] Thus there appears to have been no investigation or continuing reportage beyond the events of June 3, 1986. Presumably, Mr. Boorstin and his editors were satisfied they had satisfactorily covered the complex of occurrences that began when Rifa Setiyono entered Dr. Howard's office that morning and ended at Elmhurst General Hospital that afternoon when the boy was pronounced dead. But on the basis of the newspaper's story, what is not known is almost everything critical to understanding the boundary or reportorial events:

- Was there an obstruction in the boy's throat?

- If so, was that related to his asphyxiation?

- What relation, if any, existed between his anesthetic medication and subsequent respiratory difficulties?

- Was the boy alone between 11:00 a.m., when the operation ended, until the difficulties with breathing were noticed at 3:30 p.m.? If so, was this appropriate dental procedure? If not, who was with Rifa and did that person see him swallow anything?

- Between 3:30 p.m. and 4:20 p.m., what did the dentist(s) do to assist the boy?

- Had Dr. Howard had similar "mishaps" in his office in the recent past, or was this his first case of anesthetic complication? Was he, in fact, certified to use these drugs in this way?

- What did the police officers want to do when they first arrived at the office? arrest Dr. Howard? transport the boy themselves?

- What, if anything, did the paramedics do while in the treatment room?

- When the unnamed sergeant arrived, what was the boy's

situation and how did he resolve this jurisdictional dispute?

It is interesting to note that the use of attribution ceases by the story's final paragraphs. The arrival of the police sergeant and the boy's hospital death are stated as fact in the omniscient "Obituary" voice. But by now it is clear that police are being quoted and that this story's power is determined by its level of official attribution. It tells almost nothing, suggests virtually everything—panicking dentists, drug overdose, police and paramedics, a concerned dental technician—but in the end, delivers only what police officials choose to release. Thus at the "attributive" stage of the journalistic level officials control both the informational content and the social and political meaning signified (embedded) in the piece.

We don't know how the boy died; what relation, if any, existed between the dental anesthesia and that death; if the dentist(s) performed competently or if this was malpractice. What we do know is that the *New York Times* said the police, the source of this story and all its information (excluding that supplied by Dr. Moss) were on the job. Dr. Moss's contribution, besides the veracity his past presidency conveys to the whole, is that anything could have caused the boy's death but that drug overdose or misuse is always a good guess when the facts are not known.

This story, which promises to inform readers about a two-year old's death following dental surgery, in fact does nothing of the kind. It describes elements of a still incomplete police investigation synthesized by Detective Friedman and Sergeant Venetucci for the reporter. They were not participants in the events and may or may not have left important information out of their summation. The story provides little information about Rifa Setiyono's death or life. It provides a great deal about the police whose interest, at this point, is primarily in the relations between the 112th Precinct's officers and the doctors and staff of the dental office. The lack of information on the boy's death is not evident to any but the most critical because this story's focus is elsewhere. It is not about Rifa's demise but rather about an subsequent event complex. It is about the police.

### Levels of Information

Again using set language, it is apparent that what this story provides is a mediated description at level N+3. As illustration 4 makes clear, the reporter's involvement is based on a summary police investigation of official involvement following the medical events. . Level N-1 is the dental surgery and subsequent events in the office prior to 3:30 p.m. N level is the period of respiratory distress and resuscitation events which end with the official demise of Rifa at a distant hospital. Set N+1 describes interaction between three police officers, an unknown number of paramedics and Dr. Howard's crew. This is the reportorial event. N+2 describes the attributive event level, including the police investigation in which information from prior

**Illustration 4**
**Levels of Information and Event: Setiyono**

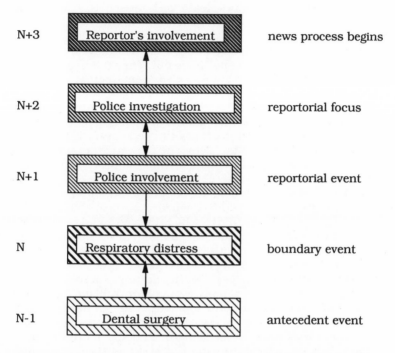

| | | |
|---|---|---|
| N+3 | Reportor's involvement | news process begins |
| N+2 | Police investigation | reportorial focus |
| N+1 | Police involvement | reportorial event |
| N | Respiratory distress | boundary event |
| N-1 | Dental surgery | antecedent event |

Arrows show information exchange between individuals involved in surgery and respiratory distress, investigation and reportage. Police have no direct involvement in respiratory distress or dental surgery but include information on it. Reporters do not investigate. This is represented by unidirectional arrow.

---

levels may or may not be recapitulated but where all data is mediated through the investigators' perspective. Finally, level N+3 is the reporter's copy, which is based only on official judgements or surmises involved in the prior level.

What is evident, again, is a break in the flow of information and a shift of story focus between event levels. This is what illustration 4 attempts to show graphically. The official, attributive set is used by Mr. Boorstin as if it were a description of and explanation for the specific, prior event. To the degree that the story was required for publication the day after Rifa's death and before an autopsy could be completed, its reliance on contemporary journalistic rules made this focus a given. If on June 6, for example, a pathologist's report was released describing death as a result of anesthetic overdose, then the information on drugs used by Dr. Howard in Rifa's sedation would become critical and germane. In that event one would also need to know the boy's weight, exact dosages used of each specific drug, and standard postoperative procedures to write a definitive story of anesthetic distress.[6] If, however, the boy's death was caused by choking on a button he pulled from his sweater, then information on drugs would be irrelevant to the story.

But the reporter, Mr. Boorstin, does not make these distinctions because, presumably, the police do not. They tell him and he tells the reader about drugs and whatever else seems pertinent to the police. Their story, to the extent they wish to release it, is Mr. Boorstin's, and through him it becomes ours. Their official narrative summarized by the detective and sergeant becomes our own and "All the News that's Fit to Print" becomes "All the News the Police Will Tell." Mr. Boorstin could have interviewed Ms. Klein, the paramedics, and participating police officers. He could have written another story after receiving the pathologist's report. But he did not. His assignment was the police investigation of a very limited set of events, and he reported very well on what the police said had happened that day.

"Who," becomes, in short, "who is quoted," and the overwhelming journalistic choice is to credit officials in a news story. The subject of the story may be nominally the death of a boy, the robbery of a storekeeper, or the vicious beating of a circuit court judge. Kipling's serving men define those parameters. But in addition a second focus, a filter, is used to focus those famous five W's of journalism. That is the need at the attributive stage to find someone who can describe the events that have occurred, because *the reporter can not speak for himself.* All his or her words must be attributed, and the more impeccable the source —"prior weight"—the safer and stronger the resulting story will be. Police officials, politicians, and "experts" mediate between the boundary event and its focus and the reporter's eventual public summary. The "who" of the attributive level describes professionals, after all, in a culture that places a premium on assumed ability and work-related titles.

Professionals are presumed to know, and thus the quote of a police sergeant will always be given more weight than that of a dental technician. The thrust of the story becomes of necessity that of a police inquest or federal investigation. Objectivity, the supposed aim of newsmen, becomes through this system a subjective acceptance of the professional's version. The message embedded in this form implies a consistent signified wedded to any signifier that comes to hand. Their sum becomes one of overwhelming bureaucratic care and omnipotence both in society and in service to the citizen. Officials quoted are the journalist's principal source of information, and those bureaucratic perspectives (by the police, the association president, the politician) will a priori prescribe and slant the information finally presented to media consumers.

If one describes the varying actors at each level and considers them as independent voices, the way this happens, especially in stories where there appears to be a concerted voice, is clear.

**N+3** Mr. Boorstin talks to: Dr. Moss, Sergeant Venetucci and Detective Friedman.

**N+2** Sergeant Venetucci and Detective Friedman talk to police officers who arrived with paramedics. Presumably they also talked to Dr. Howard and Ms Klein but it is also possible those interviews were conducted by the officers who arrived on the scene.

**N+1** Ms Klein calls police assistance which dispatches officers who call paramedics. Both officers and paramedics interact with Dr. Howard who, apparently, is the individual who barred their way.

**N** Ms Klein, Dr. Howard, Rifa Setiyono and perhaps Bambang Setiyono.

**N-1** Dr. Howard, Ms Klein, Rifa Setiyono.

This can be graphically illustrated using arrows to describe flows of communication. The story does not provide a record of every exchange, so this must be surmised on the basis of personal experience as a police reporter and on the information the story provides.[7] What is clear from illustration 5 is that the center of the complex of events --if not necessarily of the news text--is the child, Rifa Setiyono, brought by a parent and told to sit in the dentist's chair. The dentist comes to work on the boy and the staff hygienist, perhaps, tries to talk to Rifa and ease his fears. Later, the paramedics work on the boy, who is in severe distress. Information flows first in a professional fashion between Ms. Klein, Dr. Howard and his colleagues, who presumably all share their skills to assist Rifa when his distress is evident.

Miss Klein, however, then calls the police on her own initiative and they call for paramedics on their own. She calls for help and the information is one-way. The paramedics work on the boy but not with him. Police officers interview the dentists and Ms. Klein, thus establishing bidirectional information flows. Certainly the Detective in charge of the case does not do all his own interviewing. Sergeants and patrol officers are present for that purpose so information flows from them to their superior.

Finally, Mr. Boorstin receives his information from the Detective and Sergeant, not from those, like Ms. Klein, directly involved in the complex of these events. Dr. Moss is further distanced from it all, commenting on what Mr. Boorstin heard from Detective Friedman, who heard from Sergeant Venetucci, who was told by the paramedics that when the police were called (by a 911 operator), Miss Klein said that the dentists were having problems with a young patient.

The story's assurance, its appearance of objective and factual reportage, is clearly a result of the relations between Mr. Boorstin and police officials operative at N+2. The story's believability and appearance of completeness come soley from the named sources of Detective Friedman, Sergeant Ventucci, and outside expert Dr. Moss. *What is*

**Illustration 5**
**Information Flow: Setiyono**

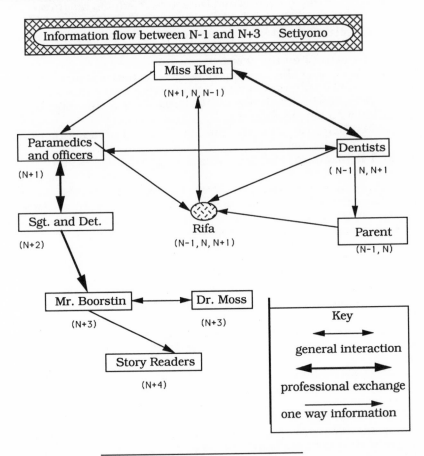

clear from this analysis but hidden from the casual reader is the degree
to which the story's subjects are, in fact, only police officials. That is
who the newsman talks to and the basis of the newspaper's report. The
story thus becomes an official version based on an official investigation using approved witnesses (who may or may not have been actors
in the boundary occurrence). We know, in short, what the police
officials tell Mr. Boorstin and what he and his editors then chose to tell
us.

It is important to emphasize that at the level of semiologic
analysis, what occurs is conjunction between signified and signifier at
each level while at the narrative level, a parallel and progressive
isolation of elements takes place simultaneously. A sign, the body of
a boy whose vital functions has ceased, signifies death. That is an occurrence of cultural note. That death is first joined at the descriptive

stage but immediately separated in the attributive stage from signified, cultural fears (professional incompetence, drugs) to create a
social and political message of professional concern and attention by
designated officials, the investigators (police officers, detectives and
paramedics), professional adepts (Dr. Moss), and finally the newspaper itself. This conjunction is balanced by the distance between
journalistic result and the boundary event.

It is not simply the distance in informational levels that separa-
tes the reader from the facts of Rifa Setiyono's demise. That distance
is an essential part of the style of the story itself. The headline tells
that a "2-Year-Old Dies After Operation In Dental Office," but we do
not know if that death was related to the dental surgery. It is implied
but suspect information. The lead paragraph quotes police, who say
that a Queens boy died hours after an operation went awry, but there
is *no surety* that Rifa's distress was in fact a result of that operation.
What went "awry" was postoperative care, perhaps, and the story's
focus seems to have been one of care in extremis. But that material is
separated from the headline by paragraphs of attributed and perhaps
unrelated text. Later, out of nowhere, Dr. Moss says that maybe drugs
played a part in the whole. Each paragraph is distanced from the
boundary event and related to the attributive stage. Because it is
"objective," short paragraph by short paragraph, nobody says (and
perhaps nobody knew) whether the dentists' attempts to revive Rifa
were correctly carried out with the proper equipment and expertise.
There are machines, like a defribrillator, and specific drugs which, in
cases of drug-related overdose and distress, can bring a patient back.
But since we do not know what caused Rifa's fatal distress we do not
know how appropriate the dentists' efforts were. Each element of the
story is thus distanced from its predecessor, and the real issues—
"why" Rifa died, "who" was responsible and "how" could that death
have been prevented—was lost in the attributive stage.

The final mediated product promises description and objective
information but the final result is rife with inuendos cloaked in facticity. There is the suggestion of drug involvement and malpractice, for
example. Also present is the hint of fear and terror by a dentist whose
young patient is in severe difficulty. Between the lines a suspicion of
panic rests on Miss. Klein's shoulders because she called the police
who in turn summoned medical assistance. But none of this tells us
how or why Rifa Setiyono died or who was responsible. It does not, in
the end, tell us what happened to the boy but suggests what might
have happened. It gives the official version of a sequence of events but
nothing, really, which leads us to or through the last of Kipling's
honest men—"why" and "how."

Thus this *New York Times* story, despite its length, manifests the
same problems as those discovered in the *Province*. It is an abstraction
of what appears to be the death of a boy but is in fact the presence of
police and paramedics at an emergency. Its signified is both police
vigilance (they were there before Rifa died) and official concern. A
detective and at least one sergeant investigate the death of a child. Dr.

Moss, a past president of his association, shows the medical community's concern by agreeing to   discuss the case (despite his lack of knowledge about it)   with the *New York Times*   reporter. That tells readers that the context and facts of Setiyono's distress are clear enough for the reporter (the public's surrogate) to seek an outside opinion. Dr. Moss's participation also eliminates any potential reader concern that  dentistry itself could have been the cause of Rifa Setiyono's death. He is a past president of his association and expresses fluency in the case's issues. At the level of the signifier this  lends an air of reassurance that physicians are generally knowledgeable and concerned about each individual's health. The reassurance comes from the conjunction of the signifier (a man quoted by Mr. Boorstin) and the signified (physician Moss, past president of the American Academy of Pediatric Dentistry) to mean professional competence and concern for the individual.

In addition, Dr. Moss's contribution is to bolster Mr. Boorstin's status both as a disseminator of information and, strangely, as a knowledgeable individual in his own right. It was as a reporter for the *New York Times* that he called the dental association's past president and gained an interview on this case. The signified is that Mr. Boorstin knows what he is writing about. If the technical association's past president does not question the facts Mr. Boorstin presents (or his right to ask questions at all), why should the reader? The newsman's power comes from his own position at the paper and his knowledge comes from the police. So the reader is seduced into accepting hearsay evidence based on police summaries from both Mr. Boorstin and Dr. Moss when in some other context—for example a court hearing—their distance from the case and ignorance of the facts would make the testimony of either suspicious and weak. But here, both are confirmed in their believability and the police are given added weight as investigators as well.

The result is the appearance that newsmen and their sources *know* and that police and officials *care*. The interrelation between actors and the juxtaposition of paragraphs all work to suggest to the reader that this report is, indeed, "All the News that's Fit to Print" about an event whose participants were not interviewed for this report. There is another  implication as well: "Drugs kill." Both Dr. Moss and the police suggested that the anesthetic drugs used in the surgery were a possible contributor to  Rifa Setiyono's death. Beneath the layers of official concern lies the implication, repeated in many ways every day in most papers, that drugs are the cause of tragedies being reported.[8] It is particularly notable here because the one thing an eyewitness, Dr. Howard, is reported to have said was that an obstruction had been removed from the boy's throat. But the story's impression is of a drug-involved crisis involving, perhaps, maladministration of anesthetics by a dentist. That, in  a nation which has made of alleged drug abuse a holy war is not, of course, surprising. When an explanation (the "why") is required for evil, drugs—even at this remove— become a cautionary tale.

## JUDGE HARRY Y. SHINTAKU

Coverage by Honolulu newspapers of the events surrounding the injuring of Circuit Court Judge Harold Y. Shintaku in 1981 was described earlier. Between October 7, the day the judge was admitted to hospital, and November 14, when the police department's hired pathologist admitted he might have made a mistake, a total of sixty newspaper stories were written by both local newspapers on Shintaku's injuries and their possible cause. Both morning and evening newspapers are published under a joint operating agreement and share a single yearly index of the combined journalistic output of both newspapers. In 1981 under "Shintaku, Harold Y." there are approximately thirty listings for each newspaper, including a few editorials and letters to the editor.

There are minor differences between the newspapers' respective story sets concerning the Shintaku case. A few stories are carried by one and not another newspaper, but the majority of library entries include under single headline summations of story content reports for both the morning *Honolulu Advertiser* and the afternoon *Honolulu Star-Bulletin*. For example:

> Circuit judge arrested and charged w/drunken driving; later found unconscious at Mokuleia residence and taken to Wahiawa Hosp. S10/7/81 A1    A 10/8/81 A1.

This entry describes two stories, one appearing in the *Star-Bulletin* on October 7, 1981, page A1 and the other on page A1 in the *Honolulu Advertiser* on October 8 of that year. Both pieces described the arrest of Judge Shintaku on a charge of impaired driving as well as his subsequent discovery, unconscious, at a Mokuleia district residence from which he was eventually transported to Wahiawa Hospital. For all intents and purposes the coverage of Shintaku's arrest and injuries, when viewed both from frequency of story and analysis of story content, was identical in both papers. The closest either came to "enterprise reporting" was an interview published October 11 in the Sunday newspaper published jointly by both newspapers.[9] It was a coup for *Honolulu Advertiser* reporter Walter Wright and published in the combined, weekend edition.[10]

Broken down into categories, the vast majority of articles concerned Judge Shintaku's decision to overturn the jury's decision at the murder trial of Charlie Stevens (twenty-five stories), including the reaction of City Prosecutor Charles Marsland to that judicial act and Marsland's views on both Shintaku's injuries and professional abilities. Of almost equal length were stories detailing the police investigation into Shintaku's injuries (twenty-three stories), almost all quoting police officials or physicians involved in the case. Approximately eight stories dealt primarily with the judge's medical condition,[11] five with his arrest for drunken driving, and six with background on the judge's professional career and history. The later material was "obituary-style," describing Shintaku's service as a lawyer and as a judge. These categories were assigned on the basis of the index's entries alone and not from a complete content analysis of each story.

There therefore appear to be three boundary events in this story complex. The first and earliest is the decision by Judge Shintaku to overturn a jury verdict in the case of Mr. Stevens and the protest that occurred after that decision. Second, there is the arrest of Judge Shintaku on a charge of driving while impaired. Finally, there is the event in which he sustained injuries requiring transportation to Wahiawa Hospital and emergency surgery. These three events offer a general perspective on the degree of interest in various aspects of the story over time. All three are referred to in the following excerpts from the newspapers' files but the emphasis in this analysis is on reportage of the cause, origin and extent of Judge Shintaku's injuries.

The judge was discovered at his beach house, severely injured, on the morning of October 7, 1981, and a story appeared that day in the afternoon newspaper. The story's first paragraphs were:

> Circuit Judge Harold Shintaku was taken unconscious to Wahiawa General Hospital this morning and was listed in fair condition in the emergency room but it was not known what he was suffering from.
> Shintaku was arrested last night and charged with drunken driving after he failed a field sobriety test and a breathalyzer test at the police station, police said earlier today.
> The judge was unconscious when taken by ambulance from a Crozier Loop residence in Mokuleia at 9:44 a.m., police said. He appeared to have no visible injuries, police said. Ambulance drivers notified police about the incident saying it may have been a situation where police need to be involved, an officer said.[12]

The rest of the piece describes Shintaku's arrest the previous evening for drunken driving. There are really two stories here. The majority of copy is given to the issue of a formal charge that Shintaku was driving while intoxicated. That was the prior event and one the newspaper had most time to prepare. The second reports the fact, attributed to police, that an unconscious Shintaku was taken by ambulance to Wahiawa Hospital for unknown reasons. It includes the tantalizing suggestion that ambulance attendants believed this might be a police case but no further details were added. The story jumped to page 5, which included another news story based on a previous day's interview in which Shintaku told reporter Pat Guy that he would welcome a judicial investigation of his decision to overturn the jury verdict in the Stevens case.[13]

The next day's lead story is crucial to understanding the set as a whole. Its headline and opening paragraphs are reproduced included on the next page to give a feeling for the whole, its style and presentation.

# Surgeon Says Shintaku Took a Bad Beating

**By Lee Games and Charles Memminger**
**Star-Bulletin Writers**

Against a background of conflicting reports and unanswered questions, police today were continuing the investigation of the apparent beating early yesterday morning of Circuit Judge Harold Shintaku.

Detective Wes Anderson early this morning was interviewing the two men who were with the judge when he was arrested on a charge of drunken driving Tuesday. Anderson was talking to Frank Kim and Michael Makibe in an attempt to determine Shintaku's movement after he left the police station where he was booked Tuesday night.

Early yesterday morning Shintaku was found injured at a beach house his family owns at 68-729 Crozier Loop on the North Shore where friends say he often went when he wanted solitude. He was seen around the beach house by neighbors at about 1 a.m., police said.

The doctor treating Shintaku said it appeared the judge received most of his injuries—skull fractures, a broken collarbone and black and blue eyes and neck—as the result of blunt blows at about 2 a.m. yesterday a few hours after he was released.

Shintaku was in serious but stable condition this morning in the surgical intensive care unit of St. Francis Hospital where he underwent more than three hours of surgery yesterday afternoon to relieve the pressure in his brain caused by cerebral hemorrhaging.

A hospital spokesman said the judge was able to say a few words this morning.

Doctors say they do not expect any permanent impairment of Shintaku's mental abilities as a result of the head wounds.

*Police said that they have not yet been able to determine how Shintaku was injured, and there are a number of other unresolved questions about the bizarre series of events involving the judge who is currently one of the most controversial in the state judiciary.* (Italics added)[14]

A problem is immediately evident. The headline states definitively that "Surgeon Says Shintaku Took a Bad Beating," but the thrust of the story is one of "conflicting reports and unanswered questions" in the midst of a police investigation. Although the unnamed physician is quoted as saying the judge's injures were "the result of blunt blows," the named police officers have apparently disregarded that view and told reporters that "they have not yet been able to determine how Shintaku was injured." To muddy the waters further and diminish the impact of the unnamed physician's apparently declarative judgment, Mr. Games and Mr. Memminger place Shintaku's injuries in the context of prior judicial events. It is, in their report, one of "the bizarre series of events involving the judge who is currently one of the most controversial in the state judiciary."

In a section excluded here, the story then goes on to quote Police Lieutenant Jerry Postman, who said that after being booked and released on a drunk driving charge, Shintaku and his friends went to a restaurant before Shintaku presumably drove home. Detective Wes Anderson said there was no sign of a struggle at the beach house and "there's been no determination on how the injuries were received." What is promised by the headline, the doctor's statement, thus is contradicted systematically by the first part of the body of the story and the attributed statements of police officials, named and unnamed. It is only toward the end of the piece, in the second column after the copy has jumped from page 1 to an inside position, that one finds the views of neurosurgeon Dr. William Won, who operated on Judge Shintaku, stated in full:

At a news conference yesterday evening after the surgery [neurosurgeon William] Won said Shintaku's injuries showed "evidence of a struggle."

"I think he was struck several times in the head," Won said in explaining the "five or six" skull fractures the judge received. He said the blows appeared to be "blunt."

Won said he first examined Shintaku at about 2:30 p.m. and said that the coloring of Shintaku's wounds indicated that the injuries were about 12 hours old.

During the operation, Won removed blood clots from both sides of Shintaku's brain. Because most of the internal injuries were on the right, or non-dominant side of Shintaku's brain, Won said he did not expect any permanent impairment of Shintaku's abilities.

But he said the judge could experience a weakness on the left side of his body after recovery. He noted, though, that after surgery Shintaku was moving both sides of his body which was interpreted as a positive sign.

Asked if the injuries could have been cause by a fall, Won said "I would think not." He also said of the injuries, "I do not believe they were self-inflicted."

Both of these those two theories [being struck with a blunt instrument and possible suicide] for Shintaku's injuries were put forward yesterday amidst feverish, if at times, misinformed, speculation throughout the city about the incident.[15]

The new and critical piece of information promised in the headline, determination by the participating surgeon that Judge Shintaku's injuries came from a severe beating, thus is inexplicably buried toward the end of the story. The text's first two columns focus almost exclusively on the police investigation and describe the context as a "bizarre series of events" surrounding a controversial judge. It implies but does not overtly state that perhaps Shintaku's actions on the bench or his arrest for drunk driving may somehow be related to his injuries in this "bizarre series of events." The origin of Shintaku's injuries, police insist, are unknown. The story describes in detail the status of the official investigation through the attributed quotes of police investigators Detective Anderson and Lieutenant Postman.

Dr. Won's clinical judgment is downgraded to a "theory" coequal with that of a self-inflicted fall (attempted suicide by hanging), which is broached circumspectly in this report. The reporter further compromises Dr. Won's assertions by stating at the story's beginning that the police (and by implication the journalists') investigation was being pursued "against a background of conflicting reports and unanswered questions."[16] The neurosurgeon's report is not conflicting and not filled with unanswered questions. Based on clinical evidence he insists the injuries could not have been self-inflicted and occurred as a result of blows from a blunt instrument to his patient's skull.

One would presume that so succinct and declarative a statement would have filled the story's opening paragraph. The neurosurgeon's information was clear, brief, and given in plain language. Further, it was the judgment of a knowledgeable, expert participant in the medical event who had seen the injuries firsthand and had the background and training to define their origin. Instead, newsmen—reporters and copy editors, the degree of involvement by each is unclear—sandwiched Won's conclusions between statements of police befuddlement over a bizarre, complex, and unclear situation.

In this and other stories consistently chose to downgrade Won's clinical conclusions and to list the series of events as "under investigation" and uncertain. What, precisely, is "bizarre"? Certainly not the bludgeoning of an individual with the traditional blunt instrument. It is a hoary form of aggression whose distinctive pathology has been observed for centuries by physicians and pathologists who, like Won, have treated skull fractures. It may be lamentable, but it is certainly not bizarre to find a sitting judge charged with impaired driving. Had it not been old news by this date, then the judge's overturning of a jury's verdict may have been considered "bizarre" by his detractors although, legally, there is ample precedent. Nor is the congruence of all these events bizarre in any legitimate sense of the word. They are, however, coincidental and might be construed as suspicious and suggestive. On October 11, in an interview with Mr. Wright, Shintaku himself suggests that his injuries were a result of his judicial actions, and implies that his arrest for impaired driving was a result of his judgment in the Stevens' case as well.

The central problem with this specific piece is clear. The neurosurgeon, Dr. Won, spoke with little doubt about what caused his patient's injuries, but his conclusions are discounted. The placement of his testimony at the end of the story beneath Detective Anderson's insistence that "there's been no determination on how the injuries were received" discounts Dr. Won's views and distances them from the thrust of the police-dominated drama. These stories make clear that Dr. Won's view, despite and perhaps because of his status as participant, were to be ignored in favor of information provided to reporters by the Honolulu police. For their part and for reasons never made public, the police from the beginning choose to discount expert medical testimony and seek another explanation for the judge's injuries. Other stories in this series—from all media—show an absolutely consistent editorial reliance on the police investigators' point of view. The day after Dr. Won stated definitively that his patient's injuries were from a "blunt instrument," for example, the *Star-Bulletin*'s page one story began:

# How Shintaku
# Was Injured Is
# Still Mystery

**By Lee Games and Charles Memminger**
**Star-Bulletin Writers**

The cause of the serious injuries received by Circuit Judge Harold Shintaku remains a mystery today and it seems the judge himself does not know exactly what happened to him before he was found Wednesday morning at his North Shore beach home.

Police said they are still unable to explain how someone could have beaten Shintaku and are not ruling out the possibility of another cause such as an accident.

But authorities have not yet been able to talk to Shintaku himself about the matter. Police detective Wes Anderson said that Dr. William Won, the neurosurgeon who operated on Shintaku Wednesday afternoon to relieve pressure on his brain due to internal bleeding, recommended yesterday against immediate questioning of the judge.

The judge was arrested Tuesday night . . .[17]

The story continues the thesis of a "mystery," holds out the promise of "another cause such as an accident," and shifts the focus of the investigation to the judge himself. It implies that police are turning to an interview with him for the key to the "bizarre" events. Won's judgment on the etiology of Shintaku's injuries is restated in the story's sixth paragraph, followed immediately by Detective Anderson's statement that "Shintaku told his brother Wednesday morning that no one had beaten him and that he did not know how he had been injured." It is difficult to understand, despite Detective Anderson's assurance, how Shintaku could have told his brother both that he was not beaten and that he did not know how his injuries were sustained. If he did not know the latter, how could he know the former? Again we find that the physician's firm conclusion is followed and dismissed, at least by inference, by reliance on police authorities pursuing answers independent of the clinical facts. If it is a mystery, then Dr. Won, who defined the injury is wrong. If the police are searching for answers and questioning individuals, it means that both they and the reporters who cover their progress don't buy the neurosurgeon's explanation.

Reporter Walter Wright's interview of Shintaku included a front page photograph of the judge, head bandaged, sitting up in his hospital bed. As new information it offered Shintaku's admission of amnesia concerning the attack and his memory of being followed on the drive to the beach house. It also included an insistence by the judge that he did not attempt to commit suicide, did not have excessive gambling debts and did not attempt to kill himself because of the impaired driving charges. The unstated implication was that police believed these were possible motives for the judge's attempting suicide. Shintaku stated firmly his belief that he was attacked because of his judicial decisions: "I wouldn't be where I am today [in the hospital] unless I was on the judiciary and did what I did [in the Stevens case]."[18]

Despite Shintaku's assertion that his injuries were the result of a beating and Won's medical judgment, which concurred with Shintaku's assumption, the newspapers followed the police investigator's line that the incident, originally filed as a "domestic disturbance," was unsolved and under investigation. In this series of stories the victim, physicians, local prosecutor and "experts" are all interviewed and quoted in turn, but the reporters consistently meekly followed the police lead, relying for information on police statements and interviews. A number of published stories included statements by the prosecutor, Charles Marsland, who was Shintaku's opponent on the Steven's case and with whom he was, at the time of the injury, engaged in a public feud.[19] Others described police demands for Shintaku's hospital records and the hospital's insistence that they were legally privileged documents.[20] In each story and in the series itself, the official, police view dominated the reportorial presentation completely, even when the official view was in direct opposition to medical supposition based on physical patterns of injury.

On November 13, Police Chief Francis Keala held a press conference to announce that police investigators had concluded Shintaku was injured in a single fall consistent with attempted suicide by hanging.[21] Keala told reporters this conclusion was based in great part on the report of an outside medical expert, University of Hawaii Medical School pathologist Dr. John Hardman. What Keala did not tell reporters was that Hardman did not really investigate Shintaku's injures at all. As reporters learned the next day:

> Hardman said police came to him with a scenario of how Shintaku tried to hang himself, and then asked him if the medical evidence that was [made] available to him was compatible with that scenario.[22]

The police conclusion thus was based not on the medical evidence of X rays and physical examination but solely on an investigator's scenario, which lacked any hard physical or medical substantiation. Like Dr. Moss's judgement in the Setiyono case, Dr. Hardman's information and thus his conclusions were based on incomplete information from parties uninvolved in the medical issues, and his opinion was delivered without the essential documents a physician would need to make an informed judgment. At the press conference, nobody questioned Dr. Hardman or Chief Keala on the basis of that judgment or its opposition to Dr. Won's informed and vocal, clinical judgment.

Dr. Won, however, immediately criticized Hardman's conclusions as having no clinical foundation and invited him to view X rays of Shintaku's injuries. After accepting Won's challenge, Hardman, identified in the text as "the Honolulu Police Department's medical expert" changed his opinion in a public statement on November 14. His new position was reported in a *Star-Bulletin* interview where Hardman is quoted as admitting that his conclusions had been based primarily on information provided by police and agreed that the X ray's showed evidence of more than one blow to the head. He then added that, while he still believed Shintaku's injuries resulted from a failed suicide, "it is possible that Shintaku was injured by an assailant."[23]

### Information Levels: Shintaku

"Even the most apparently simple description is, in reality, highly dependent on a whole series of major and fundamental analytic assumptions that are usually implicit."[24] The assumptions in this series was that the police were speaking the truth and providing full information and that their view of the events should be given primary emphasis. Even Dr. Won, who was a participant in the surgery and could speak with clinical certainty about the nature of Shintaku's injuries, was virtually dismissed to the degree that his conclusions differed from those of the police. The "who" of a story's focus is not necessarily dependent on the experts, therefore. The "force of prior weight" does not necessarily give credence to involved professionals but focuses instead on those socially charged with supervision or investigation of an event.

Dr. Hardman, "the . . . Police Department's medical expert," was given greater weight and more credence in these stories on the strength of his official status, but like the reporters, he received information solely from the police and was given the option only of affirming or rejecting their conclusion. Like Dr. Moss in the previous example, he accepted the untenable position of making a supposedly objective, clinical judgment based on clearly incomplete information (no X rays, no interview with Won, no examination of Shintaku etc.). He was frank about this. It was neither hidden nor covered up. Reporters simply accepted and reported uncritically Dr. Hardman's statements both when he spoke as the police "expert" and when he admitted his information came from a police-generated scenario. The reasonable conclusions were not raised in print or on television by Honolulu newspeople that Hardman was used by police and as a professional should never have made a clinical judgement without the necessary clinical data. Nor is that surprising since reporters find themselves in a position similar to Hardman's all the time. News professionals spend their careers commenting on events of which they have no personal knowledge, data, or experience. While one might question Hardman's "scientific" posture in accepting Chief Keala's assignment with its obvious proscriptions, one does not question the reporter who writes from a similarly uncritical posture. It is simply what a newsperson does in the daily coverage of urban events.

Illustration 6 describes the event sets of this series and the flow of information between participant groups at varying levels. It differs from previous examples because at least two antecedent events have possible but not clear relations to the most critical focus of the story— Shintaku's injuries—although their position as background is confirmed by the newspaper index summaries in toto.

Here the antecedent events (N-1) of the Stevens case and Shintaku's arrest for drunk driving have no necessary or clear relation to the judge's injuries. Judge Shintaku suggested that he was beaten because of his actions as a judge and, elsewhere, that his arrest for drunk driving was police retribution for his actions in the Stevens case. Reporters included these events as part of a series that included the physical injuries. Thus they are boundary events whose causal relation to the specific boundary, the injuries, remains unclear. The injuries drew police involvement when police dispatchers were called by Shintaku's family and sent both the ambulance and police officials, who began an official investigation into his injuries. Medical participation included the phalanx of physicians, nurses, paramedics, and "experts" like Dr. Hardman. involved in the judge's treatment or in discussing the injury's etiology.

The police investigation is headed by officials to whom reporters speak directly and, presumably, from whom they can garner gossip. Hardman's information is presented to the public either through the police—at Keala's press conference, for example—or directly to newspeople who accepted his judgement as much for its official status ("police expert") as for any technical expertise Hardman's analysis might demonstrate. Other physicians with more information and

**Illustration 6**
**Shintaku Case Information Levels**

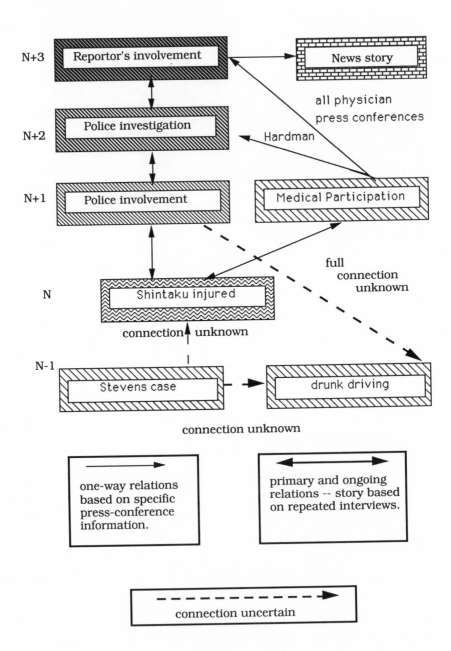

knowledge about the case could and did speak more directly as free
agents. But since they were without police sanction their judgement,
whatever its basis, was never given equal weight.

Again one finds that reporters are involved through the police investigation and at virtually no other level of this event. That is not a
given, of course. For example, reporters could have talked directly to
Dr. Won, asked police investigators why they were ignoring Dr. Won's
clinical judgment and questioned Hardman about the basis of his
conclusion before reporting Keala's conclusions. They could have
asked for copies of Shintaku's X rays and sent them to an independent, forensic pathologist. What they did instead was follow standard,
reportorial procedure and let the news copy mirror the official version
of antecedent events. That, after all, is the reporter's job. The rules of
the profession do not require that newsmen and newswomen evaluate
and analyze to the degree that scientists are required to test their conclusions. Truth and objectivity are transformed, here, into the record
of what individuals said at a given moment, and the weight of that
record is dominated, at several levels in this case, by the official view.

### Prior Weight

Finally, the closure of the case by Police Chief Keala is an
example of the "force of prior weight" introduced in the previous
example. By his title, Chief Keala is presumed to be an expert, and the
weight of his position is bolstered by reliance on the information of
another expert, Dr. Hardman. There is an assumption inherent in
these stories that the conclusion of an official, even if he or she is far
removed from the boundary or investigative levels, is to be given
prominent attention. Keala's views are given prominence over those of
Dr. Won because *he* called the press conference to announce *his* department's conclusions based on the evidence of *his* medical expert,
Dr. Hardman.

Because of *who* he is, there is a journalistic inertia proportional
to the prestige of Chief Keala's position. His views quite simply outweigh those of participants like Dr. Won and Judge Shintaku, who
have the clear weight of evidence on their side. It is instructive that nobody thought to grill Chief Keala after Dr. Hardman viewed the X rays
and modified his conclusions. In retrospect one would assume that reporters would grill police officials who so clearly prescribed the information available to department experts and closed a case on the basis
of "facts" (a single blow) that changed the next day. But as *Chief,* Keala
could say and do what he wanted without criticism or questioning
from the newspeople in his city or state. The weight of his position,
apparently, was greater than that of the actual facts.

### Reportorial Focus

Certainly, these stories that make of multiple skull fractures an
improbable attempted suicide raise serious questions: Why did not
the police immediately accept the surgeon's judgment of an attack,
based on the physical evidence? Why didn't reporters accept Won's

medical diagnosis, which was based on the physical evidence? Why didn't Hardman's admission that his assumptions were based on incomplete evidence and an unsupported, improbable suicide scenario send the newspeople into a frenzy of enterprising investigation?

Unless one accepts the thesis that Honolulu journalists were bought off and covered up en masse or that the city's reporters are particularly incompetent at their job, the only reasonable answer is that these stories *were not about Judge Shintaku and his injuries.* That event was peripheral to the journalist's institutional  focus (N+2). From the start the journalistic event in this series of stories was the police investigation into the "bizarre events" surrounding Shintaku's "alleged beating." The  boundary events, including the judge's injuries, were not the subject of this reportage or of serious journalistic inquiry at all. By dismissing Dr. Won's testimony, news professionals guaranteed police a free hand to say and do anything the investigators wanted without question or interference. Thus Dr. Hardman's conclusions, based on no clinical observation, were challenged not by reporters but by Dr. Won. The tip-off was that the congruence of boundary events was, in the early stories, called "bizarre." No necessary relation existed between boundary events, no logical ties were sought to translate the unusual into the mundane. If it was "bizarre," it was outside of normal precedent and reporters could wait for the police to decide what, in fact, happened.

News reporters did not care, objectively, about the facts of the attack on Circuit Court Judge Harold Y. Shintaku. From the  first they distanced themselves from describing elements of the boundary events (set N-1) or Shintaku's injuries (level N) for the security of police handouts (level N+2).  The police, for reasons unknown, latched onto the scenario of attempted suicide despite the lack of physical evidence (rope, rope burns, high spinal damage, larynx damage, etc.). In the face of clear medical evidence to the contrary, an "expert" was brought onto their side and fed just enough information to provide the minimum of support for the official investigation—and the news file — to be closed on a clear fiction.

## NEWS AS COMMUNICATION

The emerging pattern is that stories that appear to describe a complex of antecedent events (N-1) typically summarize instead the official investigation (N+1) into those occurrences. Information that may be critical to a complete description of the antecedent events can and may be either discounted or dismissed to the degree that it challenges the officially sanctioned position. Further N+1 is characterized by one or more individuals who, by dint of their official position—here called the "force of prior weight"—will have the ability to define, in great part, the official position and the direction of general, daily news summaries. There is a consistent, parallel disjunction between the alleged focus in these two stories—Shintaku's injuries and Rifa Setiy-

**Illustration 7**
**Markov Chain**

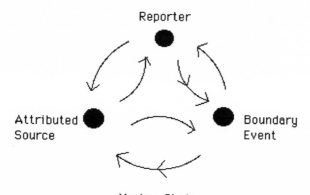

Reporter

Attributed
Source

Boundary
Event

Markov Chain
Information flows equally between all three.

ono's death—and the real focus, which was what police officials said
may have occurred. This appears to be a systemic, institutional
pattern to which all levels of editorial news personnel contribute. It is
perpetuated by reporters trained in the attributive quote and schooled
in the assumption that "objectivity" means writing down what officials
say and, at best, "balancing" those statements with divergent views.
This system is reinforced by the editors who assign newspeople to the
"field" and by others whose job it is to refashion raw copy into an acceptable form fit for the newspaper's page. The work of Boorstin, Horwood, and Memminger and Games was mediated, in each case,
through a phalanx of news desk editors, copy desk editors, rewrite
personnel, page 1 editors, and city or state editors, to list the minimum requirement of support staff.

What this cooperative effort fashioned, in each case, is an institutional shift of focus from the event to the perception of an event on
the part of officials. This can be described generically in terms of communication theory as a broken or interrupted Markov chain.[25] A traditional chain describes a three-way communications system in which
information flows between all elements of the system. Describing the
assumptions of news with this chain connected would suggest a clear
flow of information between the boundary event and its principals,
police and investigators who come later, and the journalist whose job
is to gather information for an "objective," complete and balanced
report.

The arrows in illustration 7 show that information flows, at least
in theory, in both directions between all three levels through question
and answer, interview and investigation for all principals. That pre-

**Illustration 8**
**Broken Markov Chain**

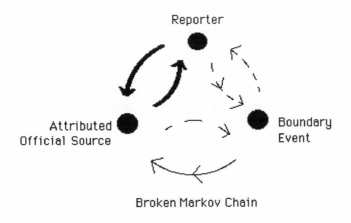

Broken Markov Chain

---

sumed free flow of information represents  the myth of journalistic objectivity  in which the reporter is an impartial investigator, a representative of the "fourth estate" seeking a description without fear or favor of events which are in the public domain. In that myth the newsperson can and would question all principals at boundary and official levels, balancing impartially information on the subject to be described. Our analysis suggests that more typical is a broken chain, represented by illustration 8, in which information between the boundary event and attributed or official sources remains operative but flow between antecedent event (N-1) and reporter is minimized. This will have the secondary effect of giving the reporter no other set of facts with which to confront and question those attributable, police based sources.

This  describes in general terms the shift observed between event levels in  stories from the *Province, New York Times*  and the *Honolulu Star-Bulletin* or *Honolulu Advertiser*  where news became information mediated primarily and uncritically through contexts dominated by official experts and investigators. Even when reporters interacted with boundary actors, the resulting information was subordinated to that of official sources. Thus reporters did interview or listen to Dr. Won, but hisjudgement  was given less weight than that of Chief Keala who neither personally investigated nor in any way participated in the prior events.  Mr. Boorstin did try to talk to Rifa Setiyono's father and to directly interview Dr. Howard. Had he been successful, however,  there is no reason to suppose the story would have been different in content or emphasis. Just as Dr. Won was interviewed in Honolulu and his comments then placed within the context of the police investigation, so too, one suspects, would Dr. Howard's contribution have been subordinate

**Ilustration 9**
**Information Flow: Setiyono II**

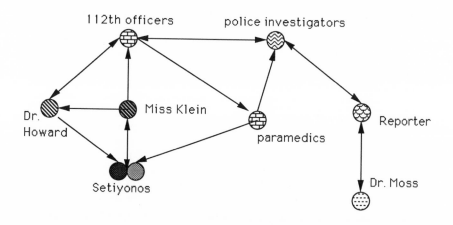

to the information garnered from the police investigators concerned with the events surrounding Rifa Setiyono's distress.

Another way to make clear what happens in these stories is with an abstracted communications diagram that shows the information flow between participants. It is a difficult task to diagram news stories because even in simple examples such as these, one does not know precisely who said what to whom. In the *New York Times* copy, for example, it is unclear if the police investigators themselves interviewed Dr. Howard and his partners or if members of the 112th Precinct who arrived in response to Ms. Klein's distress call had that privilege. We know there was interaction between police, paramedics, and the dentists but not whether that flow of information was through Ms. Klein as well. What we do know is that the reporter, Mr. Boorstin, received his information from the police supervisors and from Dr. Moss, whose total knowledge of the case came from Mr. Boorstin.

One can see, in Illustration 9 the degree to which information flows between participants, with the Setiyonos, Dr. Howard, and Ms. Klein interacting during the period prior to the emergency. Ms. Klein's call to the 112th Precinct bridges that series of events with the boundary event of Rifa's physical distress. A second triangle appears in which police investigators, police officers, and presumably paramedics exchange information so that the investigators can determine what occurred. The reporter's information comes from police investigators and shows no relation to or information from those individuals involved in the early sets of activity. Dr. Moss is even more removed, offering comments on information Mr. Boorstin received from police investigators, who received it in turn from the actors involved in level N-1.

## NEWS AND COMMUNICATION

It would seem at first a simple thing to create an index by which story focus and balance could be accurately quantified and measured. In structural anthropology, matrix analysis has been applied to accurately describe the degree of distance or centrality between participants active in clearly defined event.[26] But the newspaper story provides a surprisingly complex, mediated process whose information content is not immediately accessible to these methods.

It is not, unfortunately, simply the number of times Dr. Howard, Dr. Moss, or Detective Friedman are quoted, for example, or the degree of distance between Mr. Boorstin and Ms. Klein that define the focus and emphasis of the individual story. The information contained in these stories is not alone sufficient to accurately describe the chain of communication. We do not know, for example, if the investigators interviewed participants themselves or only received reports from attending police officers and an unnamed sergeant who participated in the reportorial event. In the Shintaku case, Honolulu police officials and Judge Shintaku both refer to Shintaku's brother, Graf, but he is never questioned by Mr. Memminger or that reporter's colleagues. The frequency of unattributed quotes ("police said," "sources said") is also too great to allow for confident quantification.

Even were all these questions to be answered, however, it still would be necessary to assume for the purposes of analysis that all respondents were of equal importance in a story, and we have seen that is not necessarily so. Although Dr. Won was a principal actor in Judge Shintaku's medical drama, for instance, his information is discounted consistently in the Honolulu story series, while Dr. Hardman, whose knowledge of the facts was meager, was given great emphasis on the basis of Chief Keala's summation. Before this material could be accurately quantified, it would be necessary to understand a number of issues if their relative importance in the text itself was to be accurately ascertained.

To describe the position and importance of a quote in each story it would first be necessary to distinguish between three different types of attribution. Each carries a different value and weight in the narrative and there is at present no clear principle stating which is most powerful to a reader. The types of attribution are:

| *Type of quote:* | *Example* |
|---|---|
| Direct Attribution | Dr. Won said |
| Generic Attribution | Police said |
| No Attribution | Rifa Setiyono died |

Failing direct observation and participation by the reporter, one would think that the direct quote by an individual participant would be most important to the creation of a news narrative, but that assumption remains untested and, on the basis of this analysis, perhaps unwarranted. Of equal importance and intimately related is the relation between individuals quoted and the events being described by a reporter. News sources can be directly involved in the boundary event, the official investigative level, or the journalistic event to the exclusion of all others. Again using Mr. Boorstin's work as example we have:

| *Participation* | *Example* |
|---|---|
| Directly Involved | Dr. Won |
| Investigation only | Detective Friedman |
| Uninvolved | Dr. Moss |

For the purposes of some form of quantified description there would also have to be a way to measure the effect of the prior weight of each actor. The outside "expert" with no direct or, as in the cases of Dr. Moss and Dr. Hardman, even indirect involvement in a boundary event may be of more importance, as we have seen, than those of active participants. What is being described here is a type of group interaction in which the final product is an abstract, sophisticated text mediated through levels of editorial production and then accepted by readers as reality. The current forms of matrix analysis used in communications theory do not answer the questions this thesis raises about the relations between actors and levels of event prior to and including the narrative's eventual effect on readers.

Also to be included in a rigorous, quantified analysis would be the origin of the interchange between reporter and source. Quotes from inquest testimony where a reporter has no chance to question the speaker and those from a personal interview in which information can flow freely may have very different weight. The legitimacy of the individual's title in an official context ("Honolulu Police Department's medical expert") may indeed be more powerful than testimony from that same individual in an ex officio role. Finally, the position of information in the story is part of the mediated process, and to fully understand that final, synthetic report, one would have to balance the previous qualifications against the following:

*Position of quote in a single story:*
   In headline
   In first paragraph
   In story body (first half)
*Positions of quote (continued)*
   In story body (second half)
   Follows prior quote to emphasize
   Follows contradictory quote to balance

The use of headlines with large type and no attribution makes a single, powerful statement which, theoretically, is supported by the copy itself and repeated in the story's first paragraphs. The rule of thumb in news is that the most important material is placed first and background or secondary information is relegated to a story's end.[27] If a statement is included only to "balance" another's statement and is not pursued beyond that single statement, this would be a "balancing quote." If, however, it is used to emphasize a point by agreeing with a prior statement, its weight is increased by dint of that proximity to another, prior statement.  This suggests the general need for one or more measures of proximity which could measure the degree to which information is contradicted by that contained in preceding or succeeding paragraphs. Thus reportage of what Dr. Won said following Judge Shintaku's surgery is preceded and followed by statements by police investigators. Those statements are bolstered by the reporter's insistence on the "bizarre" events and their prominence in the story's opening paragraphs. The physician of record's statement thus virtually disappears because of the weight of police statements which squeeze Dr. Won's contribution out of any position of consideration.

To quantify all these variables would be possible, at least in theory, but it is unclear to me that the exercise, given this book's limited goals and aims, would be worth the trouble at present. The result of such an exercise would not necessarily make more overt the degree to which the reportorial description is distanced from the level of the boundary event or the degree to which official views are given special consideration through the force of prior weight. Nor would a quantifiable paradigm make clearer the relation between the information shifts and specific social messages which they emphasize. Further, while one may not at present be able to quantify the precise shift between event levels, it is clear that a consistent pattern exists in the narrative examples used in this text. Through  simple set theory, a recurring substitution of journalistic event for description of boundary occurrence has been discussed and described. All this speaks directly to the subject defined in chapter 1: the description of an institutionalized pattern through which standard reportage, while promising objectivity, instead delivers inaccuracy and incompleteness. How does this happen and what does it mean?

The answer suggested here is that it occurs through a systematic shift between event levels such that a story purporting to describe objectively a specific occurrence instead describes the official description of abstracted investigations. Further, journalistic reliance on the attributable, quotable official has in these cases led to the shift away from each story's human, individual focus (on Mr. Graham, Rifa Setiyono, Harry Shintaku), which is the form's supposed subject. The result is a change, in Barthes's language, from an apparent sign—the boundary event—through the levels of meaning to a social message signifying official competence, journalistic vigilance and bureaucratic concern.

This reliance on official versions of specific events offers in even the most terrifying of situations a comforting myth. Consider briefly what Shintaku's injuries seemed to signify when the story began to unfold. As a*Time* magazine article published the week after his injuries occurred made clear, attacks on members of the judiciary undermine the order of judicial law on which society rests. If judges are fearful of attack, their rulings can be influenced and attacks of this nature show a blatant disregard for the law that is supposed to protect us all. Stories that quote diligent police officials showing vigilance in their investigation of a judge's injuries offers the reassurance that police will punish the guilty, protect the judiciary, and by implication, the system itself. Thus the sign is transformed from one of danger and lawlessness to one of protection and reassurance.

More frightening than an isolated attack on a single, controversial judge would be an open skepticism of the police department's role in that investigation. Thus not only would the arbiters of the rule of law be endangered, but society's protective arm would be seen to be, if not corrupt or incompetent, at the very least under suspicion itself. Reliance on police testimony changes the sign from one of danger to one of assurance to the text's readers and creates a signification of protection for all under not only the law but the several estates of modern society.

In the medical stories, a similar message is presented. Dr. Moss's function is to assure readers of his profession's concern and competence even if the boundary event may involve suspicious or uncertain acts by a member of his medical fraternity. It appears that his very distance from Rifa Setiyono's distress is, in the end, his greatest advantage to Mr. Boorstin. Dr. Moss's function in the piece is to assert the myth that the physicians—of whom he as past president of a medical association is a symbol—care enough to comment and know enough to speak intelligently about even so anonymous an event as the death of a small boy in Queens. Any question about professional incompetence or malpractice is immediately deflected by his general comments which are based on nothing but fourth hand knowledge. The sign thus changes from that of confusion, uncertainty, and perhaps incompetence by professionals in a specific case to one signifying confidence in and the omnipotence of the profession at large.

In all these stories, the journalist is transformed from an uninvolved and not necessarily astute observer to a knowledgeable and potent substitute for the reader and society at large. After all, Mr. Boorstin briefed Dr. Moss, who apparently based his conclusions on the reporter's summary of events. Mr. Memminger and Mr. Games described for readers the words of investigators and participants in the Shintaku complex of events. But they, like other newspeople whose work has been described here, emphasized the official view, assigning added weight to the police investigator's comments and less to the observations of even the most critical of participants. The effect is both to project the chimera of objective description and to align the news organ itself with the power of officialdom. Like bank tellers who handle vast sums of money but earn little themselves, reporters are granted the appearance of knowledge and power to the degree that they focus on members of officialdom without questioning too closely the expert's or bureaucrat's view. Thus the myth news professionals ultimately present through the body of their work is one of objectivity, and what it signifies is knowledge, trust, and responsibility for representatives of the fourth estate in relation to the society as a whole. But journalists typically have little knowledge about the boundary events they report. Their relations are with official spokespeople and their objectivity limited to what each is told in any single context—however ludicrous that information may prove to be. In the end, journalists thus function as a tool of legitimization for professionals and officials who are the media's attributive source and, through that affirmation, the whole enforces social rules. Each part confirms the other and each myth is mutually reinforcing. All of this follows, ultimately, from the shift in levels which has been described in the preceding section.

## POLITICAL REPORTAGE

It may be useful at this point to extrapolate from the current discussion of nonpolitical reportage and speculate on the degree to which both shifts in reportage of different event levels and the force of prior weight affect other types of reportage. In chapter 1 issues of political reportage were introduced, and the question remains whether the current analysis can be informed by or add to the critique of others, like Noam Chomsky, who have concerned themselves with issues of political and international reportage. To the degree that the form is consistent, news should be homogeneous, and similar shifts theoretically should occur whatever the subject of a specific news piece. The following tentative application of this critique suggests that what has been observed in the arena of mundane medical and police reportage may be a factor in the presentation of information by journalists active in the arena of international and political reportage as well. It is recognized that the exercise has focused so far on the description of a specific narrative form used by urban journalists reporting on local events (obituaries, wire briefs, police reportage, inquest coverage). The current critique should describe political reportage as well, but that possibility can only be suggested briefly in the next few pages. The hope is that others will consider this approach to have sufficient merit to warrant further work. For the sake of continuity, examples used here are those first raised in chapter 1.

At the time of the Soviet incursion into Afghanistan, reporters quoted the outrage voiced by then President Jimmy Carter and largely adopted, through attribution and direct quote, the language and position American officials used. When the then U.S. president decided to boycott the Olympic games in protest of Soviet actions, the question asked by news professionals was not if the U.S. and allied condemnation was appropriate but rather if the announced boycott was itself sufficient. Certainly the reaction of President Carter, Prime Minister Thatcher, Prime Minister Trudeau and other world leaders was news. But in each case, reporters "objectively" accepted the condemnations of the Soviet incursion as an example of Russian duplicity without question. Reporters covered, with clear attribution and strong editorial support, the statements of western world leaders who all strongly condemned the Soviet's actions in that country. The whole context of that chorus of U.S. and allied condemnation was the implication that the Soviet incursion in Afghanistan was symptomatic of communism's natural aggression, was antithetical to the actions of civilized, democratic nations, and proof that the "Russians" were not to be trusted. The unspoken, reportorial context to these statements portrayed the Russian incursion as a structurally unique event and this resulted in what earlier was called a "false truth." The situation was similar to that in Honolulu, where reporters treated Shintaku's injuries as unique rather than one of a class of head injuries resulting from the traditional blunt instrument.

Reporters covering the White House did not say "Excuse me, Mr. President, isn't the Russian justification for its Afghanistan incursion precisely the rationale Americans used in Vietnam?"[28] News professionals in North America did not ask historians about the number of times U.S. troops (or those of other allied nations) had been sent to bolster one or another "friendly" regime facing a civil war. Nor, naturally, did reporters bring to the U.S. President's attention the number of small civil wars being fought at that time with U.S. military equipment or support elsewhere in the world. Just as Mr. Memminger quoted Dr. Hardman without closely questioning him, so too did White House and state department-based reporters quote officials whose positions may have been equally self-serving and suspect. Thus what the attack signified to President Carter—that Russians were an aggressive, militaristic and untrustworthy people—was accepted as editorial fact by newspaper editorialists in general. That American involvement in a number of countries over the last four decades has been at least as aggressive, militaristic and morally questionable was not an issue either the president, his subordinates, nor those journalists who covered the administration saw fit to address. At this level both the force of prior weight and the shift between event levels conspired to define what the news could be and what it would signify.

Remember the figures quoted in this work's first chapter—over 70 percent of the news in the principal newspapers comes from official sources. Reporters covering the Afghanistan conflict (or Vietnam, Nicaragua, China, etc.) primarily quote state department officials, official sources and, whenever possible, the president. As with Mr. Boorstin in New York City, it is their job to cover the official statements of government officials, although the resulting copy may appear to describe the foreign, boundary events. Just as it was not, apparently, Mr. Memminger's or his colleague's function to question Police Chief Keala's statement that Judge Shintaku's injuries resulted from a single fall—however bizarre that determination was—it also was not a reporter's job to dismiss as certainly naive and perhaps disingenuous then President Carter's outrage at the Russian incursion into Afghanistan. He was president and could say anything he wanted without fear of having his honesty or his knowledge of events treated with skepticism.

It is not simply the shift between boundary and reportorial events but the "force of prior weight" at work in this as well. A sitting president is the ultimate authority and his views—as policy maker and national leader—carry enormous peremptory power. Certainly reporters can and sometimes do report independently of those perceptions, but it requires a massive and consistent effort to effectively challenge the "who" of authority at this level. Thus in another conflict, presidents Lyndon Johnson and Richard Nixon continued to assert the American presence in Vietnam as a viable and necessary political and military policy despite overwhelming evidence to the contrary from field reports.

Reporters must attribute the quotes and statements in their stories. The "who" of a story is more important, in both political and general reportage, than what is being said. Prior weight—defined here as a political or official office—gives credence to whatever the individual so appointed might say. The greater the office, the more credence its official will be given and the less rigorous the journalistic questioning will become. Lewis H. Lapham described the shift perfectly in a small aside about former President Gerald Ford and the translation of his importance from congressman to president:

> Prior to his appointment as Nixon's successor, Gerald Ford was known as an amiable but not very bright congressman from Michigan. Once arrived in office Ford was assigned, together with the Marine guard and the Great Seal of the United States, a reputation for sagacity. Not even the *New York Times* went quite so far as to describe him as a philosopher-king, but suddenly the paper's Washington correspondents recognized in Ford the lineaments of the homely wisdom traditionally ascribed to rural folk and the singers of country songs.[29]

President Reagan's ability to cheerfully dismiss facts for fancy relied on an acute and perhaps intuitive understanding of both the "prior weight" of the office and the office's power (through weekly radio broadcasts, for example) to shift the focus of news from one event level to another. He was the "Teflon president" to whom nothing stuck precisely because he could define journalistic events in whatever way he chose and know that his view would be reported as attributed fact. Reagan understood that his comments, not the events he purported to describe, were the journalist's job.

Certainly many reporters who covered the Central American wars (as well as Vietnam, and Afghanistan) knew it was not so simple a situation, and their field reports were dutifully carried by national newspapers. Similarly, in the Vietnam period many reporters worked hard to move beyond the official posture to describe the complex and deteriorating position there. But their views, like those of Dr. Won, were outweighed by the voices of authority, the "who" whose power resides precisely in the ability to shift event levels and define a story's "what," in any manner that "who" or ultimate official (chief of police, past president of an association, president of the United States, Chief Justice of the United States, university president, etc.) may choose.

It is no leap to move from former presidents to police investigations and coroner inquests. The narrative shift in political reportage—and its concurrent, myth-making result—is structurally no different from the acceptance by reporters of Police Chief Keala's assertion that Judge Shintaku's injuries were the result of a single fall or of the Vancouver physician's confident insistence that an unconscious patient extricated his own breathing tube. The shift from boundary to journalistic event appears to be consistent at various levels of reportage. This fact, even placed in the language of event sets and communication diagrams, can be applied to a number of different examples in reportage and tested as a consistent pattern of American news. One result of this narrative form is that two of Kipling's serving men, "why" and "how" are consistently given short shrift in the copy of daily journalism."Why" Mr. Graham died and "why" or "how" Rifa Setiyono died are questions not asked and, certainly, not answered. "How" Shintaku was injured, was answered but in a misleading way. "What" his injuries were is clear (skull fractures, a broken clavicle, etc.) but "how" he received them (from a single fall or from a beating) is so treated in that narrative as to have a negative news value because Chief Keala's conclusions, reported by the media were not consistent with the facts. Kipling's honest men, who were once assumed to serve the boundary event, have come to be the "who, what, when and where of the official investigation and the attributed quote. The more important the official, the more valuable the attribution, and "who" appears to be weighted as much by its social function as by the event a story purports to describe. "What" becomes what Police Chief Keala said and not an objective sifting of the facts of Shintaku's injuries.

There are simultaneously two event levels operative in these representative stories, both subsumed under the form's definition, which promises objectivity in the description of a boundary event but provides instead a culturally weighted description of the officially sanctioned journalistic event. Working in conjunction is the embedding of culturally potent signs which, at progressively abstracted levels, present a unified and consistent social myth. This occurs through a concentration on the journalistic event and at the cost of any understanding of the prior, boundary occurrence. A cost of this system is the progressive isolation of the original signifier, described here as occurring at the event level N-1. This is evident in the distance imposed on reader and reporter alike from the supposedly significant cultural event—death of a citizen—and prohibition of any real understanding of the context of that death.

**NOTES**

1. Robert O. Boorstin, "Two-year-old Dies after Operation In Dental Office," the *New York Times*, June 4, 1986, B2.

2. The combination of anesthetic and tranquilizing drugs in dental surgery is called "conscious sedation" and has been the cause of a number of deaths in North America. For a newspaper story describing a death from conscious sedation see Ann Japenga, "A Dental Sedation Death Casts Doubt on Procedure," *Los Angeles Times*, July 7, 1987 Part 5, p.1.

3. Lewis H. Lapham, *Money and Class in America* (New York: Ballantine Books, 1987), 52.

4. The search was carried out using CompuServe's IQuest database gateway which allows for the search by identifying phrase of newspapers on the Vu- Text database system.  The search phrase used was "Rifa Setiyono or Bambang Setiyono," to identify stories dealing with the child or parent.

5. The computer search was carried out on the WestLaw legal database. Two searches were conducted. One sought any court  cases involving a Setiyono and the second, topical search was for court cases in New York in which anesthetic or anesthesia played a role.

6. Drug overdoses in pediatric situations are not uncommon. Besides simple error on the part of medical professionals, they result from the necessity to administer smaller amounts of a drug than normal with the exact amounts dependent on the patient's weight, general health, and other factors. For a discussion of anesthetic administration in general and problems of administration to children and the elderly  see John C. Sun, *Manual of Anesthesia*, 2d. Ed. (Boston: Little Brown, 1982) or W. K. Hamilton, "Unexpected Deaths during Anesthesia: Wherein Lies the Cause?" *Anesthesiology* 50 (1979),  381-383. A *Pediatrics* article (June, 1986) described a series of drug overdoses affecting patients at the Hospital for Sick Children Toronto, Ontario.The article was useful background but not immediately relevent.

7. The author worked full time as a reporter at the *Springfield Union*, Springfield, Mass. from 1972 to 1974; as a bureau reporter for United Press Canada) in 1978-1979, and, from 1979 to 1984, was a senior reporter and assistant city editor for the *Province* in Vancouver, Canada. In addition, from 1976 to 1984 he worked  as a  broadcast newsman for various Canadian Broadcasting Corporation radio shows and was a CBC correspondent to the 1984 Olympics in Los Angeles, California.

8. News reportage on the issue of  chemical addiction is addressed in Chapter 4.

9. "Enterprise reportage" is a term used by some to describe news work

where the reporter shows initiative beyond the straight reportage of official statements and simple interviews. It thus resembles but is believed by some to be different from "investigative reportage," which will be discussed in the next chapter. The term "enterprise," while ill defined, is used here to describe Wright's successful attempt to enter hospital and talk directly with Shintaku.

10. Walter Wright, "Shintaku: Car Followed Me/Injured Judge Speaks Out in Hospital Interview" *Advertiser & Star-Bulletin*, October 11, 1981, A1. The Sunday edition is a joint production of both newspapers.

11. The first such report was by the *Advertiser* which ran a second-day story on October 8, 1981, describing Shintaku's thirteen years as chief legal advisor to state senate Republicans and his tenure, beginning in 1974, as a circuit court judge. Honolulu Publishing Company Index: 1981 (Honolulu: Honolulu Publishing Co., 1982), 264.

12. Charles Memminger, "Shintaku Taken Unconscious to Wahiawa Hospital," *Honolulu Star-Bulletin*, October 7, 1981, A1.

13. Pat Guy, "Probe of Incident With Stevens Would Be Welcome — Shintaku," *Honolulu Star-Bulletin*, Oct. 7, 198, A3.

14. Lee Games and Charles Memminger, "Surgeon Says Shintaku Took a Bad Beating," *Honolulu Star-Bulletin*, October 8, 1981, A1, A3.

15. Ibid.

16. Ibid.

17. Lee Games and Charles Memminger, "How Shintaku Was Injured Is Still Mystery," *Honolulu Star-Bulletin*, October 9, 1981, A1.

18. Walter Wright, "Shintaku," p. A3.

19. For example: Walter Wright, "City Prosecutor Marsland Attacks Editorials re: Judge's Alleged Assault," *Honolulu Star-Bulletin*, October 10, 1981, p. A3. Quoted from Newspaper Index.

20. See Wright, "Shintaku" A3.

21. Jim McCoy, "Shintaku Injuries Result of a Fall, Police Say," *Honolulu Star-Bulletin*, November 12, 1981, A1.

22. Charles Memminger and Lee Games, "Shintaku Controversy Continues Unsettled," *Honolulu Star-Bulletin*, November 13, 1981, A1.

23. Lee Games and Charles Memminger, "Pathologist Alters His Views," *Honolulu Star-Bulletin*, November 14, 1981, A1.

24. David R. Caploe, "Max Weber and a Dialectic Theory of Objectivity", (unpublished manuscript, Duke University, 1987), 7.

25. Technically, this is a stationary chain defined as a network in which the value of each line is a positive number. As a chain, it can be linked to others. For a discussion of Markov chains see Frank Harary, Robert Z. Norman, and Norwin Cartwright, *Structural Models: An Introduction to the Theory of Directed Graphs* (New York: John Wiley & Sons, Inc., 1965),171-2.

26. See Per Hage and Frank Harary, *Structural Models in Anthropology,* (New York: Cambridge University Press, 1983),145 and Harary, Norman, and Cartwright, ibid. for separate discussions on issues of the quantification of communication.

27. The reason for this is twofold. Reporters are told this is primarily because readers normally do not read long columns but lose interest after about nine paragraphs. The closer to the headline, therefore, the more likely information is to be read. Another explanation is that when stories ran overlong in the days of "hot type," editors and compositors in a rush would simply discard the last inches of lead type from a story until the story fit the allotted news hole.

28 . The Soviet justification for its actions was an official request for military assistance and aid by a sitting government faced with a growing and insurgent domestic force of "rebels". At this time, of course, the United States was supporting Ferdinand Marcos in the Philippines, Israel in the Middle East and would within the decade spend billions of dollars to support the "Contras" rear guard action against a legitimate regime in Central America.

29. Lapham, *Money and Class in America,* 53.

# 4

# The News as Form

It is now possible to describe with some authority the mechanism by which the "objective" news is drained out of the news report and replaced with ideology and propaganda. The consistent shift from boundary to reportorial event and the force of prior weight make clear two ways in which this occurs. By detailing the steps by which supposedly objective news is transformed into officially sanctioned reportage, we can make manifest the way in which events are coded within a specific cultural perspective. But before Barthes's semiologic critique can be fully integrated into this discussion, one further question needs to be raised. Is the shift of focus from boundary to reportorial event—from objective reportage to official description—a necessary and immutable component of daily journalism's contemporary narrative form?

## INVESTIGATIVE JOURNALISM

What is currently called "investigative journalism" may be offered by some as one possible exception to the narrative pattern in which these informational shifts occur. The term "investigative reporter" is a new one, coined in the post-Watergate environment of the 1970s. It is a loosely defined perspective used interchangeably, by some, with the terms "enterprise" or "public affairs" reportage. Whatever it is called, the result is a descendent of Nineteenth century muckraking and gained wide currency in the early to mid-1980s as television stations formed "I-teams" and newspapers set up special units whose job was purported to be the stringent and uncompromising description of social, political and corporate wrongs. Investigative reportage is defined in *The Reporter's Handbook* as:

> the reporting, through one's own work product and initiative, matters of importance which some persons or organizations

wish to keep secret. The three basic elements are that the investigation be the work of the reporter, not a report of an
investigation made by someone else; that the subject of the
story involves something of reasonable importance to the
reader or viewer; and that others are attempting to hide these
matters from the public.[1]

It is a curious definition in many ways, unpleasantly limiting and
critical by inference of the profession at large that it purportedly serves.
Do most reporters write stories which are not of "reasonable importance
to the reader or viewer," and if so, why do they bother? How much of
contemporary journalism is not the product of the newsperson's own
effort? Does this assume most reporters crib from the work of others?
Implied throughout is the assumption that  basic news does not do its
job and so journalistic super sleuths are required.

Even more curious is the insistence that the investigative report
be based on information which "persons or organizations wish to keep
secret." In the Shintaku story  some officials may  have wanted specific
details or perspectives on events obscured but Dr. Won, other physicians, and Shintaku himself, all were anxious and willing to talk to any-
body and everybody about those aspects of the case. It was not that Dr.
Hardman wished actively to participate in a cover-up but that,  until the
final press conference, no reporter asked the pathologist what his precise  assignment had  been. Had a Honolulu reporter built a series of
stories on the medical evidence and not simply reported on the official
investigation, would that have been investigative reportage?

In the infamous series of articles now regarded as the "Watergate" story, now  regarded as the sine qua non of investigative reportage,[2] The *Washington Post*"s coverage of official cover-ups was made
possible by a high-level government source (publicly identified only as
Deep Throat) interested in revealing facts to newsman Bob Woodward.
It was the *Washington Post* 's stated rule that all facts had to have at
least two substantive attributions before they could be printed. This
meant that other individuals had to confirm Deep Throat's statements
to reporters. The resulting stories thus owed as much to the desire of
one or more individuals to have a specific truth revealed as they did to
the then sitting government's desire to have that same perspective
hidden.

What those sources revealed to the Watergate reporters of the
*Washington Post* were the results of a series of ongoing investigation by
government agencies of the day. The investigative work of  Bernstein
and Woodward owed less to original research than to their role as a con-
duit for material developed by lawfully constituted governmental agencies whose research led to conclusions being denied, at that time,  by
the then sitting Nixon administration. Their work thus was not, at least
by Ullman's description, truly investigative. As Edward Jay Epstein
noted in 1974 about Woodward and Bernstein's book describing their
coverage of the story:

In keeping with the mythic view of journalism, the book [*All The President's Men*] never describes the "behind-the-scenes" investigations which actually "smashed the Watergate scandal wide open"—namely the investigations conducted by the FBI, the federal prosecutors, the grand jury, and the Congressional committees. The work of almost all these institutions, which unearthed and developed all the actual evidence and disclosures of Watergate, is systematically ignored or minimized by Bernstein and Woodward. Instead, they simply focus on those parts of the prosecutor's case, the grand jury investigation, and the FBI reports that were leaked to them.[3]

Thus "investigative journalism" may more accurately be defined, on one level, as the editorial identification and selection of sources contrary to the official perspective. On another it may involve simply reading reports prepared by dissident or opposition officials rather than merely accepting the unsubstantiated word of one or another administrator. Somehow, though, these definitions do not satisfy the myth of the investigative muckraker. To see how closely this definition defines the journalist's investigative approach, consider two other, less famous examples.

### Investigative Journalism: Examples

In the mid-1980s the *Fort Lauderdale News and Sun-Sentinel* published an "investigative" series of stories describing problems and abuses in U.S. hospitals serving veterans of the American armed forces.[4] The series began in 1980 when reporter Fred Schult began questioning officials about the Miami Veterans Administration hospital heart unit after a local veteran complained to the newspaper that the unit had been closed because of multiple patient deaths. The research and the story grew from that specific focus to a more general series describing widespread abuses, specific incidents of malpractice and financial inefficiencies throughout the 119-hospital, federally funded veterans care system.

Much of the most damaging material within the series came from official reports on and federal audits of the Veterans Administration system and thus were, in fact, based on prior, official investigations carried out by government officials themselves and not on the independent research of a courageous, lone reporter. The information was not hidden. On the contrary, the Fort Lauderdale investigative team had to sift through thousands of pages of publicly available material involving legal suits against specific veterans hospitals, federal audits of the whole veterans health-care system, and official documents concerning specific cases of mismanagement. The rule of investigative reportage is to find documentation, official when possible, to establish a "paper trail" of malfeasance or misdeed. To do this, Fort Lauderdale reporters were assisted by scores of individuals—including officials and former patients who were willing to be interviewed—for their series. The information may indeed have been important, but it was not hidden. It was available in excess. We want to believe this type of series is different from normal journalism, but whatever that difference is, the *Reporter's Handbook*'s definition of investigative reportage quoted earlier does not adequately describe it.

One further example will suffice to show the limits of the established definition of "investigative journalism." In 1983 the *Anniston Star* (Alabama) published a story on "Deaths in an Army Hospital."[5] Following the deaths of three individuals at the Ft. McClellan, Alabama, army hospital, the newspaper reported that "the civilian oxygen supply contractor failed to meet safe  industry standards and  the requirements of the federal contract. The army failed to monitor that firm's contract work. Army personnel failed to use equipment at hand that would have detected the absence of oxygen even as the patients who died struggling for air [sic]."[6] Information for these stories came from the following sources: a U.S. Army Health Service command report, autopsy reports, hospital operating room schedules, Food and Drug Administration inspection records, FDA analyses of gas tanks (all obtained through official channels), counsel to plaintiffs in three legal actions and both Army and civilian investigators.

The story thus was based on two separate sets of information which were neither hidden nor original. One area was documentation and official reports compiled by officials within the military and federal bureaucracies. Of at least equal importance was information received through the largess of lawyers representing in civil legal actions the families of those who had died. It can be assumed that in order to build as strong a case as possible, those lawyers may have been eager to share their research with newspaper reporters who would be able to present the clients' case in the press.

In submitting this series to an Investigative  Reporters and Editors competition, *Anniston Star* newspeople described its crucial investigative element as the "fight against the army's information policies and the information office at Fort McClellan, where the real purpose is to ensure that only innocuous information about the Army be told."[7] The series' power thus rested, according to its authors, on the editorial decision not to credit military public relations officers with omniscience. The investigative technique involved having news reporters read official reports themselves and then talk with lawyers representing opposing parties in a lawsuit.

News professionals often run—sometimes without any but cosmetic changes—the public information releases produced by public relations departments in both the public and private sectors. These are typically used with minimal or no attribution and no further research by those who assume each release objectively states factual occurrences that require no independent confirmation. Independent investigation requires time and critical expertise. The release is on an editor's desk and requires no further work. The assumption is one of fact outside context, the presumption that a corporate or official statement is objective and can be published as is.

The decision to question data provided by army public information officers suggests that there is something special about this category of public agency information because it is the army, an official agency. In fact, however, the context is no different from that of any reporter who chooses to disregard the releases of any corporation or government body. Press releases—from the U.S. Army; Time Life, Inc;, Health and Welfare Canada; Exxon; and so on—are written by individuals whose function is to make the employing agency or corporation look good. While in theory public information officers in both the public and private sectors are supposed to facilitate the dissemination of objective information, they are by definition press agents whose professional futures are based on the ability to present data in such a way as to reflect well on their superiors.

That this story involved a branch of the U.S. government makes it no different from one attempting to discover the reason for anesthetic deaths in a private U.S. hospital or, in Canada, in an institution supported by a provincial health-care system. That *Anniston Star* editors saw the divergence of factual information between public relations officials and a larger context as commendable. But that it was seen as a special and not a systemic problem highlights the general problem of both investigative and general reportage. The issue remains one of the relation between news professionals and information, the form in which supposedly objective data is collected, evaluated, and presented.

Investigative reportage may offer a distinct type of information but neither the official definition nor these sanctioned examples of investigative work make its difference clear. Investigative reportage seems, whatever else it may be or do, to include the substitution of minority or outsider perspectives for those of a larger official body: Deep Throat's vision was weighted against the posture of White House disclaimers and then confirmed by official investigators; plaintiffs' views were advanced against those of U.S. Army public relations officials. But flipping from one perspective to another does not necessarily correct or decrease the distance between boundary and reportorial event. It may, however, redefine the event at a reportorial level, substituting one adversary's vision and information for the other's, but that is hardly a revolution in reportorial technique.

At least as it is currently defined, investigative reportage usually does not a priori alter the shift from one to another event level, although it may allow that shift to focus on the views of nonofficial sources. What may distinguish what is now called "investigative" journalism from mundane reportage (like the Shintaku series and other examples noted earlier) is its insistence (at least in these examples) on the reading of official reports by news people. In the *Anniston Star* and *Fort Lauderdale News* cases, reporters read the audits, official summaries, and legal depositions themselves. They did not merely listen to a summary of those documents at a designated news conference. Watergate reporters searched through thousands of documents looking for information and did not simply listen to the disclaimers of state department or political party spokesmen.

This "paper trail" does result in a shortening of the distance between boundary and journalistic event. Hospital deaths in Alabama were investigated by army officials and depositions were taken by lawyers from individuals involved in the death and its official investigation. By reading the official reports rather than simply listening to army disclaimers, *Anniston Star* reporters removed one level of distance between the boundary complex of patient deaths (N-1) and the official summation of a completed investigation (N+3). What is currently described as "investigative journalism" may be more accurately termed "administrative journalism," the active perusal of official reports rather than reportage relying absolutely on an official summation of those reports.

This practice does not necessarily change the narrative form or inevitably lead to a change in content in a specific context, however. Nor does it guarantee that any report will more closely describe the "why" or "how" of a discrete occurrence. It may simply shift the focus of the reportorial event from that of official statement (army officials) to those of official adversaries. To the degree it requires reporters to read official reports (level N+2), it may decrease the distance between boundary and journalistic event without necessarily redefining either.

### Kipling Redux

One can argue that the shift from boundary to reportorial event and thus the criticisms of those who see contemporary journalism as a form of propaganda is rooted, at least in part, in the narrative form of the news. This is as true of investigative as daily journalism. This narrative form is, in turn, an outgrowth of the modern daily journalist's reliance on Kipling's active assistants: "who," "what," "when," and "where." The definition of a news story introduced in chapter 2, with its exclusion of "why" and a substantive "how," has been shown to result from the shift in attention from objective occurrence to official description. It is the primary task of this chapter to demonstrate the degree to which the contemporary form and its inherent informational shift are both based on those apparently simple story rules and thus are alterable through conscious manipulation of their definitions.

To do this, one more series of newspaper reports will be introduced. As before, the distance between the objective context and the officially sanctioned view of those boundary events will be discussed. Then the categories of story definition introduced in chapter 2 will be changed and the potential effect of those changes on these specific stories will be examined. Thus this chapter presents a case study of the relations between the narrative form, defined by Kipling's serving men, and the informational shifts that can be generated by consciously changing the definition of that form. One result will be the decrease of distance between information levels such that the reportorial event is coequal with level N or N+1.

**THE NEWSPAPER CASE**

Marvin Eric Loewen died June 19, 1987, during dental surgery at the Abbotsford Dental Group clinic near Vancouver, British Columbia. His death and the subsequent inquest into its cause were reported by three local television stations[8] the *Province*, the area's morning newspaper; and its afternoon sister publication, the *Sun*. Both newspapers are published under a joint operating agreement by Pacific Press Company. and share a single newspaper library. On June 20, the *Sun* reported both the teenager's death and the announcement of a preliminary investigation into its causes by a British Columbia coroner:

# Death Probed after Teen's Heart Stops during Dental Surgery

Abbotsford RCMP and Chilliwack coroner John Urquhart are investigating the sudden death of a 16-year-old Clearbrook youth whose heart stopped beating Friday while he was under general anesthetic during a dental office surgery procedure.

Medical officials attempted to revive Marvin Eric Loewen for approximately 80 minutes before he was pronounced dead at Matsqui-Sumas-Abbotsford Hospital about 11:35 a.m., Urquhart said.

An "implant" procedure on Loewen at Abbotsford Dental Group clinic on Marshall Road began about 9:45 a.m.

Urquhart said the youth began experiencing difficulty about 10:15 a.m. and "he simply went into cardiac arrest."

Urquhart identified the doctors in attendance as Vancouver oral surgeon Dr. Peter Nelson and Burnaby anesthetist Dr. Leonard Archer.

He said an autopsy did not reveal why Loewen, of 32651 Chehalis Drive, died.

Nelson refused to comment and Archer could not be reached for comment.

Loewen's mother, Alwina, said he was in the process of having two false molars implanted and had received general anesthetic in two previous visits with no side effects.[9]

The story is written mostly in "obituary" style with minimal attribution beyond acknowledgment that the information on this death came from a regional coroner. In a follow-up story on June 22, Mr. Urquhart was quoted as saying that "Pathologists will conduct further tests this week to determine the exact cause of death."[10] He further cautioned that until those tests were completed it would be "a little premature" to say whether an inquest would be ordered. This story's tone was more reportorial, overtly attributing statements to Urquhart. It included as well a statement by Loewen's mother, "voice breaking with emotion," that her family would miss the boy terribly and that, prior to his death, Marvin "was very normal and healthy, a big boy, [an] active boy."

Excepting the detail's of Alwina Loewen's grief, information in these stories clearly originated from one source, the regional coroner whose job in British Columbia is to administer the bureaucratic detail of investigations into suspicious or unusual deaths. Mr. Urquhart is neither a physician nor a pathologist. He is instead a lay coroner and administrator. Preliminary reports to his office came from Royal Canadian Mounted Police officials, who have jurisdiction in the Abbotsford-Chilliwack area; the hospital where the boy died; and pathologists, who completed an apparently inconclusive gross post mortem.[11]

Thus the unnamed reporter who wrote these stories was not primarily interested in Marvin Loewen, the dentist who operated on him, the anesthesiologist who cared for him or research into the medical procedures the boy underwent. The news reporter summarized instead the statements of an administrative, lay coroner who said, in effect, that the public would be told at an official inquest if something unusual had occurred. At this point the journalistic product is distanced from level N-1 (the dental procedure) by events surrounding the cardiac distress (N), medical attempts to revive the boy (N+1), police investigations, and primary pathology (N+2). Information from all these sources will be used, Urquhart makes clear, to determine if an inquest is to be held (N+3). Thus from the beginning the reportorial focus is on the official summation of antecedent, official investigations into the boundary event of Loewen's death.

An inquest was ordered and opened on October 26, 1987, with the revelation that "Vancouver dentist Peter Nelson says three out of '10 to 12' European-style implant operations he has performed have ended in death."[12] In that story the participating anesthesiologist, Dr. Leonard Archer, testified that after he administered general anesthetic (halothane), Nelson injected a local anesthetic whose active ingredient was adrenaline. "If you inject the adrenaline and you've already got halothane on board, you've got problems," Dr. Archer told the inquest. There was no indication in his reported testimony that Dr. Archer, who had worked with Dr. Nelson before, either objected to or protested his colleague's use of this drug during a general anesthetic. Dr. Archer also told the inquest, and the *Sun* emphasized, that Loewen's death may have resulted from a rare condition—carotid sinus syndrome—in which pressure on a patient's jaw in turn depresses the carotid artery and thus the patient's heart rate: "It appears to be a congenital thing."[13]

The next day's story included testimony of the executive director of the British Columbia College of Dental Surgeons. He said that a general anesthetic was in fact not required for an implant procedure and that a local anesthetic would have been easier and safer.[14] That statement was buried in the copy beneath the more critical information that the anesthetic gas machine used in Loewen's dental surgery was malfunctioning. Stephen Gorelik, a biomedical technologist who examined the clinic's equipment, testified that both the respirator's oxygen analyzer and oxygen sensor were inoperative. Gorelik explained and the *Province* reported that "without those . . . anesthetist Leonard Archer wouldn't know what gas quantities he was giving Loewen."

Further, the respirator, which breathes for a patient during an operation, had five leaks and a sticky exhalation valve and "could have caused Loewen to inhale his own waste carbon dioxide." Finally, experts testified that the clinic's defibrillator, which is to be used in a cardiac emergency, was inoperative. It had two blown fuses and a dead battery. On the following day, another local anesthetist, Dr. Douglas Graham, called for a moratorium on general anesthesia in B.C. dental offices because, in his own words: "There's a problem here, there's a big problem," he said. "I'm led to believe that this situation is widespread— faulty equipment, not following guidelines regarding monitoring."[15]

In its findings, the inquest jury agreed. The six-person jury recommended a number of changes in dental anesthetic practice, including a moratorium on the administration of general anesthesia and intravenous sedation in dental procedures performed outside of hospital facilities.[16] Under the provincial Coroner's Act, findings by a jury are not binding and have no legal force. The jury also ruled that Marvin Loewen's death was the result of hypoxia and ruled that death accidental. On the same day the mother of the deceased was quoted by reporters as saying she hoped that something positive had come out of her son's death. "It was a senseless death but, hopefully, some good will come of it. I know God does not make mistakes. I know we will meet again. I know he is in heaven."[17]

The newspaper files contain one more story on Loewen. Following the inquest, the British Columbia College of Dental Surgeons reviewed Dr. Nelson's procedures in the case and announced the findings of its inquiry to the press. The college absolved Dr. Nelson of any malpractice and "found nothing wrong with his work." Its executive director informed reporters of this and noted that "unfortunately, he [Dr. Nelson] suffered as a result of the publicity [resulting from the inquest]." In the same story. a bitter Nelson announced his departure from British Columbia because, he said, his reputation had been "distorted and ruined" by biased press coverage of the inquest. Patients apparently no longer had confidence in his abilities because of the deaths that had occurred in his dental chair that year. His practice had been destroyed by publicity resulting from the inquest, Nelson said, and he was leaving town as a result, presumably to start a new practice elsewhere.

Neither Dr. Nelson, college officials, or provincial reporters who handled this story pointed out that patients might have become chary of going to Dr. Nelson because more than 25 percent of the patients for whom he had proceeded with implants had died as a result of that operation in that year. Nor did any suggest that people concerned about their health might choose not to attend a clinic where the defibrillator is inoperative, the anesthetic respirator broken, and the choice of anesthesia questionable. Certainly nobody asked the College of Dental Surgeons, Dr. Nelson or, one suspects, the presiding coroner if there were other bodies in Dr. Nelson's closet. It was enough simply to quote Dr. Nelson's bitter adieu and Dr. Thordarson's affirmation of a colleague.

The pertinent paragraphs of that story are included here:

## Media Ruined Reputation, cleared dentist says

**by Pat Leidl**

A Vancouver dental surgeon who has been cleared of malpractice after three of his patients died while under anesthesia says the media have ruined his reputation.

"Why do you want to know my story now, after the media distorted and ruined my reputation?" Dr. Peter Nelson demanded of a reporter Wednesday night before hanging up the phone. "Why are you calling me now after my career is ruined?"

Last Friday, the College of Dental Surgeons cleared Nelson of any negligence in the deaths of three people during oral surgery in his office between November 1986 and June 1987.

Dr. Roy Thordarson, executive director of the College of Dental Surgeons, said Nelson won't reopen his practice because of the "bad publicity" surrounding the coroner's inquest.

"We found nothing wrong with his work and we feel it's very unfortunately he suffered as a result of the publicity," Thordarson said. "It's probably better he's not reopening his practice in B.C. . . .

Last October, a coroner's jury ruled the death of Loewen was accidental.

Two other patients, Ronald Mason, 50, of Prince George, and Margaret Dac, 48, of Abbotsford, also died of cardiac arrest while under anesthesia earlier in the year.

Thordarson said the coroner's jury determined the patients died of hypoxia (abnormally low levels of blood-oxygen) because of a faulty anesthesia unit.

"It was in the control of the anesthesiologist," Thordarson said."It wasn't related to the dental treatment."[18]

At this point and despite the days of inquest testimony followed by an inquiry by the provincial College of Dental Surgeons, newspaper readers and presumably reporters knew little more than they did on June 20 about the death of Marvin Loewen. What was known was that he died following the administration of anesthesia in a supposedly safe dental procedure performed in Dr. Nelson's Abbotsford clinic. Newspapers reported that the anesthesiologist blamed Loewen's death on either a very rare physiologic syndrome (carotid sinus syndrome) or the dentist's use of a specific adrenaline-based drug during a general anesthetic. The dental college, in turn, shifted blamed to the anesthetist. Dr. Nelson then blamed the press for ruining his professional reputation.

The finding of the coroner's inquest jury was that Loewen died of hypoxia. That may be "what" he died of but not "why" or "how" he died. Hypoxia is a decrease of oxygen in the blood. "Why" this occurred and "what" caused it was as unclear at the end of the newspaper series as it was on the day Coroner Urquhart announced his office's concern with Marvin Loewen's death. "How" the death could have been prevented—and thus responsibility for its occurrence—was also something treated by neither the newspaper stories or, really, the inquest on which they reported. The only real new knowledge gained, the substantial revelations of the inquest reports, was twofold. The most crucial fact was that two others beside Mr. Loewen had died within a single, twelve-month period while undergoing implant procedures in Dr. Nelson's office. Secondary but also of potential interest was the information that the anesthetic machine used by Dr. Nelson was defective and the defibrillator, a machine to be used in cardiac emergencies, inoperative.

### Changing the Rules

The focus of these stories was first on "who" and secondly on "where" and "when". "Who" at the boundary was Marvin Loewen but reportorially included the coroner, witnesses at the inquest and Dr. Thordarson in his final press conference. It was the teenager's death that the inquest investigated and the inquest officials whose testimony local journalists reported. Even after the deaths of Mrs. Dac and Mr. Mason were introduced into inquest testimony, they were seen as separate and discrete events to be treated at another time and place. "When" was reportorially a time frame of no more than two days—the time required to transfer official statements, public announcements or inquest testimony into newspaper copy or television film. "Where" was, for these stories, the official context of press conference and inquest hearing room. Information was proscribed from the start by a journalistic event that was limited to a single, discrete, discontinuous boundary occurrence—Loewen's death on June 19, 1987. Media coverage of that death was, in turn, bounded by the journalistic events of coroner inquest and official statement by recognized players in the official context (Dr. Thordarson, inquest witnesses, etc.).

At any point from the June 20 story to the final bitter address of Dr. Nelson, a reporter could have investigated the case by changing the rules of the story. To do this would have meant asking not simply "what" caused Loewen's individual death but, more importantly, "why" had the death(s) occurred and "How" could it (they) have been prevented? "how" did one explain the hypoxia that was a result of some other, antecedent occurrence or condition? To tentatively answer these questions would have required a reporter to decrease the distance between the boundary and journalistic events and look critically at the data presented to the world on June 20, 1987, and later  during the inquest itself.

All that was known to newspeople in June of 1987 was that a teenager died under anesthesia during dental implant surgery at a private British Columbia clinic If this was an isolated, atypical, unique occurrence  there was nothing, really, a reporter could have done to substantially improve newspaper coverage.  But if this was part of a pattern, the fifth or fiftieth death in which molar implants, dental anesthesia, Dr. Nelson, or Dr. Archer were involved, then this specific death might better be seen as part of a pattern, and a story or series would result. That, after all, is how the Fort Lauderdale newspaper's series was born: a single case led to a pattern of national abuse and mismanagement in the Veterans Hospital Administration.

The newspapers' files contained no prior and incriminating stories involving Dr. Nelson and Dr. Archer. Neither had been convicted of murder or manslaughter. No records of suspension by their professional organizations were listed in the  newspaper's morgue. No feature story had sung the praises or condemned as dangerous molar implant procedures. But had the focus been changed from that of the unique principals in the Loewen case  to the issue of British Columbian deaths occurring during the administration of anesthesia during dental surgery" a wealth of information would immediately  have been available. The following cases were immediately  available to any reporter interested in these issues on the day Loewen died. They are summarized from the files of the *Sun* and the *Province*  newspapers:

- On February 19, 1980, four-year-old Darcey Leo died of anesthetic complications following dental surgery in a Greater Vancouver Dental clinic. An inquest jury into that death handed down a total of thirteen recommendations. Some, including the recommendation that anesthesia be prohibited in non-hospital settings, were identical to those made seven years later by the Loewen jury.

  The jury recommendations made clear that lack of appropriate anesthetic monitoring equipment and failure to adequately monitor the patient were critical factors contributing to the death of Leo.[19]

- On November 6, 1984, Murran Bedell, 3, died following dental surgery in hospital because of low blood pressure and poor respiratory ventilation that went unmonitored during and after routine procedures carried out under general anesthesia. Drug dosages and the specific mix of anesthetics used were also factors in this death. Experts testified there was inadequate and inappropriate monitoring of the patient's vital signs before, during, and after the operation.[20]

- On November 22, 1984, Julie Ann Heagy, 14, died following dental surgery in which anesthesia was used. She shared the same anesthetist, Dr. Laurens Niebor, with Bedell and the inquest findings—and criticisms—were virtually identical to those describing the Bedell girl's death.[21]

- Charlie Nooski, 83, died following dental surgery at a Vanderhoof, British Columbia, dental clinic following an overdose of anesthesia. There was no inquest, but a coroner's inquiry determined that Mr. Nooski died of anesthetic drug overdose. Provincial coroners have the option to hold an "inquiry" in which a report on the death is filed with their service or to hold a public inquest in which a jury is impaneled.[22]

    Following a British Columbia College of Dental Surgeons inquiry into the case, Nooski's dentist was ordered to take a refresher course in anesthesia but allowed to continue his practice. The family objected to the media. The College's Dr. Roy Thordarson told reporters that, while he sympathized with the family's concerns over the dentist's continued practice, he believed the matter had been handled fairly.[23] Lack of anesthetic monitoring equipmen or inappropriate anesthetic procedures were not mentioned in the newspaper story but could be deduced from its description of Nooski's death.

Thus the day after Marvin Loewen died and long before journalists discovered that his death was one of three occurring in a single dental clinic in suburban Vancouver, the following information was available:

    (a) Since 1980 there had been at least three inquests and one inquiry into deaths resulting from dental procedures in which anesthesia was involved.

    (b) In 1980, an inquest jury recommended a prohibition on anesthetic-related dental procedures in clinics for safety reasons relating to anesthetic administration. Later deaths occurred, however, both in clinic (Leo, Nooski) and in hospital (Bedell, Heagy).

    (c) In all cases, a critical factor was the lack of appropriate patient monitoring during and after administration of general anaesthesia. Of import in these cases was the amount and type of drug administered and the degree to which a patient's vital signs were monitored during anesthetic procedures.

    (d) Even in cases where the dentist was directly responsible for a patient's death, the provincial College of Dental Surgeons took no strong disciplinary action.

    (e) The official cause of death in these file cases typically was listed as "hypoxia" but that is more properly seen as the result of, at least in the cases cited here, medical misadventure involving the administration of anesthesia. To say a person died of hypoxia says nothing about "why" he or she died, or "what" caused the fatal biologic condition. It is a signifier to which no causal meaning is attached. "Hypoxia, in the journalistic context, is like the pattern of dots which only becomes a sign, a structure with meaning, when the image is interpreted.

These four cases do not describe all anesthetic-related dental deaths in British Columbia from 1980 to 1987, but only those deaths that went to inquest or, in Mr. Nooski's case, where inquiry information was made public by the victim's family. They present a pattern in which the absence of appropriate patient monitoring equipment during dental anesthesia prevented the early detection of anesthetic-related problems and thus contributed to the patient's death.

Even without any further research, a reporter at this point had a subject worthy of active inquiry. He or she could have framed two hypotheses to be tested by interview or perusal of autopsy and postmortem reports. These lines of inquiry were that: (a) failure to adequately monitor a patient under anesthetic is a primary or contributing cause of anesthetic-related dental deaths and (b) private dental clinics are not an appropriate location for procedures serious enough to require anesthetic administration.

Because it had been seven years since a coroner's jury first had recommended prohibition of anesthetic procedures in a dental clinic, the efficacy of inquests themselves may have been considered as an issue. These hypotheses could have been focused, for example, on Loewen's case. Did Dr. Archer use appropriate anesthetic drugs during the procedure, appropriately monitor his patient and have the correct equipment available? Why have another inquest if nobody listened to the recommendations and even clearly culpable dentists were not disciplined, whatever an inquiry or inquest's revelations?

It is important to stress that these questions remove the reporter from a reactive position in which he or she must take only that information offered by officials and makes of that journalist an active investigator into the systemic elements of the specific boundary event. This active and "investigative" posture results from changing the definition of a news story. "Who" is not restricted to the actors involved in the official boundary event or the principal officials setting the inquest agenda. Rather, "who" becomes a series of events in which death occurred during dental surgery. The boundary location has been enlarged from a single Abbotsford clinic to the provincial borders, and the time frame from a specific, narrow one to the decade in which Loewen died.

With this perspective and armed with the facts of these previous cases, a reporter in June 1987 could have asked Mr. Urquhart what monitoring equipment had been in use in the Abbotsford Dental Clinic and what type of anesthetic drugs had been administered. What precisely did the autopsy and postmortem information say, and what was the precise wording on the death certificate? Questions about the efficacy of the inquest system, whose repeated recommendations had not been followed, could have been raised as well at this time.

The newsperson interested in these issues then could have expanded the definition of his boundary event and spent another hour on research. Since the common denominator in all the cases—from Leo to Loewen—appeared to be the administration of anesthesia to patients, the next logical step would be to see if anesthetic-related dental deaths differed from those involving anesthesia during general surgery. In other words, was the administration of anesthetic drugs the central issue or was the story to be, in fact, more narrowly defined by the dental context? The following stories describing coroner inquest or court testimony involving problems with anesthesia in general surgery also were available to a reporter interested in these issues:

- Patrick Doucet, 17, died September 6, 1980, of hypoxia following surgery on his leg at Vancouver General Hospital. The cause of his death was, according to inquest testimony, mechanical failure of an anesthetic respirator and failure by the operating room physician to carefully monitor his patient and check the equipment before surgery.[24]

  Medical experts said at time time of the inquest that thousands of deaths or injuries occurred each year because of anesthetic problems. Further, physicians admitted that many professionals "have an interest in not circulating the fact that a patient died " because of anesthetic mishaps.[25]

- Kari Lynn Boivin died May 30, 1986, following the administration of a general anesthetic during "routine" surgery. Inquest testimony described inappropriate administrative techniques, a lack of monitoring equipment in the operating room, and general uncertainty about what to do in the case of an emergency. "No one was in control in there," a nurse testified at inquest.[26]

- Robert W. Graham, 64, died on October 8, 1985, of anesthetic complications during surgery.[27] This case was described in chapter 2. Again, lack of monitoring was a factor preventing early diagnosis of the patient's problem.

- Anita Pike, 39, died during routine surgery at Peace Arch Hospital in suburban, Vancouver in 1981 during routine surgery. A civil case seeking damages was heard in British Columbia. Supreme Court in May, 1985. Testimony in that trial described the anesthetist as incompetent for not adequately monitoring the patient during the operation.[28]

What began as reportage of the isolated, discrete event of June

18, 1987, now appears to be one of a series of at least eight provincial deaths in which a coroner's inquest or court testimony showed that improper anesthetic administration was the critical factor in the death of otherwise healthy patients. Because only a fraction of deaths result in a British Columbia coroner's inquest or inquiry, a reporter could assume as a hypothesis that these were representative and not peculiar events. Was this a problem unique to British Columbia or symptomatic of a larger, perhaps North American problem? To test the theory that improper anesthesia contributes to or causes death in many geographic areas, a reporter could have expanded the geographic definition of the story and searched for information from a wider context. A reporter simply could have telephoned all chief coroners and medical examiners in Canada's other ten provinces to ask if they had handled anesthetic-related deaths occurring in dental or general surgery.

Another way would have been to check newspaper files in California or some other densely populated region of the United States. Canada's population is one-fifth that of the United States, and it is not uncommon for Canadian newsmen to ask if what is happening in one jurisdiction is present in the other. The simplest way to do this, at least as a preliminary step, would have been to search the newspaper files of a major U.S. newspaper for stories describing deaths involving the combination of dental or abdominal surgery and anesthesia. These files are generally available through computer searches[29] newspaper indexes,[30] or telephoning newspaper librarians or city editors and requesting information as a professional courtesy. For the purposes of this study, the *Los Angeles Times* newspaper index was searched by computer (search phrase: "anesthetic" or "anesthesia" and "death" or "injury" with the following results:

- Kim Andreasson, 23, died in 1982 as a result of a lethal combination of anesthetic drugs chosen and administered by Dr. Tony Protopappas.[31] *At least sixteen other alleged victims and survivors claimed damages against the dentist in separate lawsuits.*

  Protopappas was convicted of murder by a California court following the deaths of three patients. In these cases, the critical issue was the inappropriate administration of specific drugs and substandard patient monitoring and care.

  Appellate Justice Edward J. Wallin said of Protopappas's performance that: "no reasonable person, much less a dentist trained in the use of anesthesia, could have failed to appreciate the grave risk of death posed by the procedures he utilized."[32]

- Jodi Safier, 27, died September 4, 1986, as a result of anesthetic administered during dental surgery.[33] The story on her death described both a lack of patient monitoring and the mixing of a local anesthetic and tranquilizer together in a procedure called "conscious sedation."

- Johnny Gray, 3, died in 1984 as a result of conscious sedation. A nurse anesthetist and Los Angeles dentist were
charged with manslaughter in that death.[34]

- "Conscious sedation," the simultaneous administration of
a general anaesthetic (halothane, for example) and a re-
laxant (like Valium), was reported to be responsible for
between ten and seventeen dental-related deaths investigated by the California Board of Dental examiners between
February,1, 1983 and September 10, 1986.[35]

The problem of conscious sedation in dental surgery is
so pervasive, an ABC radio report on the subject noted,
that twenty-seven U.S. states had passed laws regarding
the training of dentists in its usage.[36] Thus it is reasonable
to assume that other cases involving conscious sedation
as an anesthetic technique have occurred in these states
as well.

Other incidents involving anesthesia related death or injury—
dental and surgical—can be found in newspapers from New York,
where Rifa Setiyono died, to Arizona.[37] In most of these stories, failure
to appropriately monitor a patient was described as a crucial factor
contributing to the patient's death or permanent injury. For the period
of January 1, 1987 to October 1, 1988, thirty-three newspaper stories
describing court cases involving anesthetic-related deaths were found
through a computer search of forty U.S. newspapers. These were only
those stories in which a legal action was instituted or where a court
judgment had been awarded and thus did not include incidents of anesthesia-related death or injury settled out of court or deaths in which
no suit was filed. Most described cases in which a hospital, physician,
or medical corporation was successfully sued for more than $500,000
because of anesthetic-related death or injury. In most cases, the critical issue was the degree to which the anesthesiologist monitored his or
her patient. A search of the legal[38] and medico-legal[39] literature uncovered more precisely documented cases. There are literally hundreds
of reported cases of anesthetic-related death or injury (involving both
dental and general surgery procedures) that can be used to build a
hypothesis and expand a story.

**THE NARRATIVE FORM**

It is important to review, at this point, precisely what has occurred in terms of changes in the definition of the story form and subsequent changes in event definitions.

The boundary "who" has been altered from principal actors in
a discrete, discontinuous event—the death of Marvin Loewen in June
of 1987—to the subjects of anesthesia-related deaths in general and
those involving dental deaths in particular. Loewen's death is no longer

the sole subject, a unique event. It has become instead the latest in a series of North American deaths which all share specific characteristics. In newspaper jargon, his death has become the "hook" for a series on preventable anesthetic-related deaths in British Columbia, Canada. or in North America at large .

"What" has been changed from a specific death ("Joe died") to a deadly context—insufficient patient monitoring or inappropriate drug administration during dental or general surgery. How this relates to Loewen's case is not clear from the material gained but is obviously a subject for inquiry and investigation.

That change has empowered the reporter, who can now ask questions on the specific event based on a pattern of consistent, prior occurrence. The ability to define and exclude information is no longer solely the prerogative of the officials and professionals involved.

"When" has been altered from June 1987 to the decade of the 1980s. No deaths occurring before January 1, 1980, were included in the summary. This was an arbitrary designation and a simple means of controlling the amount of material as it accumulated.

This is true both at the boundary, as multiple cases from the decade are examined, and at the attributive stage. Reporters could ask the presiding coroner outside the hearing why recommendations made again and again are not heeded. Was the issue really one of professional competence and regulation? Dr. Archer could be asked why, as the expert anesthesiologist, he did not check the respirator before surgery (also an issue in the Doucet case, among others)? If he did not approve of a combination of local anesthetic with halothane, why did he not protest as was his obligation?

"Where" can be broken down into several categories depending on how the story is to be written. The context can be either Greater Vancouver, British Columbia, Canada or North America. The original limiting geographic boundary, an Abbotsford clinic death which is the subject of an official inquest, has become one element in a wider context.

Whatever the specific cause of death ("hypoxia," "cardio-pulmonary collapse," etc.), the failure by anesthesiologists to monitor a patient appropriately is, according to the newspaper and literature reviews, "why" people are dying in these cases. At the very least, these file stories suggested adequate monitoring would have allowed for early detection of patient distress and assured the rapid application of corrective procedures that might have prevented death.

Precisely "how" death occurred precisely is now a real issue, as is the responsibility for that death. If anesthetic equipment was not working, if the patient was not monitored according to standards described again and again in prior cases, then his faulty anesthetic administration will have been a contributing or principal factor in the boy's death and the anesthetist will share responsibility for the boy's demise.

**Story Basics**

The following information thus was available, with clear documentation, to B.C. reporters in June of 1987. The "paper trail" shows clearly that:

1. Marvin Loewen's death was not an isolated case. Others had died in British Columbia since 1980 following the improper administration of anesthesia during dental surgery performed in both B.C. dental clinics and B.C. hospitals.

2. Deaths involving anaesthesia and dental procedures carried out in hospitals and clinics have occurred in places other than British Columbia. This is not, therefore, a peculiarly local problem.

   a. In fact, twenty-seven states in the United States had passed laws prior to June 1987 regulating the administration of anesthesia by dentists because of the dangers involved.

   b. *As early as 1980, a British Columbia coroner's jury had recommended that dental procedures requiring anesthesia be performed only in hospital because of perceived dangers of the clinic context in the event of anesthetic complications.*

3. Other British Columbians had died since 1980 as a result of the improper administration of anesthesia during general surgery performed in hospital.

4. Anesthesia and general surgery resulted in still more deaths in the United States. These cases often resulted in large malpractice awards being levied against the participating physician or physicians.

5. A critical element in almost all these cases, whatever the jurisdiction, was failure by the anesthetist to monitor the patient before, during, and after the scheduled procedure. Minimal standards of monitoring were defined, in most file stories, as checking a patient's vital signs through use of a stethoscope; blood pressure cuff; an EKG machine, electrocardiogram (which measures electrical activity of the heart); pulse oximeter (which measures oxygen saturation of arterial blood, heart rate and arterial pressure); and other equipment. The need for appropriate emergency equipment, preoperative examinations and postoperative monitoring were also described in most cases as the responsibility of the anesthetist.

### Anesthesia and Patient Monitoring

At this point a reporter could have asked the coroner what equipment was used by Dr. Archer in Dr. Nelson's clinic. The Pike inquest made clear that appropriate standards of anesthetic procedure required the monitoring of blood pressure, pulse, and heart rate. Deaths resulting from an inquest at Peace Arch Hospital blamed a patient death on failure of operating room personnel to know what to do in emergencies and to have present adequate emergency equipment. Issues of equipment maintenance—the inoperative defibrillator and the broken respirator (as in the case of Patrick Ducet)—have been covered here.

The cautious journalist would, perhaps, have searched further for specific information on appropriate monitoring before beginning to interview  specific subjects. For this background he or she could have called a recognized authority in anesthesiology or gone to the library. The University of British Columbia has both a medical and a dental school where individuals instruct in this area. Had those experts not been forthcoming, the library provides a great deal of information for the layman, coroner, or journalist.

While medical information is often highly technical, the basic issues of patient monitoring are clearly written and very accessible. Articles on anesthesia can be found, for example, in technical indexes that list all medical journal articles by subject,[40] in medical textbooks dealing with anesthesiology, and in legal journals where questions of liability relating to malpractice are presented.  An hour's research at the library following a computer-assisted search for articles on "anesthesia and injury or death" turned up the following facts which strengthen the hypothesis and advance the story:[41]

1. Incidence of anesthesia-related death can be drastically reduced by forcing anesthetists to follow accepted procedures, including appropriate monitoring of a patient before, during and after the anesthesia is administered.[42]

2. Proper monitoring is not expensive and use of  proper procedures with appropriate equipment could reduce operating room deaths an estimated 50 percent.[43]

3. When  anesthesia-related problems occur, "the error in almost all cases was the lack of proper monitoring of the patient."[44] Both this source and the previous one define what is meant by proper monitoring and describe appropriate equipment.

4. "Ultimately, prevention and correction of equipment malfunction depends on the anesthesiologist, who must understand the function of each piece of equipment and remain ·eternally vigilant."[45]

   "Before commencing any general or local anesthetic,

there should be a thorough check of all the equipment which may be needed. This has been likened to the check performed by a pilot before taking off in an aircraft."[46]

Thus the issue of anesthesia-related equipment and its condition in surgery was specifically Dr. Archer's professional responsibility.

### Story or Series

Questions the reporter could pursue in coverage of the specific event are now clear: What monitoring equipment did Dr. Archer have in Dr. Nelson's office? Was appropriate emergency equipment available and functioning? Was the patient examined before the procedure to assure proper dosages were given (an issue in the Boivin and Nooski cases)? Was an EKG used during surgery? Were blood pressure and heart rate monitored continually (a failure in the Pike case according to court testimony)? How quickly and appropriately did the anesthetist and dentist respond when a medical crisis began? If these questions were not answered to the reporter's satisfaction in the inquest, the daily newsperson could raise them independently through interviews with the coroner, pathologist, and other principals in the case.

The fact that more than six British Columbian inquests into issues of anesthetic death had resulted in recommendations which were not followed also would have raised questions about the efficacy of the provincial inquest system itself. After all, a 1980 inquest jury investigating the death of Darcey Leo had strongly recommended prohibition of anesthetic-related dental surgery in private clinics because of a death. Why had that not been followed, and did the Coroner's Service still support it? A series of inquests and inquiries all had pointed to the consistent failure of anesthetic administration as a factor in dental and surgical deaths, and yet those deaths appeared to be continuing.

Finally, there is the interesting issue of the British Columbia College of Dental Surgeons and the B.C. College of Physicians. Under provincial law, they have the sole authority to discipline and regulate their members' actions. From 1980 to 1987, no physician or dentist involved in an anesthetic death, even where gross negligence was determined to have occurred, had been suspended or reprimanded. If that was not to be a subject of journalistic inquiry, it would surely argue for caution in accepting at face value the statement of, for example, Dr. Thordarson.

Hypothesis which have been generated by these stories included the following:

(a) Anesthetic administration was a contributing or critical factor in the death of Marvin Loewen. Further, the failure, if one occurred, was likely either inappropriate monitoring of the patient by the anesthetist or inappropriate drug dosages.

(b) Inquiry recommendations, if any are made, will not be followed. From 1980 to 1987, the subject had been treated by the provincial coroners without significant effect on incidence of occurrence.

c) The B.C. College of Dental Surgeons and the B.C. College of Physicians and Surgeons will not adequately censor or discipline its members—whatever the facts of the case. Even where members have been clearly responsible for a patient's death, college officials have minimized the incident.

## TESTING THE HYPOTHESIS

A skeptical reader at this point might object that there is no evidence of a relation between anesthetic administration and the deaths of Marvin Loewen, Ronald Mason or Margaret Dac in Dr. Nelson's dental clinic. It is true that  published newspaper stories concerning the death of Marvin Loewen do not appear to have any relation to the stories of anesthesia-related deaths described here. Further, it is true that the governing board for provincial physicians, the College of Physicians and Surgeons of British Columbia, did not investigate the performance of Dr. Archer in the Loewen case. There is no evidence, at this point, to suggest they were delinquent in their oversight responsibilities. The same can be said about Dr. Nelson's organization and its findings concerning his performance. The structure of conjecture built up here seems, on the basis of the *Sun* and *Province* reports, to have no real relation to the deaths of Mavin Loewen, Margaret Dac, or Ronald Mason.

But that does not mean that anesthetists involved in these three cases were blameless or that their performance—and that of the dentist himself— did not contribute to patient deaths. What it means is that the issues either were not raised at the public inquiry or that, if raised, they were not reported by the *Province* or the *Sun*.

### Judgment of Inquiry—Anesthesia

In November 1988 coroner Diane Messier signed and filed two official *Judgements of Inquiry*, one on the November 6, 1986, death of Ronald James Mason and the other concerning the September 17, 1987, death of  Margaret Estella Dac. Both judgments included information on the death of Marvin Loewen, and treated all three as a single event.  These rather lengthy and very complete reports were not presented at a press conference and their findings were not reported either by provincial newspapers or by television stations.[47]

Television's Dr. Quincy, the crusading medical examiner of the 1970s, would not have rested until the information they contained had been widely disseminated.[48] Fictional newsmen like television's *Lou*

*Grant* would have been equally dedicated to the disclosure of all relevant facts in these three deaths.[49] Where there is a preventable pattern of unnecessary death, the erstwhile medical examiners and reporters of fiction fight unceasingly to get the information into the public domain in the hope that public controversy will help to prevent future unnecessary deaths. But this was the real world, and the case had ended. The story was over and all three individuals dead in Dr. Nelson's dental chair—Marvin Loewen, Mrs. Dac and Mr. Mason—had been buried long before. Reporters' notebooks were officially closed when Nelson bid British Columbia and its news reporters his bitter adieu. Messier did not call a press conference and scream her conclusions or force Loewen's case to be reheard.

That was a shame, because information contained in these inquiry reports confirmed the hypothesis that anesthetic-administration was a contributing factor in all three deaths. Further, these inquiries confirmed the supposition that lack of patient monitoring, failure to handle emergencies correctly, and failure to follow standard anesthetic procedures were an issue in three deaths:

> In each case, conduct of the anesthetists and interventions when things went wrong were less than optimal. Current standards of practice were ignored. Furthermore, if more suitable monitoring had been used (ECG, BP, pulse oximetry, end-tidal capnograph),[50] earlier detection of the air emboi might have been realized and treatment undertaken.[51]

Three different dentists were involved in these specific cases: Dr. Archer attended Marvin Loewen, Dr. Klassen attended Ronald Mason and Dr. Trelor attended Mrs. Dac. We know from inquest testimony that there was minimal patient monitoring of Loewen by Archer, a severely compromised anesthetic machine was in use, and a broken defibrillator was inoperative during the emergency that ended with the teenager's death. We know from our reading that, "Ultimately, prevention and correction of equipment malfunction depends on the anesthesiologist, who must understand the function of each piece of equipment and remain eternally vigilant."[52] In the Dac and Mason judgments, the following failures by attending anesthesiologists and Dr. Nelson were noted as being contrary to current standards of practice:

- No evidence of preoperative physical examination/assessment, contrary to the current standards of practice.
- No preoperative measurement of patient vital signs to use as a baseline during surgical monitoring.
- No evidence or record of measurement of patient blood pressures.
- No evidence of patient monitoring in accordance with accepted standards of practice.
- No evidence of an anesthetic record kept by physicians.

• No evidence of prompt action in the case of a medical emergency. Paramedics were not called, according to Messier's "Judgements," until either ten minutes (in Mason's case) or thirty minutes (in the Dac case) after cardiac arrest had occurred. "Much confusion was present in the dental office at the time of the arrest and this was noted by the paramedics when they arrived [following Mr. Mason's distress]."[53]

Since Leo's death in 1980, these failures had been cited in case after case as contributing to the death of other British Columbian citizens during dental and general surgical procedures involving anesthesia. Further, most were mentioned as elements contributing to the death or permanent injury of patients in cases cited from California to New York. There, however, the testimony was largely from court cases in which physicians and dentists faced either charges of murder or malpractice suits the families of the victims.

### Judgment of Inquiry—Implant procedures

Messier's official but unpublished reports also described precisely "why" these three individuals died. Further, they described the cases of two more individuals injured but not killed during implant procedures performed in Dr. Nelson's office. The problem, she concluded, was not with the technique itself:

This implant procedure is a safe, atraumatic procedure. No other deaths associated with implantology could be thus far found either in extensive literature search nor requesting information from coroners and medical examiners offices in *L.A. County, Boston or New York.* (italics added).

Dr. Nelson did 11 implant procedures. Three patients died, one patient suffered a cardiovascular collapse and a fifth patient suffered massive subcutaneous emphysema during the procedure. This complication rate makes a statement.[54]

The statement it made, she continued, was that if anesthetic administration procedures prevented detection of life threatening problems, Dr. Nelson's technique was directly responsible for the deaths:

Ronald Mason, Marvin Loewen and Margaret Dac all died from air embolism incurred during dental implant surgery. Embolism was produced because the surgeon, Dr. Peter Nelson, used a mixture of air and water for both external and internal irrigation of the drill. Flow of air and water down the cannon drill passed through the vascular system of the mandible to the facial and pterygoid plexus veins and

then to the superior vena cava and right atrium. . . . This resulted in embolised air and rapid cardiovascular decompensation.[55]

The finding of death from an air embolism insinuated into the patient during the procedure was based on postmortems and pathologies
done in each case immediately following the death of the individual victims. Mr. Mason's was performed in 1986[56] and Mrs. Dac's in September of 1987.[57] It also explained the subcutaneous emphysema and non-
fatal cardiovascular collapse of Nelson's two other cases, Messier
concluded. "How" these people died was as a result of "cardiovascular
decompensation" caused by Dr. Nelson's drilling into the porous jaw
while using air pressure and water on the operation site. "Why" they
died was because of dental technique *and* a failure by the attending
anesthesiologists to follow accepted procedures whose purpose is the
prompt detection and correction of problems during surgery.
    Dr. Thordarson was right when he told reporters the public in-
quest did not blame Dr. Nelson but wrong when he suggested his colleague was blameless in these deaths.
    In the simplest terms, Dr. Nelson inadvertently injected air into
his patients' blood streams, and that air reached the patients' hearts
and lungs, causing death or injury. Had the anesthesiologists monitored their patients in accordance with accepted standards of practice,
it is possible that earlier detection of the problem could have prevented
one or more of these deaths. "Why" this happened had nothing to do, as
Archer suggested under oath, with rare carotid syndromes, or the
combination of adrenaline and halothane anesthetics.

It would be stretching the limits of chance to have three
patients under the care of one dentist all succumb to a
similar so-called 'idosyncratic' drug reaction. The timing of
the arrest of three patients was too long after injection of the
drugs for the local agents to be implicated. Furthermore,
combinations compared "favorably to standard practice".
Many patients, similar to Mr. Mason, Marvin Loewen and
Mrs. Dac undergo general anesthesia or sedation with local
infiltration without coming to harm.[58]

"How" these deaths could have been prevented involved, among
other factors, patient monitoring during anesthesia by the anesthesiologist. Simply, the dentist *and* anesthetists shared responsibility for
these deaths, just as they had in previous cases lying unread in the
newspaper files.

**Reporting the Context**
    The information Messier used to arrive at her judgement was, in
large part, available to any provincial reporter interested in the story.
A search of provincial and then North American newspaper files uncovered no other articles concerning death during implant procedures. Nor

did the dental literature provide any indication that the procedure itself, which has been used over 180,000 times in Europe and North America, was inherently dangerous in itself. A search of the dental literature on air embolisms and subcutaneous emphysemas, information available from the autopsy and post mortems, did find several articles suggesting that air insinuated into the body through the jaw could cause these life-threatening occurrences. This literature was found using computer databases and the search words "embolism" and dental" through CompuServe's IQuest gateway system to medical databases.[59] Other articles were found using the phrase "subcutaneous emphysema" and "dental."

Not surprisingly, it is this literature that Messier also cites in her report. Thus the reporter who had asked in 1987 to see the final pathology reports, autopsy reports, or death certificates might have discovered that an air embolism was the cause of the cardiovascular distress that resulted in hypoxia. Searching the literature at that time would have uncovered the likelihood that the dental drilling technique and equipment used by Dr. Nelson could have inadvertently caused air to be forced into the patients' jaws and from there into their vascular systems. Three died and two were injured as a result.

Dr. Nelson was not ill treated by the British Columbian news fraternity. In fact, he was treated very kindly and cautiously by reporters, who limited their treatment and research to that of the officially sanctioned inquest.

### Search Results
Depending on the geographic and temporal scales at which the respective journalist might chose to work, stories dealing with the following issues could have been generated following the death of Marvin Loewen and during an inquest into his death:

(a)    An epidemic of patient deaths involving anesthesia. In researching this material I developed a database of a hundred stories detailing approximately sixty deaths involving dental or surgical anesthesia. The search was not systematic but concentrated on examination of stories and articles from one Canadian province (B.C.) one U.S. state (California) and a random examination of stories from Texas, Ohio, Maryland,[60] other Canadian provinces and U.S. states. These deaths were the direct result of the failure of anesthetic administrators to follow accepted professional procedures.

A series on this topic could have focused either on the British Columbian. material alone or been expanded, with interviews, into a Canadian or Canadian and American regional expose.

(b)    The failure of the provincial Coroner's Service to correct problems despite repeated and expensive inquiries into specific deaths. From 1980 to 1987, inquests into anesthetic deaths involving dentistry and general surgery had similar testimony and made similar recommendations time after time. If the inquest service is impotent, that is a legitimate area for reportorial examination.

(c) The failure of professional organizations in British Columbia to monitor and discipline their own members. Dr. Thordarson's group exonerated Dr. Nelson despite the clear and unequivocal findings of Messier's Judgements that his procedure was responsible for patient deaths. The dentist who accidently killed Mr. Nooski with an overdose was not disciplined. In none of these cases, in fact, was a member of the College of Dental Surgeons or College of Physicians and Surgeons penalized. Nor were their rules or procedures changed.

Since these professional organizations have absolute control over the licensing and regulation of their members, the efficacy of that system—using these cases— would have been a logical place for a reporter to turn.

It is perhaps unfair to single out British Columbia journalists for these failures. Their reportage  was  no worse if, in the end, no better than that of reporters covering similar events in other jurisdictions. Reporters at the *Los Angeles Times*, the *Globe and Mail*, the *New York Times*, the *Knickerbocker News*,[61] the *Arizona Star*  and dozens of other newspapers had multiple anesthetic-related deaths (dental and surgical) in their files. A journalist from any of more than twenty jurisdictions could have used the death of a citizen in his or her region to build the case described here. Even those news organizations boasting "I-Teams" or investigative units did not think to apply their resources and expertise to these "mundane" events.

### "Investigative" Journalism

The procedure described here  could be called "investigative" in the sense that a reporter inquires systematically into the antecedent context of a specific event. More properly, it might be called "critical" reportage because it involves the formulation of a hypothesis, based on elements in a single event, and seeks to test that hypothesis through the creation of a class of similar occurrences to which it may be structurally related. If, as Judson suggests, there is no fact without a theory,[62] then critical reportage allows the news person to place the elements of any specific boundary event into the framework of a theory that can be tested, investigated and changed. It is profoundly "active," as opposed to the "passive" reportage described in chapters 2 and 3. The reporter, like the pathologist, searches for information beyond the bounds of what officials or participants say occurred.

The distinction being made here between "administrative" and "critical" reportage is twofold. In the former, for which the *Anniston Star* stories can be an example, definition of the boundary event remains unchanged and the reporter, with the aid perhaps of the plaintiff's lawyer, reads the official reports himself. It relies not on what officials say but bases its text on what the opposing pantheon of legal discovery, pathologist reports and and adversarial lawyers say as well. "Critical" reportage goes one step further, redefining the subject of the story and the information sources to be used at the level not of N+1 or N+2 but at the N level itself. It is not simply the death or deaths in Dr. Nelson's office which are the subject. They become subsets of the failure of the British Columbian Colleges of Dental Surgeons and of Physicians and Surgeons, of the  Coroner's Service, and the provincial Ministry of Health to adequately police medical professionals who are responsible for unnecessary anesthetic-related deaths. At another scale, one could ask pointed questions about  medical associations in both the United States (the American Medical Association) and Canada  which supervise physicians in general as well as  federal supervising bodies like Health and Welfare Canada  which are charged with national standards in Canada and the U.S. respectively. "Administrative" journalism would stop at the  three deaths in Dr. Nelson's clinic while "critical journalism" would  make of those three deaths a wider platform in which the failure of medical supervision became the issue.

The result in this case was especially satisfying. What began as description of an isolated, discrete event became a potentially important series in which a pattern of unnecessary death occurring across North America—deaths in which improper anesthetic administration was an element—was identified. Most editors would agree that a headline "Hundreds Die/Doctors Blamed" is superior to "Boy Died after Dental Procedure."

Using the language of set theory introduced earlier, what this method did was to remove reliance on both the official investigative summaries (N+3) and the specific technical summaries of an individual case (N+2) through the changed definition of the boundary event. Pathology materials in the Loewen, Dac and Mason cases important but through this method their relevance and interpretation is removed from official perspectives and placed firmly in the journalist's control.

To the extent that this is an "investigative" method it does not assume material is being hidden by one or more individuals or that the "paper trail" must follow official documentation to the exclusion of other information. As illustration 10 makes clear, it shifts the level of reportorial focus from reliance on the official investigation to an independent journalistic examination.This suggests that truly "investigative," "enterprise," or "public affairs"  journalism might be better defined as occurring at the critical level of reportage. A better definition of truly critical, "investigative journalism," based on this anlysis, can be  proposed:

**Illustration 10**
**Levels of Reportage**

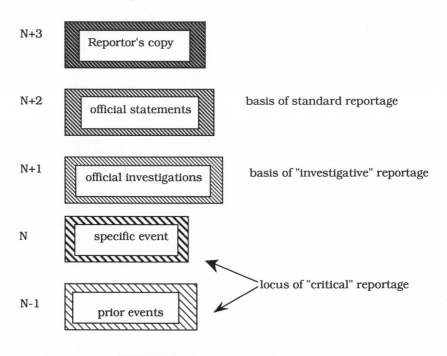

N+3    Reportor's copy

N+2    official statements          basis of standard reportage

N+1    official investigations      basis of "investigative" reportage

N      specific event

                                    locus of "critical" reportage
N-1    prior events

---

Reportage in which the subject is consciously redefined to
allow an apparently single, discrete event to be placed in a
larger context. This new boundary will allow the reporter to
place the trigger event into a pattern of repeated occur-
rence.The critical elements of that pattern can be substanti-
ated through existing documents or by interview. The result
of this will be an active story or series which, while perhaps
paralleling the work of official investigators, does not rely
exclusively on their information in the creation and testing of
a theory as to an event's cause or definition.

The benefit of such a procedure is not simply that it gives to the
reporter a flexibility that traditional reportage denies. By introducing
Kipling's last two serving men and describing a means by which official
statements can be tested, it provides to the news professional an independence that is the essential component to any notion of objectivity.
Freed from reliance solely on the information presented by officials in
a journalistic event, the journalist is empowered by a level and type of
information approximating that of the official investigators (Messier,
Urquart), and greater than that of participating actors (Nelson, Archer),

to investigate aspects of the boundary event. This new definition requires a conscious and fundamental change in the form of the news story. It decreases the importance of the discrete event (Marvin Loewen) by broadening the "who" definition and by modifying spatio-temporal boundaries to include different time frames and multiple locations. It reinstates Kipling's "why" and "how" as active participants in journalism. The relation between "standard" reportage based on official statements, investigative or, as it is here called, "administrative" reportage, which relies on official reports with an officially determined boundary, and "critical" reportage is shown in Illustration 10 using the set theory boxes describing information levels.

One can now answer with some precision the question that opened this chapter. "Investigative" journalism, as it is currently defined, does not necessarily alter the accepted narrative pattern of contemporary news. It typically conforms to the definition of story subject as an isolated, discontinuous event and includes a shift from journalistic to boundary event. The distance between these levels is shortened by at least one step in what is currently called "investigative" journalism. But by redefining a story's boundary, by restating the "who," "what," "when" and "where" in a manner different from the official definition, a very different narrative  result  can be obtained. These changes allow for the journalist to emphasize Kipling's existential serving men—"why" and "how"—in an active way while preserving the  "paper trail"  needed for substantial documentation.

### Force of Prior Weight

These changes in story definition and thus reportorial procedure have another, significant result. By decreasing reliance on the official context, they allow reporters to question the principles on which  official statements rest. The power of the force of prior weight is based on the authority of an individual's office and the assumption that officials—police chief, coroner, director of a professional association, prime minister or president—speak from knowledge. The authority of an official position carries the presumption of informed opinion. That assumption, however, is not necessarily accurate. Police Chief Keala's judgment in the Shintaku case did not fit the medical facts; the coroner's inquiry did not describe the full context of Loewen's death; Dr. Thordarson was incorrect in saying Dr. Nelson's technique was blameless; American presidents who confidently predicted the early success of American military activities in Vietnam were issuing political hopes and not accurate assessments of the situation.

To the degree that news officials define a story in terms of the  reportage of an  official statement or report, the resulting story will of necessity be biased. Information in that typical context becomes, in short, what the candidate, professor, or appointed administrator says it must be. Thus Police Chief Keala could redefine attempted homicide as failed suicide  with impunity,  Dr. Thordarson could trumpet the innocence of Dr. Nelson despite the weight of medical evidence; and Dr. Moss, in New York, could be cajoled into uttering inanities about a case of whose facts he was in fact ignorant. To the extent that the journalist is a passive "reporter," he or she is at the mercy of an official's suppositions because he or she is terminally distanced from the facts of the event or events being described. The first value forfeited when this happens is the ideal of objectivity, because without independence there can be nothing beyond a mere recitation of the facts as presented by an expert or official intimately involved in the definition of the events to be described. Passive reporters become like the army information officers criticized by the *Anniston Star*, parrots reciting information provided to them without any critical examination or thought.

But when the form changes and a story is redefined to deemphasize the dominance of the official context or statement, then everything is up for grabs and it becomes surprisingly easy to challenge erroneous but official suppositions. The reporter becomes an investigator capable of thought and action. Far from being a necessarily adversarial approach, this allows for a greater objectivity in which what were isolated events become related components in a system of occurrences; and where information is drawn not from a single, sanctioned source but from a broad context of sources, diminishing the weight of each actor's input—including that of the news reporter.

## OTHER TYPES OF REPORTAGE

### The War On Drugs

It may be useful at this point to use an example from a very different area to demonstrate the degree to which this altered posture can significantly alter the information presented by daily news. A superb example is the daily news reporter's coverage of the "War against drugs" first declared by U.S. President Ronald Reagan after his election in 1981. The chemical addiction of U.S. citizens to controlled substances— primarily heroin, marijuana, and cocaine—was throughout his tenure trumpeted as a critical danger to the national body. The eradication of drug use through the use of military, police, and judicial resources became a primary goal of Mr. Reagan's eight years in office. Between 1980 and 1988, the U.S. spent at least $22 billion to interdict narcotics during transportation to their market and to prosecute those responsible for the sale and preparation of the drugs prior to sale.[63] These monies were allocated during a period of systemic federal cutbacks in funding for social programs and services.

The war against drugs has been covered at each step by daily journalists who typically report the arrest and trial of dealers in their jurisdictions, lament the continued presence of drugs in their areas, and laud efforts to remove the scourge from the body of the American politic. This coverage is consistent despite the fact that American policies to stop the use of controlled substances have been as great a failure as was

Prohibition sixty years before. An American Bar Association report, issued in 1988, found that:

> Police, prosecutors and judges told the committee that they have been unsuccessful in making a significant impact on the importation, sale and use of illegal drugs, despite devoting much of their resources to the arrest, prosecution and trial of drug offenders. . . . These extraordinary efforts have instead distorted and overwhelmed the criminal justice system, crowding dockets and jails, and diluting law enforcement and judicial efforts to deal with other major criminal cases.[64]

The crucial question is neither "who" was arrested nor "what a police chief, president or elected official says about drugs but, rather, "why" do people take drugs at all? To understand whether drug use can be stopped, if indeed it should be, "how" is what is critical. The popular assumption is that drug use is addictive and people take drugs because of a chemical dependency forcing them into extreme actions. A search of the pharmacology and psychology literatures suggests that this is not true in most cases.

In 1979 I began researching a story on heroin addiction in British Columbia. At that time I discovered that local health officials and addiction researchers were unanimous on two points. One was that chemical dependency was not a critical factor in either heroin or cocaine use. The second point was that prohibition of use, while satisfying social strictures, could and would not be effective in the curtailment of drug use. The story was based in part on the research of local psychologists at Simon Fraser University who had spent years testing addiction hypotheses using animal research.[65] Their conclusion, that sustained drug use was a response to social conditions, confirmed studies done on U.S. veterans addicted during the Vietnam War. U.S. military personnel addicted while in that country overwhelmingly and voluntarily stopped using controlled substances after their return to the United States.[66] Support for this thesis came from hospital experiments in which patients allowed to self-administer morphine following surgery not only did not become addicted but in fact used less narcotic than physicians had proscribed.[67]

The conclusion of these and other researchers was that individuals did not take heroin, marijuana, and cocaine ("crack" was not an available drug during this period) because of chemical dependency but because of stress and tensions in their personal lives. U.S. military personnel in the 1960s and early 1970s used drugs because their quality of life in Vietnam was intolerable, but when their tours were completed, most voluntarily and freely became drug-free because their lives had returned to relative normalcy.

The clear conclusion was that to decrease drug use it would be necessary to create a program that supported lives so diminished that narcotic use was a viable alternative. Prohibition had historically failed to stop the use of alcohol and would, researchers predicted, be totally ineffective in stemming the use of heroin or cocaine, because interdiction did not address the social structure that fostered drug use. This story was published in 1982, and its conclusions were correct.[68] U.S. interdiction policies have been an utter failure, in part, one suspects, because of cutbacks in the social programs that could have materially aided the lives of those who choose to use controlled substances.

If "why" people take drugs depends on "how" an addict's life needs are not met, then billions of taxpayer dollars indeed are being consciously wasted by public officials who know their policies do not address the critical issues. But to challenge the official posture would require a reportorial stance in which it is seen as necessary and appropriate to question the assumptions of officials whose announcements and pronouncements are typically recorded without question. It would require an active and critical approach within a form where events are seen not as discontinuous but in context.

### Economic Reportage

A similar case can be made in areas of contemporary news far removed from medical issues. Addiction, forensics, and anesthesiology have as a boon, for this analysis, a large body of detailed literature against which specific boundary events and individual news examples can be measured. But even more amorphous and less clinically exact subjects can be shown to utilize a consistent, narrative form to produce an ineffectual result. A recent discussion of the degree to which Washington based reporters appropriately or adequately cover economic affairs is an excellent case in point. Deborah Baldwin questioned in general "whether the media has the ability to interpret economic policy accurately in Washington's politically charged, pressure-cooker atmosphere."[69]

The thrust of her report was that the analysis of economic policy choices and decisions is too time-consuming for reporters who cover the Federal Reserve System and other critical areas of American financial policy. From this perspective the problem is not, as Ullmann suggested in his introduction to *The Reporter's Handbook*, that journalists do not have the training or education to understand the issues but rather the complexity of the subject itself.[70] The issue is not, from this perspective, a prescribed form but rather the temporal constraints of a profession where deadlines rule. Reporters cover a rise in the prime rate through appropriate quotes from the Federal Reserve Chairman, an economist, and a daily market trader, the argument goes, because there is little more to be done.

But rates have been raised and lowered countless times in the past. Former Federal Reserve Board chairman Paul Volcker, like his predecessors, testified repeatedly in open Congressional hearings on the effects of actions and decisions the board had made. Nor was this testimony limited to official hearings. For example, the battle against inflation, which was a top priority of the Reagan administration in the early 1980s required a change in interest rates which resulted in lower produce prices adversely affecting U.S. farmers. In 1985, the Federal Reserve Board chairman told a group of farmers who argued passionately for lower interest rates that while they were adversely affected and thus unhappy, other eastern and nonagricultural sectors—his constituents one might say—had benefited greatly from board decisions.[71]

The point is that changes in the complex of Federal Reserve Board mechanisms (interest rates, money supplies, etc.) have a long history of explicated cause and effect, and this history is accessible to reporters who are not illiterate. To report on any single change or affect as part of a recurring pattern—to redefine a boundary event from that of a single event to one of a series of events—would not be a difficult or extraordinarily time-consuming task. To report on relations between Federal Reserve Board actions and the resulting effects those actions had on varying parts of the country would require perhaps a week of sporadic research and reading at the level of a freshman economics course.

To do this research require not simply time "in Washington's politically charged, pressure-cooker atmosphere" but as well a perspective which made of events such as changes in money supply, rises in the prime rate, and programs of dollar support in the foreign markets a boundary complex from whose perspective the most recent example could be described with precision. If in 1980, 1972, and 1954 one found agricultural areas in recession because of a specific tightening of interest rates to combat inflation, then a similar action in 1987 could in fact may be seen as part of a series of events. If the crash of October 1987 was an artificial "liquidity crisis" caused by specific Federal Reserve Board policies, as many believed at the time, then it was not a unique event or one necessarily related to the crash of 1929.

In fact, several financial newsletters took this position following the crash and argued that it was caused in great part by consciously conceived Federal Reserve Board actions which would be quickly reversed by its officials to forestall a serious, long-term crisis. the *Wellington Letter*,[72] for example, published in its October and November 1987 newsletters an analysis and subsequent recommendations (The headline following October 19 was "Crash! Panic! Buy!") based on this theory which, in retrospect, appears to have been correct. During this period I edited that newsletter and had the opportunity to compare daily newspaper reportage on the crash with the information disseminated by a number of widely read, specialty newsletters. The difference was instructive. Those whose profession was the analysis of market conditions quickly formulated theories that they tested against both market indicators and past events to explain, as clearly as possible contemporary conditions.

News reporters covering the same market crash, on the other hand, interviewed administration officials, federal reserve and stock market officials. The boundary event was the crash and, in the days following October 19, 1987, the issue was confidence in the market as defined by Reserve Board, Stock Market and administration officials. Other individuals who were expert in the field, disassociated from the official view, and able to place the events of those pr- and immediately post-crash weeks in perspective were rarely interviewed. When their perspective was solicited it often appeared on the op-ed page and typically was treated like that of Dr. Won in the Shintaku case. It was interesting, possibly germane, potentially relevant and immediately forgotten beneath the burden of official assurances that flowed consistently from Federal officials.

In short, it appears that financial reporters, like those previously discussed, focus on a journalistic event defined by officials and not on a either a boundary complex or the reports written by experts and professionals who, in this case, would be the practicing investment counselors and analysts. It would be an interesting exercise to trace precisely the information sources used by newspaper reporters during and after the late 1987 market crash. These could be compared with the simultaneously presented information from independent sources and tested against both subsequent events and previous economic examples. Most of the required information, including news letters and reports like the *Wellington Letter*'s Dohmen-Ramirez, is available on one or another electronic database.

### Local Events and New Technologies

The method used here works when local events fit into the context of a systematic pattern of occurrence. To the degree that a specific event in fact may be unique and local, this approach would not be of value. A great deal and perhaps most of what is reported as crucial by the news media is clearly of a recurring nature and thus amenable, at least in theory, to this contextual posture. Almost all stories pertaining to the economy, political occurrence, medical treatment, structural fault— indeed anything for which legal, academic, or journalistic precedent exists—can be reported as within a context. Several brief examples will help to make the point:

*The Homeless* — Most news outlets have, in recent years, run stories on individuals homeless in their respective regions and, typically, point out that the problem is exacerbated both by federal cutbacks in housing support and by early release regulations on the part of institutions whose funding has not kept pace with either need or inflation. The focus of such stories is neither the factors that have accelerated the problem nor the relation of the local to a regional or national problem but usually the efforts of a local volunteer (often a pastor) to provide some services for the needy.

*Urban Infrastructure* — Where a city or state maintained bridge collapses, the tragedy may be local but a search of computer records of other, similar occurrences will often indicate it is one of a widespread and geographically dispersed category of problems defined by the increasing inability of local and regional governments to maintain adequately critical areas of the region's physical infrastructure. Again, the issue is one of the use of tax monies and financing for necessary but unglamorous repairs. In many areas, deaths occurring during natural disasters (hurricanes, tornadoes, and violent storms) may be blamed on the failure of federal weather services to adequately predict the track and severity of weather systems. Increases in this type of natural disaster, in turn, have been predicted by user groups concerned with federal cutbacks in financing for satellite and other tracking stations.

Automobile Accidents and Muggings — Further, news professionals typically emphasize muggings and street crime as an urgent problem of civil distress while ignoring the ramifications of automobile accidents. The latter are reported like the weather and the former are described as breakdowns in the moral order. This suggests an inability to look at even these most prosaic of situations in any structurally integrated fashion. As Helene Hanff noted in relation to Central Park:

> The park is more fun with a dog, and these days safer. I have never personally seen anyone or anything menacing in Central Park in all the years I've been going there, with or without a dog, you understand, but the newspapers' lurid accounts of muggings have made me cautious. If the newspapers printed—which they never do—equally lurid descriptions of car-crash victims, you'd learn to be cautious about your killer car. As it is, you probably know that cars kill and maim six hundred times as many people as muggers do, but you go on driving your car.[73]

The reflexive reportage styles of street crime—both mugging and automobile related—is in no logical relation to the number of incidents or the severity of injuries incurred. One would expect that a responsible press, concerned for its readers, would be diligent in searching for the causes of the category of event which is six hundred times more frequent and whose injuries are more severe, especially since it is an endemic problem found in all American cities. And yet the issue of the automobile as a costly, inefficient, and dangerous form of transportation that kills and maims hundreds of thousands of individuals each year is largely ignored by North American media representatives. Muggings in any area, luridly described bring forth editorial calls for increased police patrols, tougher sentences for offenders and, sometimes, stricter immigration policies. Reportage of the causes and costs of automobile use as a structural problem are almost never considered.[74]

*Labor Reportage* — Structurally related stories are not bounded, necessarily, by regional or national jurisdictions. Labor reportage, for example, provides an excellent example of the absolute barrier between the description of apparently discrete, local events and general, structural or systemic issues. Americans, for example, generally have applauded the success of Poland's Solidarity party and argued for the increasing democracy that success supposedly augers. At the same time, however, many citizens and news professionals have argued against organized labor in their own regions, often endorsing the antilabor position of "right to work" legislation. If labor is to be supported as an international political instrument, then the attempt by North American employers to break the power of their unions logically should be considered in this same editorial light. And yet, that is rarely the case. Even in the most flagrant examples—for example the Pittston coal strike[75] and a grape boycott by the United Farm Workers of America[76]—coverage typically emphasized employer statements and without regard for issues of basic health or rights to representation. Had these labor battles occurred in Hungary, Poland or Rumania, Americans would have seen them as examples of systematic Communist repression but, as activities occurring on the U.S. labor scene, their relation to systemic problems (both as examples of biased reportage and as contexts themselves) were largely ignored.

*Medical Issues* — Labor, like medicine, provides a clear example of the means by which "objective" fact is bent by the constraints of contemporary journalistic forms. While this text uses anesthetic-related death as case examples, other areas of medicine would have served equally well. An examination of mortality rates in any hospital system would reveal other and structurally similar problems. In California, for example, many hospitals which do not do the minimum number of open heart surgical procedures required to maintain basic proficiency have, as a result, double digit mortality rates when they attempt those operations. Approximately 85,000 carotid artery operations, a procedure generally acknowledged to be dangerous and often of questionable necessity, are performed each year. Medical journal reviews have estimated that one third of all those are clearly inappropriate and another third of uncertain therapeutic value.[77] And yet few reporters or editors chose to examine the problems these and other equally life threatening aspects of the American medical system represent.

It is tempting to suggest that what today is considered news is either at root systemic and therefore amenable to a structural approach or, if it is unique, then the event described is merely trivial. Indeed, I am at present uncertain what would be a crucial and critical but truly local story that is at the same time unique. The issue is placed unresolved at this point in the hopes that it will engage others concerned with issues of public journalism.

*Political Events* — Although this work's focus is mundane urban reportage, it is germane to cite in passing a case study which analyzes an event complex at the scale of international affairs. In his study of reportage following the 1983 downing of KAL flight 007 by the Soviet Military, Rachlin contrasts the reportage in major U.S. newspapers and news magazines with that of Canadian publications and the *Nation*.[78] *Washington Post* managing editor, Leonard Downie, Jr., insisted after the event that the Post "like other major newspapers and TV networks investigated the flight of KAL 007 within an inch of its life". That coverage largely followed the official U.S. line which insisted American agencies did not know KAL 007 was off course and that civilian airline flights were never used by America or its friends to gather military intelligence.

Writing in *The Nation*, however, David Pearson demonstrated that U.S. military and intelligence agencies had to have known before its destruction that the civilian flight was off course and in Soviet airspace. Thus U.S. military intelligence apparently could have averted the tragedy if it desired.   Pearson's sources were not government spokespeople, the traditional sources of *Washington Post* and *New York Times* reporters, but rather an extensive technical literature on military command and control systems available to the interested resporter or researcher. Support for this position—and thus possible United States responsibility in the KAL 007 downing—was found as well by Rachlin in general Canadian  news coverage of the incident.

The *Washington Post*, (*Time* magazine, the *New York Times* etc.) reported the statements and positions of U.S. officials as well as the denials and disclaimers of Soviet officials. The investigation "to within an inch of its life," however, was all at the level of reportorial event and not at the level of  documentation. Pursuit of information at that level by Pearson presented a very different picture and one at odds with mainline American journalism's description of the event which was based on the statements of American officials who dominated by definition the journalistic event. Canadian journalists, by definition somewhat distanced from Washington, and thus freed from the perspective of its official sources, also found and presented information which, while generally available, differed from that of U.S. officials and its front line publications.

## ELECTRONIC NEWS GATHERING

The means here  used to uncover information relating to structurally similar occurrences was electronic. Some may argue that the "investigative" method advocated in this chapter was made possible only through the use of  sophisticated computer databases which became generally available for the first time in the 1980s. The ability to search hundreds of technical journals, dozens of newspapers, and scores of magazines with incredible specificity and at previously impossible speeds clearly facilitated the research on anesthetic deaths described in this and previous chapters. But the technology is no boon if it is not applied appropriately, and the basic intellectual stance its use requires—the most critical tool—has been long available but  applied rarely by newsmen and newswomen.

The use of technical and popular journals as information sources has been taught for generations in both high schools and universities across North America. It is the means by which term papers and research projects have traditionally been done. Indeed, the "investigative" approach argued  in this chapter is little more than the application of what students are told is  the "scientific" method of "critical" thought. The balance and testing of events to find a pattern is part of most contemporary junior high school curricula and the means by which it is typically taught is library research.

What has been done in this chapter has been to apply those hoary lessons. The technology facilitated but did not define the method. Libraries across the United States shelve as a matter of course both local newspaper indexes, like those cited for the Honolulu Publishing Company, and others for major newspapers like the *New York Times* and the *Washington Post*. Larger libraries also will carry sources like *News Bank*, which organizes by subject and year the stories of a hundred U.S. newspapers. As well, there are available to journalists situated near any good library specialized indexes to topical journals in fields like medicine, law, and engineering. Specialized medical or legal libraries maintain extensive journal collections whose individual publications are usually indexed yearly and by subject. These, in turn, are included in larger subject indexes that attempt to organize the data in any field over time. The *Index of Legal Periodicals*, for example, organizes data from all U.S. legal journals, just as *Index Medicus* includes author and subject information on articles published in English language medical journals from around the world. This is the primary "print" data that computer databases access online. The new technology at best makes easier the searching of these resources, which have long been available.

What the computer does, I believe, is enable and empower the reporter to search widely and with incredible efficiency for the context in which a specific event is to be understood. That search can include the technical domains of officials and professionals traditionally closed to the general reporter whose time is limited and academic background insufficient. Further, by allowing the reporter in any one city to search through the collected body of work by other newspeople active in separate circulation regions, the procedure creates a general base for the exchange of information and provides a context in which officially defined, isolated events can be seen to be parts of a social pattern.

In theory this could be done without electronic aids, but in practice it has been attempted only rarely because of limits of time and money imposed on daily journalists. Because the form defines the reportorial context as that of the journalistic event, the need to allocate resources to the newsman or newswoman interested in seeking structural contexts for supposedly unique events is rarely considered by news editors. The weeks of correspondence and waiting which would be required to compile by nonelectronic means the file of newspaper stories and journal articles that were used in this project, time newspapers would have to compensate the reporter for, would make it impossible for most newsmen to pursue a similar medical event within their circulation area. That research time is cut appreciably through use of the technology.

There has been little perceived need on the part of most journalists for reportage in which the news professional defines the context of events because news professionals have been presumed to describe specific journalistic events whose definition was believed to be objective and overt. The creation—by electronic or other means—of a context separate from that defined by officials and bureaucrats, is an outgrowth not of the electronic database technology  but rather of a critical stance in which facts, even attributed ones, are to be defined by the reporter in a context that is not necessarily a given. The relation of fact to context and form to function is the central point and one generally applicable to all individuals interested in thoughtful analysis. As Norman Cousins observed:

> Unobstructed access to facts can produce unlimited good only if it is matched by the desire and ability to find out what they mean and where they might lead. Facts are terrible things if left sprawling and unattended. They are too easily regarded as evaluated certainties rather than the rawest of raw materials crying to be processed into the texture of logic.[79]

The sprawling, unattended fact has been the traditional refuge of officials who could define and distort it to their own needs. The narrative form of the news has  provided a convenient handmaid for that refuge through a supposedly objective reportorial stance which in fact focused on isolated journalistic events and not the promised but politically more dangerous  boundary occurrence. The computer may assist in providing the information context, raw data for Cousin's "texture of logic," empowering the newsmen who choose to avail themselves of the electronic resources currently available. But it is not a necessary result.

It is important to note that contemporary newspapers, radio and television stations are not at present isolated disseminators of information. Almost all subscribe to wire services (Reuters, United Press International, Associated Press, the New York Times News Service, etc.) whose function is, at least in theory, to assure the widest possible diffusion of information between jurisdictions and, upon request, to assist in a client's search for specific bits of information. Further, almost all U.S. broadcast stations belong to one of four news networks (CBS-TV, NBC-TV, ABC-TV, CNN) that provide national and regional coverage to discrete jurisdictions. Each of these wire or network organizations provides, at least in theory, an infrastructure through which the individual newspaper, editor, or reporter can ask about event classes and seek assistance in researching a particular event.

Finally, most newspapers of any size (and most broadcast stations as well) are owned by one of a handful of information conglomerates which, at least in theory, are concerned about the information their subsidiaries present. As Ben Bagdikian laments, "The daily newspapers of the United States are being put in chains, newspaper chains. Of thirty-five dailies sold in 1982, thirty-two were absorbed by newspaper groups. . . . At the current rate, there will be no single, family-owned dailies by the year 2000".[80]   Gannett Corp, The Washington Post Corp, The New York Times, Knight-Ridder Newspapers and several others are integrated corporations owning up to 150 news outlets a piece. These are large information conglomerates whose purpose is the production of news for profit.

These corporate linkages provide, at least in theory, an infra-structure in which the exchange of information between individual members and the joint reportage by geographically separated reporters could be encouraged and facilitated. And yet it is rare for any news or-ganization to have its members pool their resources and concentrate as a unit on a class of recurring events. They do not provide effective mechanisms through which a reporter in Washington, D.C., can ask colleagues in other cities if they have seen medical deaths or felt the results of specific policies in their respective areas over time. The sus-picion is that the focus is on the "bottom line" and that the isolation of fact and context, of boundary from journalistic event so clear in the form is replicated in the isolation of news components in a specific corporation from the cultural issues raised by "the news" itself.

Perhaps the computer technology's ease and power does make a difference. Certainly it can easily and inexpensively empower a repor-ter by placing at his or her disposal information resources that are often equal to or greater than those which officials have at the ready. Using a combination of on-line medical, news, and legal databases, for example, it was possible to develop sources equal to Coroner Diane Messier's and to focus that information by pinpointing a pattern of British Columbian deaths. To have searched the medical literature by traditional methods (*Index Medicus* and specialized journal indexes) would have taken several days to find and access the relevant literature in library. Using *PaperChase*,[81] an on-line version of *Medline*, the critical articles were found in hours. Searching *VuText* produced a series of stories describing similar cases in the United States and *WestLaw's* legal database showed that in the U.S. both legal authorities and medical experts placed the responsibility for anesthetic mishaps directly in the hands of the anesthetic practitioner.

To the extent that a news reporter seeks freedom from the official view, he or she must rely ever more heavily on the evidence available from other sources. Given the journalist's traditional lack of expert knowledge, the "pressure-cooker atmosphere" in Washington, and the failure of news corporations to provide an informational infrastructure for reporters, resources are limited. The ease with which information can be accessed at a nominal fee by computer does offer reporters a po-tential for independence and informational riches which, in the past, were practically unavailable. But this will be of no benefit if the correct questions are not asked and if the distance between boundary and jour-nalistic events remains absolute. That is a structural issue and one which cannot be changed by any piece of technology, no matter how formidable it may be.

## CONCLUSION

The shift of reportorial focus from boundary to reportorial event
—from "objective" reportage to official description—is not a necessary
or immutable aspect of daily journalism. It is an outgrowth of the narrative form that defines the daily journalist's focus as a discrete, discontinuous event. Further, the context in which that event is reported
must typically be based on  acknowledgment of its occurrence by an
elected or appointed official whose franchise assures him or her a
credibility that may not be deserved. What is currently called investigative journalism does not necessarily alter this form, although it may
decrease the distance between boundary and reportorial events.  But
the narrative form can be changed, and through those changes the distance between boundary and journalistic events  as well as the weight-
ing of official positions can be significantly decreased.

What is described here as "critical" investigative is what most
North Americans are taught in high school as an adaption of the
scientific method, a type of reasonably objective  analysis that, at least
in theory,  can  be used by all adults interested in attacking specific
issues or problems.  It is rarely applied by daily reporters to their work,
although most would pay lip service to the principles of objectivity and
impartiality the scientific method is supposed to assure. The reason for
the continued reliance by daily newspeople on a passive, reportorial
stance in the description of  discrete, isolated events is not a lack of
alternate narrative forms. Rather, it must itself be seen in the context
of the function of the news within the sociopolitical structure.

## NOTES

1. John Ullmann and Steve Honeyman, eds., *The Reporter's Handbook*
(New York: St. Martin's Press, 1983), vii-viii.

2. "Watergate was a classic example of investigative reporting." Ullmann and Honeyman, ibid.

3. Edward Jay Epstein, "Did the Press Uncover Watergate?" *Commentary*, July 1984.

4. These stories were first published as a single series and then as a
collection: "VA Hospitals: A Question of Quality" (*Fort Lauderdale
News and Sun Sentinel*: Fort Lauderdale, Florida: 1986). This collection was made available to participants at the Investigative Editors and
Reporters annual meeting in Phoenix, Arizona, in 1986.

5. "Deaths in an Army Hospital," in Steve Weinberg, Ed.,*The IRE Book*
(Columbia, Mo.: Investigative Reporters and Editors,1984), 23. This is

a collection of stories done by IRE members. By being included in the "morgue" of Investigative Editors and Reporters, Inc., a story presumably becomes ipso facto an example of investigative journalism.

6. Ibid.

7. Ibid.

8. CKVU is a member of the Global Television network; BCTV, a member of the CTV network; and CBC-TV is the local outlet of the Canadian Broadcasting Corporation.

9. "Death Probed after Teen's Heart Stops during Dental Surgery," the *Sun*, June 20, 1987, A2. The newspaper's name was changed in the 1980's from *Vancouver Sun to the Sun*. Both are used here, reflecting the masthead name used on any single date.

10. "Pathologists to Conduct More Tests as Teen's Death at Dentist Probed." the *Sun*, June 22, 1987, B2.

11. A preliminary postmortem looks for overt causes of death. In many cases, this is all that is needed. The trajectory of a bullet, path and definition of a knife wound, or clear evidence of some pathology are sufficient to determine the cause of death. In those cases where no overt cause presents to the pathologist it is common to pursue more time consuming and more sophisticated tests including toxicologies and microscopic investigation of specific organs. That, apparently, was what occurred at this time.

12. Ian Austin, "Dental Probe Opens," the *Province*, October 27, 1987, B7.

13. Brian Morton, "Rare condition cited in dental deaths" the *Sun*, October 27, 1987, A7.

14. Ian Austin, "Gas Machine Flawed, Dental Inquest Hears," the *Province*, Oct. 28, 1987.

15. Ian Austin, "Inquest Hears Plea for Halt," the *Province*, October 29, 1987, 3.

16. Ian Austin, "Docs Face Probe" the *Province*, Oct. 30, 1987, 3.

17. Lisa Fitterman, "Mom Hopes some Good Comes of Dental Death," the *Sun*, October 30, 1987.

18. Pat Leidl, "Media Ruined Reputation, Cleared Dentist Says," the *Sun*, May 19, 1988, A1.

19. "Delay in Treatment found in boy' death," the *Sun*, May 31, 1980. Also see Martha Robinson, "No guidelines' in Boy's Death, Coroner's Jury Told," the *Vancouver Sun*, May 30, 1980. No page number was included on the library file clip for this and several other Vancouver stories. Thus, with apologies, no page number has been included in these endnotes.

20. Gerry Bellett, "Evidence Conflicts at Inquest on Tot," the *Sun*, February 26, 1985.

21. Gerry Bellett, "Drugs Caused Circulation Failure, MDs Say" the *Sun*, February 27, 1985. For a summary of this case and the Bedell case see, Gerry Bellett, "Anesthetist Quits Hospital Job During Inquests into 2 Deaths," the *Sun*, February 28, 1985.

22. Mark Hume, "Dead Man's Kin Urges Action Against Dentist" the *Sun*, March 25, 1986, A1.

23. Ibid.

24. Phil Needham, "Hoses 'Worried' Staff,'" the *Sun*, February 10, 1981.

25. Tom Koch, "Inquest to study surgical oxygen loss," the *Province*, February 9, 1981. Because British Columbian inquests do not make legal findings of guilt or innocence in a death, reporters in that jurisdiction have the freedom to interview witnesses before they testify at an inquest and to write without fear of contempt proceedings being brought against them.

26. Gerry Bellett, "Doctor Admits Administering Anesthetic Despite Warnings," the *Sun*, October 15, 1986, A1.

27. Holly Horwood, "Fatal Slip Unnoticed," the *Province*, February 11, 1986.

28. Larry Still, "Gross Medical Negligence Cited in Death of Woman," the *Sun*, May 18, 1985, A1.

29. Searches were carried out on WestLaw's database for all cases involving "anesthesia and death or injury" for the period of 1980-1988 and on VuText's newspaper database for stories using the same search parameters for the years 1987-1988. The latter's global search command is active only for that period.

30. The *Los Angeles Times*, like many papers, publishes a hard print index of its stories. Its recent files are also available to computer searching through VuText or the CompuServe "IQuest" gateway. Finally, *Los Angeles Times* stories are indexed, as are those of 100 other

newspapers, through the yearly *News Bank* index, which lists stories by subject. Finally, some newspapers can be searched through microfiche files.

31. "Victim's Mother Testifies in Dentist's Civil Trial," *Los Angeles Times*, June 19, 1986, 6.

32. Philip Hager, "Dentist Loses Appeal in Murder Conviction," *Los Angeles Times*, August 22, 1987, 1.

33. Ann Japenga, "A Dental Sedation Death Casts Doubt on Procedure," *Los Angeles Times*, July 27, 1987, V1.

34. Ibid.

35. The number of deaths depends on the official quoted. Low figures of death resulting from conscious sedation were contained in a letter to the author by Larry C. Ballard, Department of Consumer Affairs, Board of Dental Examiners, *Personal Communication*, Sept. 10, 1987. Higher figures were broadcast in an ABC (Radio) News report, Mike Silverstein, "Deadly Dentists," *ABC (Radio) News*, August, 1987. Mr. Silverstein, writer and producer of the four- part series which focused on the Safier death, graciously provided me with a transcript.

36. Silverstein, "Deadly Dentists."

37. See, for example, Michael Murphy, "Review of malpractice verdict denied," the *Phoenix Gazette*, February 27, 1987, B6.

38. See, for example, "Medical Negligence: Damages: Loss of Adult consortium," *American Trial lawyers Association Reporter Law Reporter*, 29, November 1986, 388-390. This describes the case of Hathaway v. Frank in which an Arizona Court of Appeals upheld a $5 million compensatory award to a 34-year-old woman made permanently comatose as a result of physician failure to monitor the patient during surgery. This class of material was found on WestLaw but could also have been accessed through databases like Nexus or Dialog.

39. See, for example, *Regan Report on Nursing Law*, a journal that each month reviews court cases and legal judgements involving nurses' responsibilities. Cases reviewed include a description of the general problem, case facts, summary of the court's opinion, and the "legal lesson" on responsibility supposedly learned from the review. This class of information was accessed through Beth Israel's *PaperChase* online service through CompuServe's IQuest. *PaperChase* searches the *Medline* database, accessible through a number of online vendors and is itself the source of other more specialized sources like *Index Medicus*.

40. These have been computerized and are available under the name of *Medline* through most major data information services. Further, a popular form is offered by Beth Israel Hospital, Boston, under the name *PaperChase.* Traditional hard copy volumes of medical indexes and journals are, of course, available in every medical school.

41. The search term was used to obtain articles from the medical database *MedLine* on CompuServe in September of 1987 and, in a second search, through the facilities of the library of the School of Veterinary Medicine at Ohio State University in October of 1988. The assistance of that library is hereby acknowledged.

42. John Eichorn, et. al., "Standards for patient monitoring during anesthesia at Harvard Medical School," *Journal of the American Medical Association* 256 (1986), 1017-1020. Also see a special issue on the subject of patient monitoring in *Anesthesia and Intensive Care,* February, 1988.

43. C. Whitcher, et. al., "Anesthetic Mishaps and the Cost of Monitoring: a Proposed Standard for Monitoring Equipment," *Journal of Clinical Monitoring,* 4 (January 1988).

44. John L. Sun, *Manual of Anesthesia* (Boston: Little, Brown, and Co., 1982), 29.

45. F. K. Orkin and L. H. Cooperman, eds. *Complications in Anesthesiology* (Philadelphia, P.A.: Lippincott, 1983). quoted in Whitcher, op.cit., 8.

46. W. M. Crosby, "Checking the Aneasthesia Machine, Drugs, and Monitoring Devices," *Anesthesia and Intensive Care,* 16, February, 1988, 32-5 This was a special issue devoted to the topic of Anesthetic administration problems.

47. This does not mean the reporters were not in the possession of news people. Province managing editor Don Maclachlin had one with an editor's note penciled on top asking if his newspaper had reported the Judgment's facts, Maclachlin, personal communication, November, 1988. John Daley at BCTV, Burnaby, B.C., also reported having a copy of at least one of the two Judgments. I also am indebted to Mr. Daley for checking television files to assure no story had been broadcast on these Judgments.

48. Quincy starred Jack Klugman, with Robert Ito as his laboratory assistant. It was superbly researched, and the publicity it accorded to specific issues and problems resulted in new federal statutes. Robert Ito, Personal Communication. July, 1984.

49. Popular in the 1970s, this show starred Ed Asner as a city editor

on a Los Angeles newspaper.

50. The capnograph is a positive detector of esophageal intubation and airway disconnection. It also measures inhaled and exhaled carbon dioxide concentrations as well as other gases. Had a functioning capnograph been used at the time of Mr. Graham's surgery, for example its alarm would have sounded when his intubation problems occurred and he might have been saved.

51. Diane Y. Messier, "Judgment of Inquiry into the death of Margaret Estella Dac," *Coroners Court of British Columbia*, November 8, 1988, 25-6. Separate although virtually identical Judgments were filed in the cases of both Margaret Dac and Ronald Mason. Both included information on the Loewen case which was far different from that presented to the jury information.

52. F. K. Orkin and L. H. Cooperman, *Complications in Anesthesiology*. Quoted in Whitcher, *Anesthetic Mishaps*, 8.

53. Messier, *Judgment of Inquiry into the Death of Ronald Mason*, 23.

54. Diane Y. Messier, "Judgement of Inquiry into the Death of Margaret Dac," *Coroners Court of British Columbia*, November 8, 1988, 26.

55. Ibid., 24

56. Diane Y. Messier, "Judgement of Inquiry into the Death of Ronald Mason," 24.

57. Diane Y. Messier, "Judgement of Inquiry into the death of Margaret Dac," 26.

58. Messier, "*Judgement of Inquiry into the death of Ronald Mason*," 8.

59. A "gateway" allows for the searching of multiple databases through a single entry service. Thus through IQuest, for example, specific medical databases like *PaperChase* and *Index Medicus* could be searched for information on these procedures.

60. See, for example, "3 Lawsuits in 5 Years Result in Investigation of Texas Physicians," *Houston Post*, May 15, 1988, B1; "$800,000 Awarded in Child's Death," *Beacon Journal*, January 16, 1987, D1; Susan Schmidt, "Review of Complaint Delayed Despite Court Request" *Washington Post*, January 10, 1988, 17.

61. John Caher, "High Court to Decide Earnings Award," the *Knickerbocker News*, March 10, 1988, A5.

62. Horace F. Judson, *The Search for Solutions*, (Baltimore: John Hopkins University Press, 1987). His Chapter 8 discusses the relation be-

tween fact and theory and uses the legal concept of "evidence" as its theme.

63. Andrew J. Glass, "Why Drug Crisis is Spinning Out of Control," *Honolulu Star-Bulletin*, March, 10, 1988. Glass is a syndicated news columnist.

64. Associated Press, "Drugs Thwart Justice, Lawyers Find," *Columbus Dispatch*, December 1, 1988.

65. Bruce Alexander, Patricia Hadaway and Barry Beyerstein, "Rat Park Chronicle," *B.C. Medical Journal*, 22 (2)(February 1980), 54-56. Alexander and his associates have published widely on the issue of addiction and habituation.

66. Lee N. Robins and John E. Helzer, "Drug Use Among Vietnam Veterans — Three Years Later," *Health World News* (October 27, 1975), 44-49.

67. Richard Bennett, et. al. "Morphine Titration in Postoperative Laparotomy Patients using Patient-Controlled Analgesia," *Current Therapeutic Research*, 32 (1) (July 1982), 45-51. This study replicated earlier tests by other researchers of patient-controlled analgesia.

68. Tom Koch, Three stories were published in a take out on Alexander's research and its implications to the then growing anti-drug crusade. See, *The Province*, October 17, 1982, A4.

69. Deborah Baldwin, "The Dismal Science," *Common Cause* (March/April, 1988).Reprinted in*The Utne Reader* (March/April, 1989), 15.

70. John Ullmann and Steve Honeyman, *The Reporter's Handbook*, (New York: St. Martin's Press, 1983), 3.

71. William Grieder, *Secrets of the Temple: How the Federal Reserve Runs the Country* (New York: Simon and Schuster, 1987) reviewed in *The Utne Reader*, ibid., 15.

72. Bert Dohmen-Ramirez, *The Wellington Letter*, (Honolulu:The Wellington Corporation, Oct., 1987), 1. A subscription newsletter,*The Wellington Letter* can be accessed through several online database vendors.

73. Helene Hanff, *Apple of My Eye*, (Mt. Kisco, N.Y.: Moyer Bell Ltd., 1977), 126.

74. These would include, in brief, stories on the visual requirements for motor vehicle operators in North America and its relation to accidents in all age groups. In all but two U.S. states, individuals with cor-

rected vision of 20/40 in one eye can obtain a driver's license. In Tennessee, the requirement is 20/35, and in Georgia, 20/60; some researchers have argued that a percentage of single-vehicle automobile accidents are, in fact, suicide attempts; the average American typically travels in any one origin to destination path less than 10 miles at a time, a distance more safely and efficiently rationalized by public transit than by private car.

75. For an interesting analysis of this in the context of the Pittston coal battle, see Denise Giardina, "Where the Sun Never Shines," the _Independent Weekly_ (Raleigh, N.C.), June 29, 1989, 5-6.

76. Cesar E. Chavez, "Nonchemical Pesticides need Encouragement," the *New York Times*, July 13, 1989. p. 18. Chavez points out in a Letter to the editor the disparities between a *New York Times* story on the United Farm Workers of America's grape boycott and crucial facts involving the issues on which the boycott was based. He further charges that Times reporters used as "objective" fact press release information issued by grower organizations.

77. Alain Enthoven, "A 'Cost-Unconscious' Medical System," the *New York Times*, July 13, 1989, 18. It is important to note in passing that most newspaper stories on medical care (excepting court cases) focus on the cost of care, not the lack of quality or inequities in its delivery.

78. Allan Rachlin, *News as Hegemonic Reality* (New York: Praeger, 1988), 70-87.

79. Norman Cousins, "The Poet and the Computer," *Phi Kappa Phi Journal*, (Spring 1989), 7.

80. Ben H. Bagdikian, *The Media Monopoly* (Boston: Beacon Press, 1983), 198. Quoted in Russell Jacoby, *The Last Intellectuals: American Culture in the Age of Academe* (New York: Basic Books, 1987). Also see on this point: Loren Ghiglione ed. *The Buying and Selling of Newspapers*, (Indianapolis: R.J. Berg, 1984).

81. *PaperChase* is a simplified version of *Medline* created by Beth Israel Hospital. See: *Your Guide to PaperChase*, (Boston: PaperChase, 1988). PaperChase is available as an independent service as well as through CompuServe gateways.

# 5

# The Myth of the News

The means by which a specific sign—the newspaper's description of a discrete event—is transformed into a socially acceptable, second-order signifier supporting a culturally potent signification is now clear. It occurs by means of a structural transformation whose general mechanism is based upon a shift between what have been called here the boundary and journalistic events. This is not a necessary attribute of the act of reportage. Rather, it is the outgrowth of a narrative form that has developed to answer specific social and cultural as well as informational needs. This chapter summarizes the nature of that shift using the language of semiology and structuralism, discusses its implications, and speculates upon its ramifications. In this task, the critical perspective of Roland Barthes, introduced in chapter 1, will be reiterated. Now, however, the precise means by which this shift occurs and, to a great extent, its effects can be described.

## STRUCTURAL TRANSFORMATIONS

The transformation from boundary to journalistic event is profoundly unary, admitting of a single and unambiguous transformation that results in a single sequencing of information. It thus transforms an event into a description, in Barthes's words, "without doubling it, without making it vacillate (emphasis is the power of cohesion): no duality, no indirection, no disturbance."[1] Vacillation would occur were that boundary occurrence seen as other than unique, were it compared, contrasted or multiplied and shown to be related to other events. There is, in short, "no disturbance" because of the unary transformation that is the heart of the narrative form. This is a profoundly existential, textual pattern in which the single boundary event stands forever isolated. Each car accident is described as if it were the only one, each arrest is unique, and each death is described as if it were the first—whatever the larger context—without pattern or form and, therefore, without reason.

By accepting a form proscribed by a unary grammar, daily journalism by definition will, to paraphrase Barthes, record facts or perceive values but forever refuse explanation. That is because explanations— "why" something happened, "how" could it have been prevented and "who," therefore, was responsible—are typically excluded from a unary transformation's discourse. Those questions require of most events an antecedent, the description of a pattern in which the specific base is seen as not isolated but rather as part of that pattern. From this difference comes Barthes's observation that a unary transformation lacks the power of cohesion.

It is unfortunate when a child dies accidentally, but it is significant when children die unnecessarily and systematically. It is sad when an individual attempts suicide because that act states the unique distress of a human being with whom we may empathize or, failing that, for whom we may have pity. But it is scary and threatening if that failed suicide is, in fact, attempted murder hidden under the gloss of official indifference because those officials are who we as a society trust to protect us against injury or, failing that, to avenge our misfortune.

To transform failed suicide into attempted murder, accidental death into a pattern of medical incompetence, or chemical addiction to systemic, social failure would require that the narrative form include a basis for comparison. To expand a narrative base from the specific to the contextual, to make of an isolated event an example, can be as simple as the description of definitive traits common in all attempted suicides or as complex as a database of sixty separate and geographically dispersed incidents that share salient characteristics with one even more recent. Any occurrence that claims inclusion in that specific class of events can be measured against an objective and consistent pattern that defines medical malpractice, suicide, or addiction. Those patterns come from outside journalism and are based on as objective a base of prior events and theory as researchers in each field have been able to describe. But where the form is defined as unary, relating only the isolated event, that yardstick cannot and will not be used by daily news reporters. Thus the single most critical element in the shift between boundary and journalistic event levels lies precisely in the narrative's persistently unary grammar.

It is the unary nature of journalism's transformative grammar that explains the periodic attention given by modern journalists to the specific, isolated but emotionally charged case. This is often as true of periodical coverage as daily news. In the late 1950s, for example, *Life* photographer Gordon Parks photographed a family in São Palo, Brazil, and the resulting story—photographs and words—on members of Brazil's impoverished favelas drew an enormous response from the magazine's readers. But the response was not to social inequities or a class of individuals whose poverty was absolute. Rather, readers responded generously with unsolicited gifts of money and offers of aid both to the family Parks featured and, in particular, to its youngest member, who eventually was brought to the United States as a result of the readers' largess. But the story did not concern itself with the causes of Brazil's impoverishment or the millions who shared the fate and future of Park's subjects. Americans responded to *Life*'s portrait whose subjects became symbols not of Latin American problems in general, Brazil's in particular, or the responsibility of the United States for Latin American conditions in general, but rather of the context of Park's subjects alone and, eventually, of the vaunted (and well reported) generosity of the American readers themselves.

The magazine's concern and reader response for a single boy in a socially impoverished environment did not focus attention on the context of that country's poverty or the complex factors that kept and keep millions of families bereft of financial and medical improvement there. It was a singularly unary and banal story whose narrative—photographic and written—made of Brazil itself a context as amorphous as Oz. By aiding and lionizing that one family, the complex of factors that contributed to the Brazilian distress could be safely and equally ignored by both *Life* readers and editors.

More recently, Americans and their media have responded with similar generosity to drought victims, children trapped in wells, victims trapped under buildings where shoddy construction in earthquake-prone regions caused entire city blocks to collapse and other victims of specific natural disasters. But while giving the impression of care and concern, this focus is unary and, because of that, ultimately impotent. It disavows the need to address the causes of or wider context contributing to a disaster (shoddy construction in earth-quake zones; the failure of federal weather watch systems truncated by budget cuts; Central American poverty, mismanagement of dikes and levees, etc.) and makes of each often remediable social situation, a narrowly defined and ultimately frivolous story. Like the *National Geographic*, which could feature Vietnam in the 1960s and never mention that a war was being waged there, daily journalism in its focus on the individual, "human" context—the "who"—can safely ignore the systemic problems that lead to the very events reporters purportedly describe.

Daily news people typically are barred from addressing social issues, the broader context, by a perspective tied to the narrative transformation and the general form of the text that is its outgrowth. The effect of this textual pattern is typically hidden from, or at least not perceived by, the actors whom a story features, however. Thus Marvin Loewen's mother, like the relatives of previous anesthetic victims, could hope that something good would come of Marvin's death. That social benefit was to result from the inquest into his death and the recommendations that were issued by the jury. Local newspapers gladly covered her statement as they had those of other relatives who, in identical contexts, previously had voiced similar hopes following inquests into the death of their loved ones. the *Sun* and the *Province* reported the statement by Mrs. Loewen but not the fact that it was a repetition on a theme and that the contextual problem—preventable anesthetic misadventure—continued without pause.

### The Studium

From this reliance on a single transformation comes the studium of daily news reports, the pervasive and consistent "feel" of stories which march across the page or roll down the television's teleprompter's screen without a sense of individual style or difference. Daily journalism utilizes a pattern of description, here described as the narrative form, that is remarkable for its lack of individuality. Stories written by a score of reporters (and edited, sometimes, by a baker's dozen of anonymous editors) are transformed through the narrative pattern into a grey continuum of copy in which a single narrative voice is dominant. Stories by correspondents from Beirut to Beijing are transformed through the studium into copy whose style, tone and perspective are constant. That there is a consistent narrative form can be seen by the stylistic similarity of stories quoted earlier from the following sources: the *Honolulu Star Bulletin*, the *Province*, the *Sun*, the *New York Times* and *Canadian Press*. All adhere to a narrative pattern whose single characteristic is the absence of a particular voice or view in the description of a specific, base event and its antecedents.

It is in this constancy that contemporary journalists see the objectivity of the press, the assurance that an individual reporter's perspective will not intrude into the columns of "fact" that are its pride. But as we have seen, the ubiquity of the form does not assure objectivity (the complete description of an event within the context of its antecedents) and the "facts" conspire to nothing more than vacuous facticity. The promise of description, of objective reportage fails precisely to the degree that the event to be portrayed is leavened by the textual frame and not enriched by a broader context. This pattern is the studium and begins with the unary nature of its grammar. Around that transformation has grown a narrative form that, at its most basic, is the obituary and that commonly relies exclusively on only four of Kipling's six famous serving men—"who," "what", "when" and "where"— the systematic exclusion of the other two: "why" and "how."

The subject is "who died?" and more important, who (what official) will speak officially in a public voice about that occurrence. The emphasis within the text is almost always on the latter. "Where" and "when" an individual died thus of necessity become rapidly less important than the location and time of a press briefing, inquest, or trial at which an official may provide sanctioned information about that death or occurrence. The newsperson, barred from analysis of prior occurrence by a focus narrowed to the isolated event, is bound to report on the official's view presented at an inquest, press conference, or in an official report and not on the event itself, much less its structural context. "What" becomes, in this transformation, not what killed or injured the individual but, rather, what an official says killed or injured a person in an event defined by officials as disconnected from any context.

The journalist's narrative pattern thus relies through its very structure on the attributed statements of an individual whose official position gives—whatever the facts—an absolute franchise to define the prior event as he or she sees fit. Reporters, to the extent that they accept the form and the perspective that is its result, must become bound to the officially designated interpretation of occurrences they are pledged to describe. Thus the analysis of a patient's injuries by the physician of record, despite extensive medical experience, will be discounted by newsmen who without question will sanction in their copy the views of a police spokesman whose task is often to present an official and prescribed (that is, unary) description of a disputed event.

The narrative's reliance on a unary transformation leads naturally to the studium's emphasis on the official context. Because an event is isolated, the range for independent initiative by reporters is minimal. If the event is discrete, there will be no other sources to turn to, no prior knowledge for the newsperson to rely on. It is not his or her job to rediscover the wheel or the medical pattern of failed suicides. "Just the facts, ma'am" becomes those of officialdom, and objective reportage typically becomes the reiteration of what officials insist to the press. In this way the studium becomes a general principle and the result is a reportorial reality based on official perceptions rather than general knowledge and consistent, verifiable patterns.

**Transformation and the Studium**

It was thus almost inevitable that, in the case of Shintaku's injuries, reporters would focus their attention and talents upon the police investigation. As reporters, their job was the promulgation of an official interpretation of the attack on a circuit court judge. Even the physicians who saved Shintaku's life in surgery, whose diagnostic perspective was contextual and objective, could not sway the published narrative from that of officially attributed surmise.

Police Chief Keala called a press conference and his word was reported as fact. Police investigators told reporters what they were considering and that, too, was stated as fact. Even where Shintaku, Dr. Won, and other dissident voices were quoted, they were "balanced" by official statements and thus buried, hidden beneath the weight of the official investigator's statements. This is the given of the narrative pattern that most reporters follow without question. News reporters never asked "how" or "why" Shintaku had been injured but rather "what" do police detectives, investigators and the prosecutor have to say at today's press conference or official briefing? For such a perspective to approximate objectivity, the stated goal of most journalists, it must first assume that those quoted officials will speak both from knowledge and without ulterior motive. This is what was earlier called the force of prior weight. To challenge Police Chief Keala's conclusions would have been to challenge the myth, the assumption of official omniscience and intelligent honesty.

The result was what earlier was termed a "false truth." It was truth to the extent that the actors were correctly quoted and their statements adequately summarized within the constraints of the narrative form. Police Chief Keala did tell a press conference that Mr. Shintaku had sustained injuries in an attempted suicide. Dr. Hardman did state that he believed (on information provided by the police) that Keala's conclusion was correct. It was false to the degree that the official explanation of "what" happened bore little relation to any objective description of "how" those injuries could have been sustained. Judge Shintaku had two major fractures of his skull, not one; he sustained none of the  physical complications typical of attempted suicide by hanging; he did sustain hearing loss consistent with what in other cases resulted from "a blow of tremendous force"; there was neither rope nor evidence of hanging found at the house from which he was transported to hospital.

A similar pattern of transformation occurred in the anesthetic cases. The *New York Times* story by Mr. Boorstin did not describe "how" young Rifa Setiyono died or "what" killed the child. Instead, the text summarized what police investigators said was a confusing situation in which paramedics and police officials were called to a dental office. The story by Ms. Horwood in the *Province*  provided no real information on the death of  Mr. Graham unless one credits the physician's suggestion, made at an official inquest, that an unconscious man actively extricated his own anesthetic tube while medical personnel rolled him around on the operating table. Marvin Loewen, Margaret Dac and Ronald Mason did not die, as the anesthetist suggested, of carotid sinus syndrome or simply expire from hypoxia, and the dentist Dr. Nelson was not ill used by the press.

In all these cases medically objective fact, conclusions built upon the widest context of antecedent evidence, was transformed through narrative legerdemain into officially sanctioned, sanitized portraits of benign and isolated occurrences. This transformation was based in each case on the reporter's reliance on a  narrative form whose  grammar resulted in a textual pattern that demanded that journalists write only what officials said to them. It is thus within this grammar and form that the sign was transformed into a myth. The signifier, a specific event,  may be a  death occurring in a dental clinic or hospital but what ultimately is signified is official concern underlined by the state's inquest procedure and the media's coverage of the state's event. The resulting message ultimately becomes that of an active and responsive fourth estate as well as overt concern for society's individuals on the part of professional and official communities. After all, the British Columbia College of Dental Surgeons  held an inquiry into the death of Marvin Loewen and announced its conclusions  to the public through the news media; the provincial Coroners Service publicly investigated the facts of Loewen's death and the deceased's mother pronounced herself satisfied with the result, hoping "something good will come of it." Regional media outlets covered it all religiously.

That the  resulting information in all these stories  was shown to have little in common with the objective, medical context of the antecedent event ultimately is of little importance, because objective truth is not the function of daily news. The purpose of the story  lies not at the level of the basic sign (cessation of bodily functions means death) but instead at the level of generated myth. As Barthes noted in a different context, "Men do not have with myth a relationship based on truth, but on use." The reportage produced was useful in each case to the degree that it publicly affirmed the official's view of his role as an interested, caring and competent public guardian. It was useful to the extent that it dampened the fear that otherwise might have been felt by patients with legitimate concerns over the prospect of surgery in which anesthesia was to be used.

The useful myth of concern and competence on the part of professionals and investigating officials need bear no relation to the facts of a case, to the objective description of a specific event through the analysis of its parts. The narrative form assists officialdom to seem able and potent even where its sanctioned explanations are demonstrably fictitious when applied to a specific boundary event: "The order of the world must be seen as sufficient or ineffable, but never be seen as significant." That is what this narrative pattern achieves all too well. The society is seen as sufficient or ineffable and its noteworthy events, unique and discontinuous, will thus never be of importance as indicators of abuse or malfunction.

The creation of a potent if inaccurate social sign in all these cases was not a necessary result. In all cases evidence was available to any daily news reporter interested in placing a specific boundary event into a context of multiple occurrence that would have allowed that reporter to describe aspects of the boundary occurrence with great accuracy. This is not to suggest that individual reporters whose work has been used here lied or consciously covered up information in their reports. Rather, they adhered to a narrative form whose result (if not its overt, conscious purpose) is the perpetuation of the myth of official concern. Officials did not need to hide information or purposely distort information. They followed the rules whose result and perhaps whose function is to sustain a culturally potent message of official competence and omnipotence. The result of the narrative pattern of contemporary journalism is precisely an inflection that favors the official version and technocratic view of events and thus of society.

While a relatively narrow class of events has been used in this study, the results apply to all other areas of reportage. The categories of medical incident used in this research allowed for the information presented in each story to be compared with a wide body of medical information and placed within well-studied classes of prior events. It is precisely the form's lack of context that is at the heart of Noam Chomsky's criticism of American political reportage. When he or other critics suggest that American reporters should have seen the structural similarities between the Russian shooting of an off-course, Korean passenger airline and the later destruction of a non-military, passenger airplane by the U.S. military in the Persian Gulf, they are arguing for the expansion of a unary event definition to include an antecedent but structurally similar occurrence.[2] To have linked them editorially would have been to expand the grammar from unary to multiple and, as a consequence, would have required editors and reporters to recognize in the later, American shooting the moral responsibility assigned by them to the U.S.S.R. in the antecedent event. That was something neither editors nor state department officials wished to do. Contras are "freedom fighters" if a sitting U.S. president says they are. The difference between virtuous freedom fighters and despicable terrorist or guerilla forces is one of who is assigning names, not defensible taxonomy. The narrative fact is that naming depends not on an insurgent group's ideology or behavior but rather on what an official says they represent. Freedom fighters become "friends" and guerilla forces are always enemies, whatever their actual behavior. From this distinction, set by officials and repeated in the news copy of the nation, flows arms, bombs, American troops, materials, and monies for the former to use against the latter.

The method of transformation is clear. The narrative form is profoundly unary and written through recourse to a simple set of existential, locational rules, "who," "what," "when" and "where" which typically give the impression—rarely fulfilled in fact—of describing "how" and "why" an event occurred. The locational rules define the isolated event and prohibit its analysis in relation to other parallel but structurally similar occurrences. The studium insists that these questions be based on a boundary event but also insists that the narrative focus only on attributed statements of officials. It discourages the independent inquiry of a reporter who seeks a different and perhaps more objective understanding of the boundary event. For that to occur the form would have to change and its emphasis shift from "who" to precisely "what" and on "how."

The reporters whose stories have been discussed in this work were propagandists precisely to the degree they presented partial and unsubstantiated information about an occurrence or fact that sustained the view of those whose press conferences they covered and whose reports they summarized in their copy. Like public relations officials everywhere, they did their job and presented as a complete assessment the incomplete summaries of events that officials (police, medical organization, the state department, etc.) were willing to release.

### The Function of the News

What does this analysis say about the role of the daily journalist who accepts and works within the proscribed narrative pattern? If news is myth and myth itself is based not on objective "truth" but on "use," then what is the function of daily journalism in modern society? Clearly the sole purpose of daily news reports is not objective description. Even in the most rigorous of sciences, objectivity is an unobtainable goal that researchers seek with the certain knowledge of eventual failure. But even the rudiments of their posture require that events be defined within a context of other occurrences and theory, something the narrative form of news disallows. Reporters do not seek independent confirmation or use a critical method to test the statements issued by officials at "photo opportunities," "media opportunities" or "press conferences." There is no real attempt to balance the official version against the contextual evidence. More than 70 percent of the stories in the nation's principal newspapers are based on the statements and quotes of government officials. It has been suggested here that this is in great part the result of an institutionalized narrative form. If the overwhelming body of material in a daily newspaper is officially generated and if its focus in even the most extreme cases is the sanctioned view, with a resulting socially conservative signification, then what, precisely, is it that daily journalism provides?

One function is clearly commercial and capitalist. Newspapers and television or radio stations are components of large corporations traded on one or another stock exchange or, less frequently, owned for the exclusive profit of a single family or private group. Media outlets exist to make money for their owners and are sustained through the sale of advertising, the commercial drive to sell products that editors and producers may neither use nor endorse. Thus at one level the function of a contemporary North American newsperson is to provide information that will increase or sustain circulation and thus improve the financial bottom line of a station or newspaper. The amount of news which any single newspaper can report is defined not by solely on objective editorial criteria but rather on the news space or "hole" left unused by paid advertisers.

But it is too simple to blame the failure of contemporary news solely on the need for revenue. It is simplistic to argue with Mark Crispen Miller, for example, that television reporters only "serve commercial television. Their aim is to boost ratings: They always tell the people what they think the people are already thinking."[3] It is not, as others have argued, a simple equation in which rich newspaper owners with powerful and monied interests conspire to constrain the flow of information.[4] Samuel Johnson, the original and self-confessed journalistic drudge, wrote well and perceptively while enriching his employer. But Johnson, fully aware of the degree to which he wrote for pay, did not simply write to tell people what they were already thinking. It is more complex than that.

More likely is the supposition that the narrative form is an outgrowth of the function of the media to promulgate the social myth of a functioning, effective and progressive democracy in which each member is safeguarded by the vigilance of a potent and omniscient bureaucracy. It is the myth itself that is crucial, and it is pervasive in contemporary North American journalism. It assures that where social failures clearly occur, the narrative form will proscribe a full investigation in favor of a limited description, resulting in a type of "damage containment." Typically this does not require of officials either conscious censorship or active disinformation. It is done automatically by editors and reporters themselves through a narrative form that assures that systematic faults will be transformed into isolated and thus unimportant events. Were the form to be changed, however, the sign of concern and safety and competence would change as well.

Were newspapers to make of a single occurrence a pattern of deaths, the resulting story would deny the prevailing myth of  professional omniscience and official concern.

The function of the news as it is presented in its currently accepted form is, in fact one of the socialization of the electorate. Jürgen Habermas  argued  that the university's critical social purpose is one of  the socialization if not the pacification of its student clients. University graduates gain through their successful tenure those qualities, characteristics and perspectives that will allow them to  perform appropriately in modern society. A principal function of the university is to "transmit, interpret and develop the cultural tradition of the society . . .   [that]  forms the political consciousness."[5] Both technical information and a critical social  perspective are secondary to this function of social indoctrination.

In the same way, the  news media become a socializing voice for the bourgeoisie, and  readers are told again and again that, while mistakes may occur, the system itself is the best in the world and works to everyone's advantage. It does not matter if a  newspaper also  writes about the  corrupt police officer,  gambling judge, crooked congressman,  venal official, or the high crimes and misdemeanors of a sitting president. In these stories the signification  remains constant. Each time malfeasance is discovered,  the isolated event will be affirmed within the narrative's own grammar as unusual if not unique, and the result, officials can say, will be that a "bad apple" was found in a good barrel of concerned officials. The newspaper or broadcasting station can and will emphasize this position editorially, insisting that the system works even if the allegedly unique abuse is so common that the facts argue for a failure in the society as a whole.

Indeed, it was precisely this observation—"the system works"— which was the editorialists' principal observation following the resignation of President Nixon before he could be tried for "high crimes and misdemeanors." From Los Angeles to New York, editorial writers concluded that the system worked and, shyly, that its maintenance was in large part a result of the  performance of the fourth estate in the investigation of Mr. Nixon's transgressions.[6] That was true, of course, but not in the way those pundits suggested. Newspaper reporters were not the independent, investigative heroes public myth and media relations experts made them out to be. It was not a purely adversarial role which news reporters played. "Watergate" was not the result of lone, courageous reporters bringing down a president who was out of control.

The system worked because, in great part, congress functioned appropriately within the U.S. adversarial system, and individuals like Alexander Butterfield and Archibald Cox made it work. Journalists were persuaded to publish information provided by dissident officials pursuing official investigations *as well as* the denials and perspectives of administration spokesmen.The emerging myth that courageous newspeople "brought down" a sitting president through independent and adversarily acute investigation is, in retrospect, perhaps as important as the myth of a functioning system able to correct its own in-equities.[7] The perception of an aggressive, active, perceptive, and ad-versarial Fourth Estate is as integral and as crucial to the American cosmology (and the sale of the news product) as is that of a respon-sive and concerned government run by qualified and capable citizen-officials.

In fact the fourth estate is not an ombudsman but a partner. Its form assures that the general parameters of official vision will be sup-ported and advanced even when individual problems are advanced. It does not examine the system or act as critique except in the most limited context. As Washington correspondent Tom Bethell said in an article on "The Myth of an Adversary Press":

> For all intents and purposes, the *New York Times* or CBS News can best be understood as departments of the federal bureaucracy. . . . In the end, the government is fine, thanks to the media; and the men in the media are heroes, thanks to their relationship with the government.[8]

This "relationship" is one based not on the observer's goal of objectivity, however, but rather on the government's absolute need for public affirmation of its legitimacy. By legitimacy is meant "the positive valuation and acceptance enjoyed by a system of power and its bearers who 'voluntarily' accept their masters as valid and deserving and their own subordination as an obligatory fate."[9] The idea of legitimacy in the political sphere was clearly described by Max Weber, who argued that the modern bourgeoisie tends to legitimate itself through an enforce-ment or reinforcement of beliefs in both the legality of its rules or codes and in the prior (legitimate) right of those who are its leaders.[10] The out-come of this absolute need for the enforcement of a society's tenants by its administrators is that "not only obedience but also internalized respect tends to be granted to the impersonal, legally founded social and political order which is more and more organized in administra-tive, bureaucratic form."[11]

It is perhaps no coincidence that the modern narrative form of the news draws its doggerel code from Kipling, who was the premier chronicler and literary supporter of England's age of glorious empire and empire's right. His writing enforced the view that it was England's right to act as colonial lord to the developing world and, in its descrip-tion of the mechanisms of dominion, enforced a vision of the cor-rectness of that exercise. So too, today, do journalists who have inher-ited his form legitimate through their descriptions the social order that is the final context in which each writes. The story's form, to the degree that it requires the attributed statements of officials and official experts, affirms their position and role in society.

Weber asserts that where legitimacy is the driving social force, "there can be no independent inquiry into the validity of the beliefs of the regime's dominated groups and the claims of their rules and their procedures to authority."[12] Reporters are thus free to write as they and their editors see fit on any specific event but, simultaneously, do so only within a narrative form whose result is to reinforce the legitimacy of their subjects. The form affirms the role of experts and officials by repeating their titles and assuring the permanence of their statements in the narrative. It is Coroner Diane Messier, Police Chief Keala, Doctor Nelson (or Moss or Archer or Hardman). They are quoted because they are officials and therefore are presumed to know.

The partnership between news and government is ultimately one of mutual legitimization. Government's authority and the roles of its officials are not easily questioned through the current narrative form, and thus the roles of officials and the official view are continually both enforced and affirmed. At the same time, the legitimacy of media representatives is established. Their access to the corridors of power and knowledge is maintained and the chimera of their independence—chimera because it is consistently self-prescribed—maintained. The continual and mutual reinforcement of these specific roles of journalist and official is the ultimate result of the signification resulting from the narrative rules prescribing the narrative form.

### A Political Example

This is nowhere clearer than in the spectacle of televised and widely reported "debates" between two candidates during U.S. presidential election years. In this process two individuals seeking to be elected president stand at a lectern before a panel of seated news reporters and during the entire period of question and answer never address their opponents. These two individuals represent the two major parties of the country but, at least in 1988, other hopefuls who are also legitimate candidates were barred from participation. Thus the fiction of a political structure allowing only two individuals as true candidates is enforced. Legitimate third parties representing other points of view (libertarians, communists, vegetarians, fundamentalists, etc.) are by definition excluded.

By convention well-known and prestigious reporters take turns questioning the two designated and "official" candidates, who are addressed only by preferred title (Mr. Vice President, Senator, Governor, etc.). They are then free to respond briefly (in 1988 the time limit was, I believe, under three minutes) before the opponent is offered the chance of an even briefer rebuttal. Then another reporter on the panel asks another equally polite question and the game goes on. Care is taken that both hopefuls are questioned equally and that the issues under discussion never get out of hand. Little if any debate, at least as the word is traditionally used, results. There is no mechanism in this process for the reporter to hammer away at a point on which a candidate is clearly at risk. Events are what the candidate says they are and reporters are too polite to challenge those definitions in any but the most prescribed and gentle of fashions.

By contrast, in 1988 the Canadian electorate was preparing to vote for a new government in which the critical issue was a controversial trade treaty with the United States. The sitting prime minister, Brian Mulroney, and Opposition Leader John Turner participated in a televised debate notable, when compared to the U.S. "debate", for its lack of moderation and its accent on the issues. Speaking directly to and in fact cutting off his opponent's rebuttals, Mr. Turner told the prime minister that he and his policies were "selling out" their country. The contentious trade treaty, Mr. Turner said as his opponent sputtered, would result in the destruction of the Canadian ethos and in general was a traitorous a program detrimental to the commonweal. This was, in fact, a real debate—a discussion on the issues between individuals holding opposing views— and stood in sharp relief against the earlier, moderated "debate" which was to inform American voters about the attributes of Mr. Bush and Mr. Dukakis.[13]

The American "debate" process is revealing and, within the context of news as it is currently conceived, perfectly consistent. Candidates can define and redefine the context in which each wants to respond to an issue or event and the moderators will not protest. Thus in 1988, then Vice President Bush lyrically responded to questions about the increasing number of homeless, the administration's disavowal of the elderly, and the failure of America to help its functionally disabled by assuring that good works by volunteers like his wife would set all problems right with a "thousand points of light." The failure of the Reagan-Bush administration to do anything but exacerbate these problems during the previous seven years was raised briefly and dropped quickly by the reporters who were the designated inquisitors of the candidates.

Further, questions posed by representatives of the press are carefully chosen to limit the level and areas of discourse. Each may be related only to a prescribed and logically distinct event or social area. When then candidate Bush accused his opponent of being a liberal and member of the American Civil Liberties Union (ACLU), it was not the reporter's place to lash out with follow-up questions. Reporters did not ask Bush if as he distanced himself from the liberal tradition he was also disavowing the political heritage of Thomas Paine, Abraham Lincoln, Franklin Delano Roosevelt, John F. Kennedy, and other heroes of that political ethos. Nor did they ask if, in condemning membership in the ACLU, he also decried the absolute support of both the American Constitution and U.S. law which is that organization's chartered purpose.

Finally, they did not ask either candidate if the restrictions placed on the format by the candidates themselves had not created such a travesty of discourse as to suggest everybody should apologize and go home. That had been the position of the League of Women Voters which refused to participate in the debates as organizers because, as spokesperson Nancy Neuman told reporters: "We have no intention of becoming an accessory to the hoodwinking of the American public."[14] But reporters could not simply refuse to participate, because the individual role of the participating journalists and of news reporters at large was equally on the line. Through it all, polite journalists were seen as participants, as powerful members of the process. But as their role was confirmed through a demonstration of the journalists' relations with and access to the candidates, the restrictions inherent in these mutually legitimating roles were unconsciously underlined as candidate functionaries, now called "spin doctors," descended on the reporting press to define and redefine the journalistic event of which the "debates" themselves were the boundary event. The whole "debate" process was a wonderful example of the degree to which the original boundary elements (the homeless, the poor, military incursion, official corruption, environment, etc.) were dismissed by officials' recapitulation and consumed in turn by reporters who passed the result on as news. It underscored the degree to which issues of objectivity and social perception have been transformed through the narrative form into a process of perhaps unconscious but certainly consistent official legitimization.

### Editors and Reporters

In this whole process reporters are like bank tellers on a busy day. For the latter, all the money flows through their hands and very little stays in the way of a weekly pay check. They learn the ways of the bank, the pattern of behavior expected of officials, and the forms by which the medium of money is exchanged. If they do well and accept the constraints of their environment, a few might in the course of time move up to account officer and, maybe to vice president of a branch. Power flows through the newsperson's hands in precisely the same way. The police reporter may drink with police officers and ride in their cars, but he does not get to carry a gun or have to salute when a captain goes by. A city hall reporters may call the mayor by his first name and explain why a proposal has not found favor, but that journalist is neither answerable to the electorate nor responsible for anything greater than twelve to fifteen column inches of copy on a busy news day.

The trappings of power without its responsibilities persist for the journalist only to the degree to which he or she adheres to the form and perpetuates the myth it embodies. When he or she contradicts the police chief, challenges the mayor, accuses the coroner—and does so with indisputable facts gained from outside official channels—then the rules change forever. Such a situation would make of a member of the fourth estate not a player with the prior three estates but an ombudsman for the peasantry who, in medieval society, were in liege to the royalty, clergy, land owners, and eventually journalists, who in their capacity as the fourth estate joined society's ruling forces.

Thus reporters addressed their respectful questions to Mr. Vice president or Mr. Governor who, in turn, replied using the questioners' familiar, first names. This signified, on one level, the familiarity and close working relations between participating politicians and journalists as well as the success of the journalists themselves. Their closeness was underlined by casual friendliness with which Mr. Bush would respond to "Dan" or "Peter's" questions. These journalists, the whole said, were known, respected and close to the nation's most powerful men. Had any reporter insisted on the right to hammer at a question, to be other than an official and respectful moderate, he or she would not have been allowed to play. Sitting with the mighty, reporters are unmasked as impotent because, really, what power do they have? None, except to the degree that each can bask in the reflected glory of the officials they are supposed to question critically. Representatives of the fourth estate at those debates could not set an army in motion, clean up Boston Harbor, counsel the homeless, or even speak indignantly about the failure of an official American policy or act. To do so would inevitably have decreased their personal access to the powerful, which is for many journalists their critical stock in trade. Thus the one power a journalist by tradition and myth must have, that of a critical and independent stance, is abdicated to the degree that newsmen become moderators for, publicists to and legitimaters of the official world. It is what Herbert Marcuse a generation ago called "repressive tolerance," the integration of critical voices to assure their acceptance of the general social order. Nowhere has it been shown to more powerful effect than in the relations of the American journalist to the system he or she is supposed to describe.

But it is unnecessary for officials to actively seduce journalists trained from their first obituary to seek official quotes and define events as isolated and discontinuous. This narrative tack is at base amenable to the official view, and to the extent that it is accepted by reporters and editors, results in copy that a priori will be slanted and restrained. When a reporter denies the form it will most likely be his own colleagues who will censor the malcontent. His or her editors, after all, were reporters themselves and were promoted because of successful adherence to the rules. Just as the bank manager may have been a teller before, so too is the managing editor likely to have been a reporter who has been indoctrinated into the economic, financial, and social milieu in which bank presidents also move. The journalistic community holds a view of propriety as strict as that of any ministry, and rebels are often disciplined more harshly than outsiders might suspect. This, of course, was a resulting caution of Janet Cooke's story, the virulent condemnation by one's fellows, who police the rules which define the stories any are allowed to write.

But then, most journalists have little real franchise and are perhaps understandably insecure about their trade. Most reporters, like bank tellers, are paid an hourly rate but insist on thinking of themselves as members of the salaried, "professional" classes. In the 1930s, when the Newspaper Guild was formed, the name was consciously chosen to distance its editorial members from the unions of hourly workers who were organizing at the same time.[15] Since then the distance and tension has remained between the reportorial perception of his or her "profession" and the fact that reportage is a largely repetitive trade in which compensation is by the hour and work is done by the minute or by the inch.

## CONCLUSION

It seems from this perspective that linguist and critic Noam Chomsky was right after all. Contemporary journalism does have as a central function the role of propagandist in a modern democracy. Further, it appears that role is mundanely fulfilled through a structural transformation based on what linguists define as a unary grammar. This results in a narrative pattern that defines events in terms of official statement and not through any critical method that would place the news in its broader context. Thus there is a consistent and generally accepted shift of information from the boundary to journalistic information levels. The result is a textual pattern whose emphasis is on the social signfication of official interest rather than on a description of the events occurring at the boundary level itself.

This is not a necessary form. There are other ways to present information. If objectivity is an impossible dream, a story's levels of information, at least in theory, can be consciously recognized and controlled by the newsman. A reporter can redefine his subject in such a way that the isolated event becomes part of a pattern of occurrence. To the extent that the distance between objective and reportorial event levels is consciously lessened by the reporter, the level of information imbedded in the news story can and will change as well. If they wished, and if editors were receptive, daily journalists could radically change the form through a conscious transformation of the form from an unary to a replicative grammar. This would require that each boundary event be placed in the context of a class of relevant occurrences and that the news reporter pursue a line of inquiry similar to that of a scientific researcher. By insisting on a form in which the officially defined journalistic event was not the sole focus of a story, news professionals could focus on what is signified at the level of the boundary event—the slowed heart and pulse that cause cessation of life for an individual undergoing anesthesia—and question the interpretation of officials who assume it is a "one in a million" chance occurrence.

One result of this change would be not only different information in the news but, perhaps more critically, a different social myth. It would deny the insistence that elected officials or medical professionals are always competent and always aware of the facts and assert both their capacity for error and the public's ability to question. That would make of the fourth estate a counterbalance to officialdom and the reporter's job one of watchdog in the arena of not only political but mundane affairs. To the extent that the fourth estate is structurally propagandist and spokesperson for its three compatriots, this would be a profoundly radical and potentially disturbing change of affairs. In addition, it would require newspeople to abdicate their often close reciprocal association with officials and adopt an independent, truly objective, and perhaps adversarial posture. This is not the role most choose, not the role graduate schools of journalism recommend to their graduates and certainly not a posture actively encouraged by the majority of editors and publishers in North America today. Like the university and the government itself, the contemporary newsperson has as his and her primary function the socialization of the citizenry. Professors concentrate on adolescents and journalists on adults in the persistent reinforcement of social myths first taught citizens in high school social studies classes. Both have as a social function within their respective forums the maintenance and promulgation of specific myths which include the care, concern, and vigilance of fundamentally interested, concerned, and knowledgeable officialdom. For the daily journalist, fulfillment of that function is embedded in the narrative form, the textual organization of the news.

**NOTES**

1. This and other quotes from Roland Barthes in this chapter were first introduced in chapter 1 to which the reader is referred. The intention is to use in conclusion those statements that assisted in the development of the argument.

2. For a very good description and discussion of the coverage of the August 21, 1983, downing of Korean Air Lines Flight 007, see: Allan Rachlin, *News As Hegemonic Reality* (New York: Praeger, 1988) chapter 3.

3. Mark Crispin Miller, "TV's Anti-Liberal Bias," the *New York Times*, November 16, 1988.

4. See for example, Lewis H. Lapham, *Money and Class in America*, (New York: Ballantine Books, 1988). As both a journalist and a scion of the monied class, he takes delight in explaining that money is the rule for all: "The media's long-standing alliance with the monied interests should surprise nobody except the youngest student at the Columbia School of Journalism. Among the 400 richest Americans memorialized in 1986 by Forbes magazine, 83 of them derived their fortunes from newspaper, television, and publishing properties. Only the oil industry, which contributed 48 names to the list, could make even a modest claim to such pecuniary glory." (p. 50).

5. Jürgen Habermas, "The University In a Democracy," in *Toward a Rational Society* (Boston: Beacon Press, 1971), 1-12.

6. See Tom Barthell, "The Myth of an Adversary Press," *Harper's*, January, 1977.

7. One can note in this regard the length of time it took both officials and journalists to become interested in the issues, the degree of difficulty reporters and prosecuting investigators had in disseminating information eventually collected, and the speed with which, after resigning voluntarily, Mr. Nixon was pardoned by his successor. The "perpetrators" did less time and less "hard time" than the average nineteen-year-old ghetto youth caught selling an ounce of marijuana in the District of Columbia or the average criminal convicted for breaking and entering in, say, Colorado.

8. Berthell, op.cit.

9. John Keane, *Public Life and Late Capitalism* , (Cambridge, London: Cambridge University Press, 1984), 224. The analysis of legitimacy as a concept used here applies Keane's general thesis to news.

10. Guenther Roth and Claus Wittich, eds. *Max Weber, Economy and Society*, (Berkeley: University of California Press, 1978). See chapter 1, sections 5-7 for a general discussion and chapter 3, sections 1-4, for a discussion of precise types of legitimate domination.

11. Keane, *Public Life and Late Capitalism*, 225.

12. Keane, Ibid.

13. Many have lamented the loss of serious debate in the body of American politic. See, for example, Russell Jacoby, *The Last intellectuals*, (New York: Basic Books, 1987) and Neil Postman, *Amusing Ourselves to Death* (New York: Viking, 1986). The former blames a variety of factors, including the professionalization of intellectuals in academia. The latter believes television is the crucial culprit in the decline of reasoned and sharp discussion within the public sphere. Chomsky's argument, at least regarding news, on the limits of dissent built into the U.S. information structure is cogent and compelling. It also has the advantage of being a general, social model tested against the offerings of daily U.S. newspapers. See the bibliographer or citations in previous chapters for references to his work.

14. *New York Times*, February 17, 1988. Quoted in Hugh Carter Donahue, *The Battle to Control Broadcast News* (Cambridge, Mass.: M.I.T. Press, 1989), 190. Donahue's chapter 2 discusses the candidate debates in 1988.

15. A.H. Raskin, "The once and future Newspaper Guild," *Columbia Journalism Review*, (September/October1982), 26-34.

# Afterword

The pervasiveness of the myth and the degree of its entrench-
ment in the journalist's society can be seen, perhaps, by the length of
time it has taken this reporter to reflect self-consciously on what has
been for twenty-one years his primary professional and critical stance.
Since 1968, when my first bylined story was published, I have reported
happily on a stunning variety of topics about which I was often totally
ignorant. When I was assigned to topics on which personal knowledge
had been gained, I rarely challenged the officials I was dispatched to
interview through manipulating the narrative form to make critical use
of that background. Had I wished to, and usually I did not, I could not
have easily changed the parameters of the stories I was assigned by
editors or informed of by official sources, who often had their own axes
to grind. Simply, it was not important to do so and not necessary for
the daily reports I was engaged to write. Over these two decades my
work, precisely attributed, has appeared in several languages through
the media of various newspapers, magazines, and radio stations. My
stories have been published or broadcast, on occasion, with exotic
datelines (Mexico, Equador, Honolulu, Canada, Taiwan, and Japan) in
publications ranging from *Black Belt* to *Yankee* magazine and from
newspapers ranging geographically from the *New York Times* to the
*Honolulu Star-Bulletin*. Despite a lavish undergraduate and graduate
education, I have reported on everything from anesthesia to zoos and
rarely thought about what a story's crucial issues were, its relation to
wider social concerns, or what its effects might be.

It is with equal parts of shame and anger that, in retrospect, I understand why the best stories were the most difficult to have published
and the ones that editors resisted most consistently. Through most of
those professionally full decades of work I believed journalism fulfilled a useful, informational function and that news professionals
were among the brightest and most enlightened of society's citizens.

Each time a person died, it seemed like a singular tragedy, and each time a military incursion occurred, it was a unique, frightening, but isolated incident—not a disease and not a symptom but an isolated if odious event. The suicide of a teenager was always tragic and incomprehensible. When psychologists called to remonstrate with me, arguing that  suicide  among the young was an epidemic resulting from  a complex of social and psychological debasements, I suggested they write a Sunday op-ed feature. In it all I worked with zest and gloried in my relations with the mayors, government ministers, lawyers and cops I quoted by title, addressed by name and knew I could reach by phone.

Only now, from the perspective of this exercise, do I understand that I was as much participant and supporter as observer and critic of the abuses I pursued with righteous passion. It is cold comfort at this remove to know that I was not alone, that most journalists are little different from other publicists sanctioned by society, and that we share, assuming Habermas is correct, with university educators the primary function of myth making and socialization. But I do not want to agree with Mark Harris that the answer is not to read newspapers and, certainly, not to write for them.

I would like to believe that others, reading this, will pursue a similar line of contextual reportage and utilize the libraries and computer databases that facilitate the task of elementary research. The collapse of a new bridge in Florida or of a shopping mall roof in Vancouver, Canada, are not unique acts of a capricious God but, typically, examples of shoddy construction work easily amenable to contextual reportage. In most reported instances of such collapse, the cause has been determined to involve shoddy construction by a subcontractor who skimped on concrete or did not put in enough structural supports. Perhaps a local inspector was bought off. But the sanctimonious and immediate avowal of innocence by participants in a preventable disaster can be quickly discounted—and such protestations are typical — when a reporter begins to ask "why," "how," and "where did this occur before?"

It is nice to think that news corporations will see the potential for making of their separate parts a cohesive informational force such that, for example,  a Gannett reporter in Honolulu, Hawaii, could use that organization's infrastructure to solicit information from other Gannett-owned media outposts on anesthetic deaths, patterns of attack against the judiciary, or the hundreds of other structural issues that, each year, are buried in the trivialization of daily news. It would make good news sense and good social sense, and perhaps such a posture can become a commonplace in the business.

I doubt that will happen soon, however. Because the issues raised here are structural, they are cultural. News is a single step in the interlocking social form that propels the greater environment. It is a reflection and a symptom, not the problem in isolation. Thus to the extent that the narrative shift is a structural fact, it involves more than a merely textual problem. The relation of reporters to editors, producers to cameramen, stations to corporations, and newspapers to conglomerates are all a part of a pattern of interlocking relations which result in the story's narrative form. Those relations, for their part, are subsets of a wider cultural perspective in which elected officials, academics and readers are joined. The style of a story—its length and its prominence—depends on the degree of advertising and "news hole" availability, which is a function of who has paid how much to trumpet what product in the news. Its content is the result of a whole social posture of which the narrative form described here is merely a single result.

To the degree that the news professional is a social participant, his function and identity are invested in his role. That role is one of legitimizer and of buttress to the advertiser who supports the medium in which each of us write, To the extent that we aim for professional advancement, we accept the rules of the game which are taught from the first obituary through the limits of police reportage until they are second nature. News professionals who have become public figures —Dan Shorr, Sam Donaldson, Peter Jennings, Dan Rather—are not going to tell a sitting vice president and state governor that the rules they have chosen for their debate are exclusionary and unjust. At least, they will not do so in the public sphere. Had the been so inclined, it is unliely any would have become the powers they are today. NBC is not going to refuse its elected officials an hour's programming because that is contrary to its role in the system as a whole.

Those who are told at their respective newspapers, radio or television stations that there isn't time or need to dig deeper are unlikely to quit over principles of in-depth versus biased news. I never quit my reportorial jobs when told a topic I wished to pursue was "too complex," "too risky [for the newspaper]" or just "not what we [at this newspaper] do." When stories I knew to be correct were spiked for reasons of political or personal and not news judgment I didn't walk off the job, both because I wanted to be a newsman and because I liked the money and prestige that came with the job. The work was never truly onerous, often interesting, and on occasion exciting as hell. It was easy in the press of business not to think about the limits that were as much a part of the atmosphere as the attributed quote.

In theory, newsmen could become public surrogates, watchdogs who did refuse to participate in debates whose structure they privately disdained. Reporters could on a daily basis insist on a role in which they questioned instead of repeated. A new function for the journalist and one distinct from legitimization and corporate sales could be lauded. But this would require a commitment on the part of all— publishers, editors, reporters, politicians, news directors and advertisers—to self-consciously consider in their respective environments the whole of the system we call the news. I do not believe this will soon occur. It is not simply because I believe that the supervisors of news conglomerates and the editors who serve them are content with the way things are. I am pessimistic because I have been an editor and, proudly, a reporter. I remember precisely how easy and how much fun it was to glibly chat up the mayor of a city, call a deputy minister for "balance," and then write a fast fifteen inches of copy or fashion an "in-depth" two minutes and forty seconds of radio news. That was my job and I did not want to change it. There was little incentive to do so and more than enough inducement (more pay, better assignments) to suggest that the future would certainly hold more for me if I stayed rather than quit. So after work, most days, I went to dinner full of pride and with my conscience clear and rarely gave another thought to the events or lives which had been reported under the by-line of Tom Koch.

# Selected Bibliography

## BOOKS

Bagdikian, Ben H. *The Media Monopoly.* Boston: Beacon Press, 1983.

Barthes, Roland. *Camera Lucida.* New York: Hill and Wang, 1981.

_____. *The Eiffel Tower and Other Mythologies.* New York: Hill and Wang, 1979.

_____. *The Pleasure of the Text.* New York: Hill and Wang, 1975.

Bate, Jackson W. *Samuel Johnson.* New York: Harcourt Brace Jovanovich, 1975.

Benjamin, Burton. *CBS, General Westmoreland, and How a Television Documentary Went Wrong.* New York: Harper and Row, 1988.

Berman, Marshall. *All That Is Solid Melts into Air.* New York: Viking Penguin, 1982.

Brooks, Brian S. et. al. *New Reporting and Writing.* Third Ed. New York: St. Martin's Press, 1988.

Chomsky, Noam. *Necessary Illusions: Thought Control in Democratic Societies.* Toronto, Canada: CBC Enterprises, 1989.

Cort, David. *The Sin of Henry R. Luce: An Anatomy of Journalism.* Secaucus, New Jersey: Lyle Stuart, Inc. 1974.

Diamond, Edwin. *The Last Days of Television.* Cambridge, Massachusetts: MIT Press, 1982.

Donahue, Hugh Carter. *The Battle to Control Broadcast News.* Boston: M.I.T. Press, 1989.

Gans, Herb T. *Deciding What's News.* New York: Pantheon, 1979.

Gatrell, Anthony. *Distance and Space: A Geographical Perspective.* Oxford: Clarendon Press, 1983.

Ghiglione, Loren, ed. *The Buying and Selling of Newspapers.* Indianapolis: R. J. Berg, 1984.

Gitlin, Todd. *The Whole World is Watching: Mass Media in the Making and Unmaking of the New Left.* Berkeley: University of California Press, 1980.

Habermas, Jūrgen.*Toward a Rational Society.* Boston: Beacon Press, 1971.

Harary, Frank; Norman, Robert Z. and Cartwright, Norman. *Structural Models: An Introduction to the Theory of Directed Graphs.* New York: John Wiley & Sons, 1965.

Hage, Per, and Harary, Frank. *Structural Models in Anthropology,* New York: Cambridge University Press, 1983.

Hanff, Helene. *Apple of My Eye.* Mt. Kisco, New York: Moyer Bell, 1977.

Harris, Mark. *Short Work of It: Selected Writing by Mark Harris.* Pittsburgh: University of Pittsburgh Press, 1970.

Hayes, Nelson E., and Hayes, Tanya, eds. *Claude Lévi-Strauss The Anthropologist as Hero.* Cambridge, Massachusetts: MIT Press, 1970.

Hill, George, B. ed. *Boswell's Life of Johnson.* New York: Harper and Brothers, 1891.

Hofstadter, Douglas. *Metamagical Themas: Questing for the Essence of Mind and Pattern.* New York: Basic Books, 1985.

Jacoby, Russel. *The Last Intellectuals: American Culture in the Age of Academe.* New York: Basic Books, 1987.

Keane, John. *Public Life and Late Capitalism.* London: Cambridge University Press, 1984.

Kernan, Alvin. *Printing Technology, Letters and Samuel Johnson.* Princeton: Princeton University Press, 1987.

Lapham, Lewis, H. *Money and Class in America.* New York: Ballantine Books, 1988.

Lippmann, Walter. *Public Opinion.* New York: MacMillan, 1926.

McLuhan, Marshall. *The Gutenberg Galaxy.* Toronto, Ontario: University of Toronto Press, 1962.

McPhee, John. *La Place de la Concorde Suisse.* New York: Farrar, Straus & Giroux, 1983.

Merrill, John C. *The Elite Press.* New York: Pitman, 1968.

Morris, William, ed. *The American Heritage Dictionary of the American Language.* New York: American Heritage Publishing, 1969.

Nagel, Ernest, and Newman, James R. *Godel's Proof.* New York: New York University Press, 1958.

Orkin, F. K. and Cooperman, L. H. eds. *Complications in Anesthesiology.* Philadelphia: Lippincott,1983.

Pember, Donald R. *Privacy and the Press: The Law, the Mass Media and the First Amendment.* Seattle: University of Washington Press, 1972.

Postman, Neil. *Amusing Ourselves to Death.* New York: Viking, 1986.

Rachlin, Allan. *News as Hegemonic Reality.* New York: Praeger, 1988.

Sacks, Oliver. *The Man Who Mistook His Wife For a Hat.* New York: Summit Books, 1985.

Schiller, Dan. *Objectivity and the News.* Pittsburg: University of Pennsylvania Press, 1981.

Schlesinger, Phillip. *Putting 'Reality' Together.* London: Constable and

Company, Ltd., 1978.

Shudson, Michael. *Discovering the News*. New York: Basic Books, 1978.

Sontag, Susan, ed. *A Barthes Reader*. New York: Hill and Wang, 1982.

Soper, Roy G. et al. *EMT Manual*. Philadelphia: W.B. Saunders, 1984.

Stephens, Michael. *A History of News*. New York: Viking, 1988.

Sun, John L. *Manual of Anesthesia*, 2d ed. Boston: Little, Brown, and Co., 1982.

Tuchman, Gaye. *Making News: A Study in the Construction of Reality*. New York: Free Press, 1978.

Ullmann, John, and Honeyman, Steve, eds. *The Reporter's Handbook: An Investigator's Guide to Documents and Techniques*. New York: St. Martin's Press, 1983.

Wain, John. *Samuel Johnson, A Biography*. New York: Viking, 1974.

Weinberg, Steve, ed. *The IRE Book*. Columbia: Investigative Reporters and Editors, 1984.

Western, J. *Outcast Capetown*. Minneapolis: University of Minnesota Press, 1981.

Whitman, Alden.*The Obituary Book.*. New York: Stein and Day, 1964.

**JOURNAL AND MAGAZINE ARTICLES**

Alexander, Bruce; Hadaway, Patricia; and Beyerstein, Barry. "Rat Park Chronicle." *B.C. Medical Journal*, 22 (2) February1980.

Anderson, Kay J. "The Idea of Chinatown: The Power of Place and Institutional Practice in the Making of a Racial Category." *Annals of the American Geographer*, 77(4), 1987.

Baldwin, Deborah."The Dismal Science." *Common Cause*, March/April, 1988.

Barthell, Tom. "The Myth of an Adversary Press." *Harper's*, January, 1977.

Bennett, Richard et. al. "Morphine Titration in Postoperative Laparotomy Patients Using Patient-controlled Analgesia."*Current Therapeutic Research*, 32 (1), July, 1982.

Bethel, Tom. "The Myth of an Adversary Press." *Harper's*, January, 1977.

Breed, Walter. "Social control in the Newsroom." *Social Forces*, 33, 1955.

Caploe, David R. "Max Weber and a Dialectical Theory of Objectivity." Unpublished manuscript. Chapel Hill, North Carolina: Duke University, 1988.

Cousins, Norman. "The Poet and the Computer." *National Forum, The Phi Kappa Phi Journal*, 69 (2), Spring, 1989.

Crosby, William. "Checking the Anesthetic Machine, Drugs and Monitoring Devices." *Anesthesia and Intensive Care*, 16 February, 1988.

Daniels, Clifton and Kristol, Irving. "The Times: An Exchange." *The Public Interest*, (7), Spring, 1967.

Eichorn, H. et. al. "Standards for Patient Monitoring During Anesthesia at Harvard Medical School." *Journal of the American Medical Association*, 256, 1986.

Epstein, Edward Jay. "Did the Press Uncover Watergate?" *Commentary*, July, 1984.

Hamilton, W. K. "Unexpected DeathsDuring Anesthesia: Wherein Lies the Cause?" *Anesthesiology*, 50, 1979.

Henry, Willam A. "The Right to Fake Quotes." *Time*, August 21, 1989, 49.

Lovell, Ron. "Triumph of the Chi-Squares." *The Quill*, October, 1988.

"Medical Negligence: Damages: Loss of Adult Consortium,"*American Trial Lawyers Association Reporter*, November 29, 1986.

Messier, Dianne Y. "Judgement of Inquiry into the Death of Ronald Margaret Dac." *Coroner's Court of British Columbia*, November, 1988.

_____. "Judgement of Inquiry into the Death of Ronald James Mason." *Coroner's Court of British Columbia*, November, 1988.

Raskin, A. H. "The Once and Future Newspaper Guild." *Columbia Journalism Review*, September/October, 1982.

Robins, Lee N., and Helzer, John E. "Drug Use among Vietnam Veterans—three years later." *Health World News*, October 27, 1975.

Scanlon, Joseph T., and Alldred, Suzanne. "Media Coverage of Disasters: The Same Old Story," *Emergency Planning Digest*, October/December, 1982.

Schwartz, Thomas A. "A Proposal for a Research Project Measuring Freedom of the Press Ideology." Unpublished manuscript, Ohio State University, 1980.

Stein, M. L. "Who Sets the News Agenda?" *Editor and Publisher*, December 31, 1988.

Van Gelder, Lindsay. "Can the Chatter, Sweatheart." *Business Month*, February, 1989.

Westin, Av. "Inside the Evening News." *New York*, October 18, 1982.

Whicher, C. et.al. "Anesthetic Mishaps and the Cost of Monitoring: a Proposed Standard for Monitoring Equipment." *Journal of Clinical Monitoring*, 4, January, 1988.

White, David M. "The 'Gatekeeper': A Case Study in the Selection of News." *Journalism Quarterly*, 27 (1950).

**NEWSPAPER STORIES**

Robinson, Martha. "'No Guidelines' in Boy's Death, Coroner's Jury told." the *Vancouver Sun*, May 30, 1980.

_____."Delay in Treatment Found in Boy's Death." *Vancouver Sun*, May 31, 1980.

Needham, Phil. "Hoses 'Worried' Staff,'" *Vancouver Sun*, February 10, 1981.

Koch, Tom. "Inquest to Study Surgical Oxygen Loss." *Province*, February 9, 1981.

Guy, Pat. "Probe of Incident With Stevens Would Be Welcome—

Shintaku." *Honolulu Star-Bulletin*, October 7, 1981.

Memminger, Charles. "Shintaku Taken Unconscious to Wahiawa Hospital." *Honolulu Star-Bulletin*, October 7, 1981.

Games, Lee, and Memminger, Charles. "Surgeon Says Shintaku Took a Bad Beating." *Honolulu Star-Bulletin*, October 8, 1981.

_____. "How Shintaku Was Injured Is Still Mystery." *Honolulu Star-Bulletin*, October 9, 1981.

Wright, Walter. "City Prosecutor Marsland Attacks Editorials re: Judge's Alleged Assault." *Honolulu Star-Bulletin*, October 10, 1981.

_____. "Shintaku: Car Followed Me/ Injured Judge Speaks Out in Hospital Interview." *Star-Bulletin & Advertiser*, October 11, 1981.

McCoy, Jim. "Shintaku Injuries Result of a Fall, Police Say." *Honolulu Star-Bulletin*, November 12, 1981.

Memminger, Charles, and Games, Lee. "Shintaku Controversy Continues Unsettled." *Honolulu Star-Bulletin*, November 13, 1981.

Games, Lee andMemminger, Charles. "Pathologist Alters His Views." *Honolulu Star-Bulletin*, November 14, 1981.

Gerry Bellett. "Evidence Conflicts at Inquest on Tot." *Sun*, February 26, 1985.

_____. "Drugs Caused Circulation Failure, MDs Say." *Sun*, February 27, 1985.

_____. "Anesthetist Quits Hospital Job during Inquests Into 2 Deaths." *Sun*, February 28, 1985.

Still, Larry. "Gross Medical Negligence Cited in Death of Woman." *Sun* May 18, 1985.

_____. "Patient Death Sparks Probe." *Sun*, October 24, 1985.

Horwood, Holly. "Fatal Slip Unnoticed." *Province*, February 11, 1986.

Hume, Mark. "Dead Man's Kin Urges Action Against Dentist." the *Vancouver Sun*, March 25, 1986.

"VA Hospitals: A Question of Quality." *Fort Lauderdale News and Sun Sentinel*: Fort Lauderdale, June, 1986.

Boorstin, Robert O. "Two-Year-Old Dies after Operation in Dental Office." *New York Times*, June 4, 1986.

"Victim's Mother Testifies in Dentist's Civil Trial." *Los Angeles Times*, June 19, 1986.

"Move to Save Lives in Operating Room/Researchers Urge Anesthesia Standards." *Sacramento Bee*, August 22, 1986.

Bellett, Gerry. "Doctor Admits Administering Anesthetic Despite Warnings." *Sun*, October 15, 1986.

"Death Sets Off Alarm." *Province*, February 3, 1987.

Murphy, Michael. "Review of Malpractice Verdict Denied." *Phoenix Gazette*, February 27, 1987.

"Death Probed After Teen's Heart Stops During Dental Surgery." *Sun*, June 20, 1987.

"Pathologists to Conduct More Tests as Teen's Death at Dentist Probed." *Sun*, June 22, 1987.

Japenga, Ann. "A Dental Sedation Death Casts Doubt on Procedure."

*Los Angeles Times*, July 27, 1987.

Hager, Philip. "Dentist Loses Appeal in Murder Conviction." *Los Angeles Times*, August 22, 1987.

Austin, Ian. "Dental Probe Opens." *Province*, October 27, 1987.

Morton, Brian. "Rare Condition Cited in Dental Deaths." *Sun*, October 27, 1987.

Austin, Ian. "Gas Machine Flawed, Dental Inquest Hears." *Proince*, Oct. 28, 1987.

_____. "Inquest Hears Plea for Halt." *Province*, October 29, 1987.

_____. "Docs Face Probe" *Province*, October 30, 1987.

Fitterman, Lisa. "Mom Hopes Some Good Comes of Dental Death." *Sun*, October 30, 1987.

Kell, Michael. "Quayle Likely to Stay in Bush's Shadow." *Baltimore Sun*. reprinted in *Columbus Dispatch*, January 3, 1988.

Schmidt, Susan. "Review of Complaint Delayed Despite Court Request."*Washington Post*, January 10, 1988.

Caher, John. "High Court to Decide Earnings Award." *Knickerbocker News*, March 10, 1988.

Glass, Andrew J. "Why Drug Crisis Is Spinning Out of Control." *Honolulu Star-Bulletin*, March 10, 1988.

"3 lawsuits in 5 Years Result in Investigation of Texas Physicians." *Houston Post*, May 15, 1988.

Leidl, Pat. "Media Ruined Reputation, Cleared Dentist Says." *Sun*, May 19, 1988.

Miller, Mark Crispin. "We Are What We Read." *New York Times Book Review*, Sept. 18, 1988.

Mittelstaedt, Martin. *"Is It Really All* The News That's Fit to Print?" *Globe and Mail*, October 8, 1988.

Miller, Mark Crispin. "TV's Anti-Lberal Bias." *New York Times*, November 17, 1988.

Associated Press,"Drugs Thwart Justice, Lawyers Find." *Columbus Dispatch*, Dec. 1, 1988.

Chavez, Cesar E. "Nonchemical Pesticides need Encouragement." *New York Times*, July 13, 1989.

Enthoven, Alain "A 'Cost-Unconscious' Medical System." *New York Times*, July 13, 1989.

# Index

## About the Author

TOM KOCH is a writer and consultant on news and information technologies and has been on the staff of *The Springfield Union and Republican, The Province,* the Canadian Broadcasting Corporation, and United Press International.